Also by T.H. Breen

American Insurgents, American Patriots:
The Revolution of the People

Marketplace of Revolution: How Consumer Politics
Shaped American Independence

Imagining the Past: East Hampton Stories

Tobacco Culture: The Mentality of the Great Tidewater
Planters on the Eve of Revolution

"Myne Owne Ground": Race and Freedom on Virginia's
Eastern Shore, 1640–1676
(with Stephen Innes)

Puritans and Adventurers: Change and Persistence
in Early America

The Character of the Good Ruler: A Study of Puritan
Political Ideas in New England, 1630–1730

The President Forges a New Nation

George Washington's Journey

T.H. BREEN

Simon & Schuster

New York London Toronto Sydney New Delhi

Simon & Schuster
1230 Avenue of the Americas
New York, NY 10020

First Simon & Schuster hardcover edition January 2016

SIMON & SCHUSTER and colophon are registered trademarks
of Simon & Schuster, Inc.

For information about special discounts for bulk purchases,
please contact Simon & Schuster Special Sales at 1-866-506-1949
or business@simonandschuster.com.

The Simon & Schuster Speakers Bureau can bring authors to your
live event. For more information or to book an event, contact the
Simon & Schuster Speakers Bureau at 1-866-248-3049 or visit our
website at www.simonspeakers.com.

Interior design by Lewelin Polanco
Maps by Paul Pugliese

Manufactured in the United States of America

10 9 8 7 6 5 4 3 2 1

Library of Congress Cataloging-in-Publication Data

Breen, T.H.
  George Washington's journey : the president forges a new nation /
T.H. Breen.—First Simon & Schuster hardcover edition.
      pages cm
  Includes bibliographical references and index.
  1. Washington, George, 1732–1799—Travel—United States. 2. Presidents—
Travel—United States—History—18th century. 3. United States—Politics
and government—1789–1797. I. Title.
  E312.B77 2015
  973.4'1092—dc23

                          2015007283

ISBN 978-1-4516-7542-9
ISBN 978-1-4516-7544-3 (ebook)

Photograph credits appear on p. 285.

As always, for Lady Susan

Contents

Acknowledgments

I learned of George Washington's journey to the new nation several decades ago while preparing a newspaper piece for a special Presidents' Day section. His diary, which figures centrally in this book, recounted his decision to stay only at public inns and taverns, even though that meant that he often had to endure bad food and uncomfortable beds. He complained about the unsatisfactory accommodations for him and his horses. Only later did I come to appreciate the larger significance of this extraordinary trip, which took him to all original thirteen states. The research for this project involved reconstructing Washington's tours of the United States, from New Hampshire to Georgia, following as best I could the same roads that he had traveled.

As my readers will discover, the president encountered many interesting and generous men and women along the way. So did I. The list of people who offered guidance includes Mary V. Thompson, a research historian at Mount Vernon, who repeatedly came to my rescue when I needed precise information on topics such as the theater in New York City in 1789 and the details of the lives of Washington's slaves. Edward G. Lengel, editor of the Washington Papers, a magnificent project that is the foundation of all modern Washington scholarship, provided insights and encouragement at key points.

Several others gave me welcome direction, often over coffee when perhaps they did not realize how much they were helping to advance the project. Although the interpretation of Washington's journey is entirely my own, I thank those who offered welcome and helpful guidance along the way: David Hancock, Christopher W. Brooks, Bill Brown, Steve Hindle, Roy Ritchie, Hermann Wellenreuther, John Brewer, Gideon Manning, Alan Taylor, Carole Shammas, Doug Bradburn, Patrick Griffin, Edward Stehle, Walter Woodward, David Cressy, Naill Kirkwood, Howard Pashman, Larry Hewes, Harvey (Amani) Whitfield, and Michael Lammert. Several people helped me locate illustrations, for which I owe them a considerable debt of gratitude: Dawn Bonner at Mount Vernon, Ashley Cataldo at the American Antiquarian Society, Joyce Baker at the Gibbes Museum of Art in Charleston, and Bea Ross of the Congregation Jeshuat Israel at the Touro Synagogue.

Northwestern University generously funded my research. I also acknowledge two marvelous institutions, the California Institute of Technology and the Huntington Library and Garden, for their support at key moments. At Caltech, Francine Tise patiently explained the mysteries of modern technology. Two gifted Northwestern students, Andrew Jarrell and Nicholas Ruge, collected valuable research materials. It was a pleasure working with all these people.

During autumn 2013, I delivered the Gay Hart Gaines Lectures at Mount Vernon. In 2014, I gave the James Marsh Lectures at the University of Vermont. I used these occasions to test my interpretation. The people who attended these events raised many excellent questions, for which I thank them. I also thank Christopher Celenza, director of the American Academy in Rome, who provided me with an opportunity to write in a splendid environment. Just when I thought I had finished the book, my editor, Alice Mayhew, pushed me to sharpen the argument and reveal more clearly the full dimensions of the president's genius. She was correct in every case, and I owe her a great debt for helping me to recount a compelling story.

Acknowledgments

Susan Breen joined George Washington and me on the full journey. Without her insights, I would have missed much of what the president was trying to tell me about the new nation.

T.H. Breen
Greensboro, Vermont
February 4, 2015

Untrodden Ground: Defining a New Political Culture

Throughout history, revolutions have usually ended badly. The course of these events is all too familiar. After success on the battlefield, a sense of solidarity born of dreams of liberation and reform gives way to disappointment and fragmentation. We do not usually think of the American Revolution in these terms. After all, our revolution did not end badly. The American people not only achieved independence, but also established a constitutional republic that has survived for more than two centuries.

We owe a lot to George Washington for this striking achievement. During his first term as president of the United States, he recognized the critical need to preserve the original goals of the Revolution. Fearful that the promise of national independence would slip away, he insisted on creating a powerful union capable of overcoming internal division. *George Washington's Journey* recounts how he devised a boldly original plan to promote a strong central government during a time of political peril.

We study Washington's journey today to recapture a sense of national purpose and unity that has gone missing from the ongoing conversation between our country's elected leaders and the American people. It is true, of course, that Washington's appeal for solidarity often fell on deaf ears. Unlike him, we know what the future held for the country after his presidency. Civil war almost destroyed the union he worked so hard to preserve. Local concerns have repeatedly trumped comprehension of the common good. Political parties have stimulated heated debate, which sometimes has led to the utter paralysis of the government. Whatever the threats to the nation have been, Washington's travels remind us, now more than ever before, of the enduring need for the American people to pull together to recover the original promise of the Revolution. For us, that is his message.

— I —

During his first days in office, Washington organized a journey that shaped how the American people perceived their relationship with the new federal government. Drawing on his immense popularity, Washington envisioned an ambitious tour of the United States as a way to transform the abstract language of the Constitution into a powerful, highly personal argument for a strong union. At a key moment in our country's history when the very survival of the new system could not be taken for granted, he took to the road to discover what was on the minds of the American people and, more, share with them his own expansive vision for republican government in this country.

By reaching out to the people where they lived and worked, Washington invited ordinary men and women to imagine themselves not simply as victorious revolutionaries or as individuals who had managed briefly to establish a loose confederation of states, but, rather, as citizens of a powerful new republic. His decision sparked a far-reaching conversation about the future of the entire country that still echoes throughout the public forum. As he explained repeatedly, the success of the new nation was in the hands of the people. All they had to do, Washington declared, was to give their full support to the union for which they had fought.

Washington's political brilliance lay in sensing the need to persuade scattered Americans, most of whom identified with the separate states, to affirm their belief in a strong federal government. It was a difficult challenge, since when he began his tour of the United States, neither Washington nor the people he encountered were quite sure what it meant to be citizens of a very large republic. They found themselves engaged in an exciting, unprecedented experiment in self-rule. As we follow Washington's coach over thousands of miles of dirt roads, we are reminded of the words of Brissot de Warville, a Frenchman who visited the United States in 1788: "The object of these travels [is] to study men who had just acquired their liberty."[1]

The tour of the new republic began early in Washington's first term as president. Between 1789 and 1791, Washington organized several separate journeys, which carried him to all the original thirteen states. Although travel by coach was extremely difficult, he covered thousands of miles and on at least two occasions was involved in potentially fatal accidents.

The first trip took him from Mount Vernon to New York City for his inauguration as president. It covered the middle states—Maryland, Delaware, Pennsylvania, and New Jersey—and while not planned specifically as a way to interact with the people or to gauge public opinion, the experience alerted him to how much the success of his presidency depended on making himself visible to ordinary Americans.

Later in 1789, Washington visited New England, then a region of the United States that, despite its celebrated Revolutionary heritage, harbored serious doubts about the power of the new federal government. He took a brief trip to Rhode Island in 1790, an action designed chiefly to solidify support in a state that had taken an embarrassingly long time to ratify the Constitution. The arduous journey to the South began in spring 1791. It lasted several months and left the daily business of government in the hands of cabinet members who were none too sure how to reach the president in case of emergency.

Washington's papers contain only terse explanations as to why he subjected himself to the hardship of travel. In a diary entry written in 1789, for example, he announced that his goal was "to acquire knowledge of the facts of the Country, the growth and Agriculture there of and the temper and disposition of the Inhabitants towards the new government."[2] This concise statement, typical of Washington's laconic correspondence, hardly communicated the broader significance of the remarkable enterprise. He wanted to obtain an accurate sense of public opinion, to free himself from the kinds of partisan, often uninformed conversations that echoed through the nation's capital. From a modern perspective, of course, we expect presidents to interact with the people wherever they happen to live.[3] Presidents are forever complaining about being trapped. They seek renewal through direct contact with the people. We should appreciate that it was Washington who initiated what we now regard as an essential element of political life.

Washington confronted an unusual political environment. For most Americans in 1789, the year he became president, the recently ratified Constitution remained essentially a statement of hope. It is doubtful that many of them had read its complex clauses. Certainly the creation of a new federal system had not directly touched their lives, and while they may have followed the contentious debates over ratification, they could not be said to have forged the emotional ties with the federal government that we might label as the effective bonds of nationalism or patriotism. Their political horizons remained intensely local, seldom in fact extending beyond the borders of their own states. By devising a practical way to bring the new government directly to the people, by performing the presidency in their own communities, Washington not only enhanced the legitimacy of the Constitution but also helped ordinary Americans comprehend that the United States was now more than the sum of its parts.

No other founding father could have taken on this task. Washington brought immense political capital to the presidency. He may have been the most charismatic person ever to hold the office. Everything about the man—his behavior, dress, and pronouncements, even his coach—became emblematic of the new constitutional order. In a profound symbolic sense, he *was* the nation. Whatever his standing as the hero of the Revolution, Washington had to discover how best to present himself persuasively to the public as the leader of a new republic.

Washington's insights into the performance of power resulted in a presidency that suited not only his own character—diffident and formal—but also the expectations of a people who had just successfully established this republic. It is important to remember that when it came to the presentation of the presidency, Washington could not control the interpretive conversation. The American people, women as well as men, had a major voice in authenticating his performance of executive leadership under the Constitution. The populist character of this conversation is important to remember, since most narratives of this period in our nation's history focus almost exclusively on a small group of familiar political and intellectual leaders—Hamilton, Madison, and Jefferson—and in this account of clashing egos, the American people are often reduced to the role of mere spectators on the creation of their own republic. In fact, they engaged fully in a process of mutual discovery about the character of the new republic. If it had not been so, if the founding years had really involved only a small group of leaders, the nation would have been more unstable than it was in fact. It was Washington's genius to engage the people in a conversation about their shared future.

At the start of his journey, the president had no assurance of success. He operated in an uncertain political environment in which every decision lacked clear precedent. No one knew the rules. Indeterminacy put a heavy burden on Washington. Even mundane acts had the potential to become precedents, binding future generations or, worse, triggering destructive faction. In January 1790, in an unusually forthright letter to Catharine Macaulay Graham, the celebrated London author of *History of England* (1763–1783), Washington confessed, "The establishment of our new Government seemed to be the last great experiment, for promoting human happiness, by creating a reasonable compact, in civil Society." With obvious trepidation, Washington accepted the responsibility. "Few," he noted, "who are not philosophical Spectators, can realize the difficult and delicate part which a man in my situation had to act." The president, who worried about the force of public opinion and strove so hard to translate the Constitution into a working national government, knew the dangers that awaited him. "In our progress toward political happiness my station is new," he told Graham, "and, if I may use the expression, I walk on *untrodden ground*."[4]

—II—

This reflective, often apprehensive Washington is not the figure with which most of us are familiar. Few historians of the Early Republic have associated him with bold innovation or daring risk. They usually depict him, especially during his first years as president, as a somewhat wooden individual—a person possessing admirable personal attributes but not one inspiring intimacy or even deep affection. He receives credit for recruiting gifted colleagues such as Hamilton and Jefferson into his cabinet and working productively with James Madison, who among other tasks was busy drafting the Bill of Rights.

In such brilliant company, Washington recedes into the background, becoming a kind of well-meaning avuncular character who did his best to keep dysfunctional cabinet members from fighting in public over complex fiscal issues. It was this genial Washington who later convinced Mason Locke Weems, otherwise known as Parson Weems, to reimagine Washington's entire life story. In his celebrated *Life of Washington* (1800), Weems, who was in fact no clergyman, tried to make his subject more exciting, more dynamic, even if that meant inventing whole-cloth tales of cutting down a cherry tree, kneeling in prayer at Valley Forge, and throwing a silver dollar across a wide river. More modern treatments of Washington distance themselves from pure fabrication, but honesty seems to make them a little grumpy, as if they wished that the real Washington had been closer to Weems's fiction than he was in fact.[5]

Any attempt to transform Washington into a polished conversationalist able to speak knowledgeably at dinner parties about music, philosophy, or literature is a nonstarter. He was no Jefferson. Nevertheless, Washington's painful awkwardness in formal social situations—dinner guests often watched him play with the silverware or drum the table with his fingers—should not diminish our appreciation of his talents or accomplishments. He was a masterful politician who could size up a potential ally or adversary within minutes.

To comprehend fully Washington's contribution to American political culture, one has to follow his feet rather than his table talk. Early in January 1790, Gouverneur Morris, a trusted friend, expressed a view of political life with which Washington was in full agreement. "As it happens somewhat unfortunately that the Men who live in the World are very different from those that dwell in the Heads of Philosophers," explained Morris, "it is not to be wondered at if the Systems taken out of Books are fit for Nothing but to be put into Books again."[6] Or, as Washington himself declared in 1797, "With me it has always been a maxim, rather to let my designs appear from my works than by my expressions."[7] This was the voice of political realism, not anti-intellectualism. To appreciate his vision for the new nation as well as his innovative strategy for reaching out to the people, we too must follow his footsteps as much as his words.

During the mid-1780s, Washington was convinced that time was running out for the United States. As if he needed instruction on how to meet the challenge, the leaders of North Carolina who had dragged their feet on ratification of the Constitution reminded Washington of how hard it was to bring the critics and the doubters around to supporting the new government. In a letter sent to Washington in May 1789, the governor and council observed, "Your Excellency will consider (however others may forget) how extremely difficult it is to unite all the People of a great Country in one common sentiment upon almost any political subject, much less a new form of Government materially different from one they have been accustomed to." They were optimistic. After all, "We sincerely believe that America is the only country in the world where such a deliberate change of Government could take place under any circumstances whatever."[8]

Washington hoped the North Carolinians were right. The preservation of a strong post-Revolutionary union would not be easy. It required constant vigilance. For him, federal unity became nearly an obsession. The Revolution for which he had fought depended on maintaining a sense of common purpose. Washington's uncompromising commitment to a strong union sometimes clouded his judgment. As he traveled the primitive roads of America, he remained blind to the corrosive effect that slavery would have on the nation. He did not want to hear about issues that threatened the union. And there is no question that his insistence on unity occasionally caused him to mistake candid criticism of government policy for disloyalty.

It was within this mental framework—one that stressed a shared sense of national purpose—that Washington organized his journeys to the people. He was prepared to sacrifice personal comfort to fulfill what he regarded as the original promise of the Revolution.

—III—

Reconstructing Washington's journeys led me to explore some of the less traveled highways of the eastern and southern states. I tried to see as best I could a lost world of the Early Republic from the perspective of a new president and the people he met on the tours. To be sure, I relied heavily on traditional sources. The president kept a diary in which he recorded the names of taverns where he spent his nights, how many miles he traveled on a certain day, or a particular community's commercial prospects. In addition, newspapers throughout the country followed his progress and often provided detailed accounts of the elaborate ceremonies that various cities such as Boston and Charleston staged in Washington's honor. For me, however, the most poignant link with Washington—getting to know the man and escaping with him from the formality of ordinary presidential affairs—owed a lot to accompanying him from place to place. I drove the modern roads that more or less followed Washington's original path.

Traveling with him was a pleasant although demanding challenge. Everywhere I went, from New Hampshire to Georgia, I encountered extraordinary change, especially in the South, where more than two centuries of war, hurricanes, and insects had radically altered the physical landscape. Much of his experience could not be recaptured. But change affected the material face of history in other ways. It appeared not only in predictable forms associated with urban growth but also in the movement of the very buildings where he stayed. In several towns, the houses Washington mentioned in his diary had been relocated two, sometimes three, times, so that what appeared at first as the house or neighborhood as he would have encountered it turned out to be the product of decisions made many decades later.[9]

Still, retracing the journeys yielded unexpected insights, even if that merely meant gaining a clearer image of a late-eighteenth-century society. Enough physical evidence has survived from his first term in office to provide the modern traveler with a palpable sense of the physical hardships that Washington endured day after day on terrible dirt roads and nights in taverns that provided dubious food and uncomfortable beds. As a man who was convinced that he did not have many more years to live—he did not die until December 1799—Washington was willing to sacrifice personal comfort in an effort to communicate to the American people his vision of the promise of a strong federal union. Whatever else one might claim, the long trips to the nation were not for the faint of heart. Even today, the road speaks to the intensity of his commitment.

For me, one moment in Washington's travels stands out. He left Georgetown, South Carolina, on May 1, 1791, heading south toward Charleston, where he had reason to anticipate an especially enthusiastic welcome. Whatever the expectations, he could not escape the fact that the road between those two cities provided little to reduce the tedium of the trip. Moreover, the sandy soil added greatly to the stress on the horses, who were pulling Washington's Great White Coach, a vehicle we will encounter several times. He went for miles not even seeing a house, let alone a proper village. As Washington noted in his diary, all he encountered were "sand & pine barrens—with very few inhabitants."[10]

Perhaps to break the monotony, Washington paid a visit to Hampton, the manor house of a huge rice plantation long associated with two of the more powerful families in the state, the Horrys and the Pinckneys. Constructed in 1730, the building was located some miles off the main road, its isolation reflecting the owners' need for a huge amount of land. Indeed, rice plantations were sites for what we might call industrial agriculture. They relied on the labor of hundreds of slaves, people who spent their days knee deep in water in fields where the plants were cultivated.[11] None of that seems to have concerned Washington as he drove up the long road leading to Hampton.

On the imposing front porch, three women greeted the president. One of them was Eliza Pinckney, who among other accomplishments had discovered a process to turn indigo into an important commercial crop for South Carolina. Next to her stood Harriott Horry, her daughter and the widow of a colonel who had fought during the Revolution. Harriott's daughter joined them. All the women wore special "sashes and bandeaux painted with the general's portrait and mottoes of welcome."

The group shared breakfast, and then, just before he set off for Charleston, Washington and Harriott Horry took a short walk through the grounds of Hampton. Perhaps to spark conversation, Harriott informed the president that she intended to cut down a large live oak tree, since in her estimation, it obstructed the view that visitors had of the house when they came up the driveway. The tree was probably then several centuries old. Washington reacted strongly, urging her to rethink the plan. According to family tradition, he explained, "Mrs. Horry, let it stay. It can do no harm where it is and I would not think of cutting it down."[12] His intervention saved the tree.

More than two centuries later, I retraced Washington's route to Hampton from the main highway. It is only a few miles. Piney woods surround the connecting country road. I saw very few houses. For a spring day, it was unseasonably warm. Emergency crews were busy dealing with scattered hot spots that testified to a recent forest fire that had destroyed much of the underbrush. The driveway to the house, now a state historic site, would probably still annoy Harriott Horry. It winds through the trees. As she warned, I was not able fully to appreciate the beauty of Hampton until after I had walked a hundred yards or so from the parking lot. But for all that, nothing had dramatically changed since the morning of May 1, 1791. The State of South Carolina has wisely not attempted to restore the building to some imagined eighteenth-century grandeur. It has stabilized the structure and done what was necessary to protect it from further deterioration. And the Washington Oak still stands in front of the porch—a survivor, beautiful, healthy, and still competing with the mansion for attention, a living link to the president's journey to discover America.

—IV—

George Washington's Journey makes no attempt to follow the president's progress in detail from town to town. Rather, the goal is to highlight broad interpretive themes that gave this long and difficult journey larger significance for the history of the United States. The president promoted a strong federal government in the name of national prosperity, military security, and territorial expansion. At every opportunity, he condemned those who aggressively defended state sovereignty. Washington called these figures demagogues, insisting that they stood in the way of national progress.

As we explore these themes, we will encounter many ordinary Americans who seldom find a voice in traditional histories of the period. The list of people Washington met includes female factory workers in New England, the spokesman for a struggling synagogue, a young girl who imagined what it would be like to have a woman as president of the United States, an inventor who constructed a strange mechanical boat that could propel itself against river currents, a young man who lost the power of speech when he first met the president, and an extraordinary slave who forced Washington to tell a lie. These men and women participated in the invention of a new political theater. They were Washington's audience. They forced him to discover how to present himself persuasively as the president of a republic in which no person could claim political power solely on the basis of inheritance or birth.

CHAPTER I

—=◦=—

The Power of Public Opinion

George Washington's departure for New England in 1789 introduces the people who accompanied him on his tours. The cast of characters included secretaries who attended to the details of travel and slaves who cared for the horses and wagons. The little cavalcade figured significantly in the creation of a new republican culture. Several months before setting out for New England, Washington had discovered firsthand the importance of public opinion, a powerful new force in the nation's political life. As he traveled to his first inauguration, he witnessed crowds of noisy, self-confident, and demanding Americans, women as well as men, many of them unable to vote, who lined the country roads and city streets. It was a profoundly moving experience for Washington. He was the product of an earlier colonial society in which the ordinary people had not enjoyed a significant role in politics. The Revolution changed all that. Washington quickly accommodated to this new, challenging political environment. He learned that by pleasing the people, he could communicate to them his own expansive vision for the country's future.

—I—

George Washington's ambitious tour of the Eastern States, as people then called New England, began with little fanfare. The prospect of rain on the morning of October 15, 1789, would have discouraged many travelers just setting out on a long journey. Washington was not such a person. The overcast skies eventually produced showers, which began falling about ten o'clock, but the weather failed to diminish the president's high spirits. He had been eagerly contemplating his departure from New York City, then the capital of the United States, for several months, and now that he had finally commenced his trip, his major concern was maintaining a tight schedule.[1]

The little procession followed the Post Road northeast toward the Connecticut line. No surviving record suggests that adoring citizens endured the rain to cheer their president, the result no doubt of the lack of public announcement that Washington was taking a significant trip. No soldiers were present, no special guards. No one mentioned that the travelers carried arms. Washington had no reason to fear the American people. He sat in an open carriage, not exactly an ideal situation for a rainy autumn day, but he did not complain. More than a year later, when he organized a much more arduous trip to the southern states, Washington insisted on traveling in a stunning new coach, rumored to be one of the most elegant vehicles in the nation, but for the present, he made do with an older carriage that he had owned since the end of the war. Four well-groomed bays pulled the vehicle.

Washington took exceptional pride in the appearance of his horses. He had a well-deserved reputation as a skilled rider. Before the Revolution, he had competed with Colonel William Byrd, a wealthy Virginia planter, for the honor of having the most impressive equipage in the colony. Contemporaries described the contest as a rivalry of "the grays against the bays." After he became president, Washington continued to monitor the condition of his animals, perhaps a little obsessively. In New York City, people referred to them specifically as the "muslin horses." Every morning at dawn, stable boys carefully brushed the horses, and when they had finished, a supervisor ran a clean muslin cloth over each horse looking for "the slightest stain." There was hell to pay if he found an imperfection. One of the stable boys went by the name of Paris. Washington had recently brought this young slave to the capital from Virginia. He is of special interest for us, because Paris and a fellow slave, Giles, assisted the president on the major trips, first to New Hampshire and later to the southern states.

Washington's favorite chargers, one of which accompanied him on the New England tour, received even more elaborate attention before public events. These were large horses of the kind that Washington had ridden during the Revolution, and many paintings from the period show the general standing next to a great white charger. According to Washington's grandson, then a small child, in the evening the president ordered the show horses "covered entirely over with a paste, of which whiting was the principal component part." The animals spent the night in this condition. It was reported that by "morning the composition had become hard, was well-rubbed in, and curried and brushed, which process gave to the coats a beautiful, flossy, and satin-like appearance." Stable hands addressed the smallest details. Hooves were blackened, teeth "picked and cleaned." Only then, as valued props in political theater, were the white chargers led out for service.[2]

The New England procession also included a baggage wagon driven by one of the six servants who traveled with Washington. The word *servant* was a euphemism. These men were actually slaves who had worked for the president at Mount Vernon. For this occasion, they wore special garments selected to impress the public. The coachmen and postilions, for example, sported blanket cloaks, new jockey caps, and fashionable boots. Like the horses, the slaves were part of the show. Their appearance reflected the taste and judgment of the president.

Behind the wagon, a slave, probably Paris, led a large charger, which Washington intended to ride as he entered communities along the way. A tall figure mounted on a spirited horse, of course, made a more powerful impression on the spectators than did a man waving from an aging carriage. At the start of the tour, Washington wore a business suit appropriate for a person of his social standing, but at some moment along the road, he elected to exchange it for a full uniform of the Continental Army. He discovered that although he described himself simply as a citizen of the new republic, the American people still regarded him as General Washington, the hero who won independence on the battlefield. And in the political theater of the new republic, what the people wanted or expected powerfully shaped the president's performance.

Riding alongside the carriage, at least for the first few miles, were several members of Washington's cabinet. Whether John Jay, Alexander Hamilton, and Henry Knox—chief justice, secretary of the treasury, and secretary of war, respectively—wanted to be out in the rain is impossible to document. They probably chatted among themselves. No doubt, they regarded a proper send-off for the president as part of their official duties.

Before setting out for New England, Washington had solicited advice from these men. He valued their opinions, and since the tour was an unprecedented undertaking, he wanted to know specifically whether they thought it wise for the president to be absent from the nation's capital for several weeks. If Congress still had been in session, he would never have proposed the trip. He took a keen interest in legislative debates. Now, however, during the recess, and with official business less pressing than usual, Washington wanted assurance from the cabinet that he was doing the right thing.

The response from these men was encouraging. James Madison could not be present for the departure, but the newly elected congressman from Virginia who had worked so closely with Washington during the Constitutional Convention informed Washington that he "saw no impropriety in my proposed trip to the Eastward."[3] Knox also gave a positive answer, as did Jay, who with astute political insight into the deep sectional differences dividing the nation warned Washington that "a similar visit would be expected by those of the Southern [states]."[4] Hamilton gave the issue careful thought. "Had conversation with Colonel

Hamilton on the propriety of my making a tour through the Eastern states during the recess of Congress to acquire knowledge of the facts of the Country," Washington noted in his diary. Hamilton concluded that he "thought it a very desirable plan and advised accordingly."[5]

An empty seat in the carriage begged explanation. John Adams, the vice president, decided not to travel with Washington on the Eastern States tour. If he had been savvier politically, he would have done so. The trip to Boston would have provided him with a much-needed opportunity to be seen publicly in the company of the most popular man in America. More important, the long hours traveling in the carriage might have sparked frank conversation between them that could have eased tensions that troubled their relationship.

Even before the first election under the Constitution took place, some of Washington's most enthusiastic supporters raised awkward questions about Adams's character. In 1788, for example, in a confidential letter to Thomas Jefferson, who was then in France, Madison explained that he regarded Adams as a potential political liability for the new administration. He hoped that the Electoral College would turn to someone with more promising credentials. "J. Adams has made himself obnoxious to many particularly in the Southern States," Madison wrote. There was more. Rumors circulated that Adams had questioned Washington's leadership during the Revolution. According to Madison, "Others recollecting his [Adams's] cabal during the war against general Washington, knowing his extravagant self-importance . . . conclude that he would not be a very cordial second to the General, and that an impatient ambition might even intrigue for a premature advancement."[6]

Although Adams did in fact win the vice presidency, he remained insensitive to political nuance. On such matters, his wife, Abigail, showed much more insight. She could hardly believe that Adams had declined the opportunity to accompany Washington. Writing from New York to a relative in Massachusetts, she observed tersely that the president "would have had Mr. Adams accept a seat in his coach, but he excused himself from motives of delicacy."[7] What counted for delicacy in this situation, she did not make clear. Adams may have been brooding over stories that he and Washington were on bad terms. It is true that unflattering tales were circulating in New England. One man in Boston demanded to know from John Quincy Adams, the vice president's son, "the truth of a Report which had been industriously spread here within this week past 'that there is so great a Coolness between the P——t & V-P——t that they do not speak to each other.'"[8] Although the two men in fact spoke regularly, Adams could never ignore a slight, real or imagined, and he probably reasoned that by traveling alone, he was acting on some high-minded principle.

Adams left New York for Boston a few days ahead of the president. Still trying to help her husband, Abigail told him on October 20, "I presume the President will overtake you on the Road [since] he set off on Thursday." You will remember, she added, what had happened in New York "the Saturday Evening when you took leave of him. On Sunday he [Washington] expressed himself anxious . . . lest he had not been sufficiently urgent with you to accompany him." Abigail counseled Adams not to let personal feelings impair his judgment. She was sure that Washington will "send you an invitation to accompany him [from Boston] to Portsmouth, which I hope you will find . . . convenient to accept."[9] For his part, Washington was probably relieved that he did not have to endure long hours in a coach with Adams.

Two other men who figure centrally in our story traveled to the eastward with Washington. Today we might describe Tobias Lear and William Jackson as special assistants to the president, but at the time they were generally known as secretaries. To be sure, Washington referred to these young bachelors who lived in his house—in New York, they occupied a cramped dormitory room on the top floor—as "family" or as "Gentlemen of the household."[10] Although Washington intended the designation "Gentlemen of the household" as a compliment, he may soon have had second thoughts about the political connotations of such a phrase. In a republic it smacked of monarchical culture, of a world of court lackeys and sycophantic placemen. However happy these men may have been working so closely with Washington—it was an honor to be asked to serve—the job was extremely demanding. They were on call all the time. Their duties included drafting routine letters for the president, carrying messages from him to members of Congress, and organizing routine household business.

Tobias Lear, Washington's long-serving secretary, never witnessed the face of battle during the Revolution. Nevertheless, soon after graduation from Harvard College in 1783, he became Washington's most trusted assistant. He owed the appointment to glowing recommendations testifying to his intelligence and diligence. Lear soon moved from Portsmouth, New Hampshire, where he had grown up, to Mount Vernon and quickly demonstrated an ability to organize household affairs not only for Washington, but also—perhaps more important—for Martha and her grandchildren. He had a good eye for numbers, and most of the personal records that have survived in his hand record the bills he paid to various merchants in Washington's name. Indeed, it is from his detailed accounts that we know that Washington purchased a stylish new cap for Paris the slave just before the New England trip.

Lear possessed the perfect temperament for a personal assistant. He had a capacity to disappear into the background as family members and political leaders made decisions. In New York, he went about his business, always competent but never intrusive, showing initiative without seeming pushy, and studiously diffident in the presence of superiors. Although one might have expected the young man to strike out on his own, he remained tied to the Washington family for the better part of his life. Lear did try his luck with business ventures during the mid-1790s, but his experiment in land speculation and in managing a canal company ended in failure. He kept returning to his patron, and in 1799 he achieved a measure of celebrity as the man who recorded Washington's last words at the moment of his death.[11] Like the other secretaries, Lear never told tales in public about what went on behind closed doors. On the morning of October 15, 1789, as the presidential party left New York City, his life still seemed full of promise. He was excited about returning to friends and family in New Hampshire.

Of all the people who traveled to New England, William Jackson remains both the most intriguing and enigmatic. He accompanied Washington on every major trip during his first term as president. He was present at Boston and Charleston, Portsmouth and Savannah, Hartford and Richmond. Few other men ever experienced such sustained access to Washington. Day after day, over thousands of miles, sharing the discomforts of the road and trying to keep up polite conversation, these two men maintained a formal relationship that seems to have been defined more by mutual respect than deep affection.

Despite years of service, Jackson never entered the inner circle of Washington's most trusted associates. It was not that the president questioned Jackson's abilities or feared indiscretion. Rather, Jackson remained an employee who carried out assigned responsibilities but was always careful not to overstep the social constraints of his position. If he had been a person of different character, Jackson might have produced a sensational book revealing aspects of Washington's life that remained hidden. But that did not happen. Long after Washington died and Jackson had become a newspaper publisher, he never offered the slightest hint that he had secret tales from the road to recount.

About Jackson's early life, little is known. Born in Cumberland, England, in 1759, he lost both parents as a teenager. Their deaths may have closed off anticipated educational opportunities. Whatever his prospects as an orphan were, he decided that they were not sufficiently promising to warrant remaining in Great Britain, and on the eve of the Revolution, he took his chances on Charleston, South Carolina. Although he lacked financial resources, he possessed considerable personal charm, which served him well in America, and as a volunteer in the Continental

Army, he quickly achieved a reputation as a brave and reliable officer. Jackson caught the eye of General Benjamin Lincoln, who during the war had earned Washington's lasting respect. Lincoln championed the young soldier's advancement. By the end of the Revolution, Jackson had risen to the rank of major, and for the rest of his life, including his years as Washington's secretary, everyone called him Major Jackson.

Not surprising for a man so eager to make his mark in America, Jackson struck some associates as perhaps a little too ambitious. He was always searching for patrons and the positions he thought they had on offer. By his early twenties, he had found ways to extend his network of powerful contacts. The list included Henry Laurens, one of South Carolina's wealthiest planters and a leading American diplomat in Europe during the Revolution. Jackson also impressed Alexander Hamilton. During the early 1780s, Hamilton had already grown impatient with the chronic inefficiencies of the Confederation Congress. The critique made a lot of sense to Jackson. His war experience had persuaded him of the need for the creation of a strong central government in the United States. His political beliefs certainly mirrored Hamilton's, and in 1783 when Lincoln appointed Jackson Assistant Secretary of War under the Confederation government, Jackson forged a lasting bond with Hamilton, who was then serving in Congress. Jackson greatly advanced his career prospects three years later by delivering an oration commemorating the anniversary of American independence. Much of the speech, later published in Philadelphia, offered little more than a standard story of great leaders accomplishing great things.

Toward the end of his performance, however, Jackson raised troublesome questions about the country's future. He doubted the ability of the Confederation to serve the financial interests of the new nation. For him, the source of the problem seemed obvious: "How far our national character shall be established on the basis of virtue—and our public credit be supported with honor—will depend upon ourselves, and can only be chargeable upon our own neglect if unattained." Although this was a truism, what he said next amounted to an appeal for a bold new start. The country desperately needed a strong central government. "With great deference," said the major, "I beg leave to offer an opinion, which suggests . . . the indispensable necessity of strengthening the confidence in our continental councils, and increasing the energy of our federal constitution, or to change the confederated system altogether, must soon become an unavoidable alternative."[12] For Hamilton, the message demonstrated that Jackson, not yet thirty years of age, had the right political views. Washington and Madison would have agreed.

Minor posts in the Confederation government apparently did not assuage Jackson's ambition. He seems to have thought that his maneuvering on the margins of real power would somehow propel him into the top group, making him if not a Madison or Hamilton, then at least a person in the new political structure to be reckoned with. But lacking special genius or, even more important, substantial inherited wealth, he never quite fulfilled his own high expectations. His frustration occasionally gave voice to complaint about not having enough money to get on in the world. In 1789 he wrote a self-serving letter to Washington that Jackson may have thought would win sympathy. "Entering into the Army, at the early age of sixteen," the major explained, "it was my lot to pass eight years, the most interesting of my life, in the service of my country—The expense, necessarily induced, to support the character of an officer nearly exhausted my patrimonial pittance, and left me no other consolation, at the close of the war, than the consciousness of having faithfully done my duty."

In this brief autobiographical account, a rare personal document in the life of this mysterious man, Jackson seemed willing to blame everyone around him for lack of professional advancement. He traced his initial failure to achieve the success he expected to his parents, who were too poor to provide the boy with the funds necessary to make a mark in his new home. And then he drew Washington's attention to his selfless commitment to American independence, which in Jackson's materialistic account of patriotism had cost him a lot more money than he had bargained for. The list of disappointments expanded to include friends who had given inadequate guidance to a young man struggling to find his calling. "Collecting the remnant of my property," Jackson continued, "I embarked in commerce, which, being neither congenial to my temper, nor favorable to my fortune, I was forced to abandon." Someone apparently should have come forward to help him avoid this waste of time. Then came the study of law on the "advice of my particular friends." Once again, after reading the law, he discovered an impediment. There was a long wait before new lawyers were allowed to practice before the supreme court of Pennsylvania, the state where he now lived, and with no inheritance, no money from commerce, and no income from the law, he turned to Washington for help.[13]

In ordinary circumstances, requests based on self-pity did not move Washington to generosity. He had no trouble rejecting appeals for support, even from members of his family. But perhaps because of Jackson's distinguished war record, his genial personality, or a good word from Lincoln or Hamilton, the major gained a sympathetic hearing. Jackson's appointment as secretary for the Constitutional Convention seemed a turning point. It was certainly an assignment that required extraordinary discretion. Day after day during a hot Philadelphia summer, he recorded one of the greatest debates in American political history. And when it was over, he never shared—at least in writing—a single secret of what had happened at the meeting in Philadelphia. He made a good impression on Washington, who chaired the convention, and he soon invited Jackson to join Lear in New York City as one of the president's secretaries.

At that moment, Jackson still possessed youthful charm. No one during Washington's first term in office openly questioned his abilities or loyalty. But Washington maintained a certain distance from Jackson. He was an associate, a colleague, but not a genuine friend, as were Lear and David Humphreys, whom we will meet later in this chapter. The major once found himself the butt of Washington's humor, not a side of Washington that many people ever witnessed, when he asked to ride one of Washington's famed chargers. The horse was hard to control, and within minutes it threw Jackson. Washington thought the incident very funny and thereafter called the animal "Jackson." There was no forgetting the embarrassment, since this particular horse accompanied Jackson and the president during a trip of several thousand miles through the southern states in 1791. Another indication of the coolness that defined the relationship was the tone of a note that Washington wrote to Jackson after he had asked late in 1791 for a letter of recommendation. To this request, Washington responded that he was willing to "declare to you [Jackson] that your deportment so far as it has come under my observation, had been regulated by principles of integrity and honor." He added that Jackson had always been a welcome member "of my family."[14]

Although polite, this was not the kind of effusive rhetoric that would open many doors. Nevertheless, even without a glowing testimonial from the president, Jackson managed to win the heart of a woman who was the daughter of a rich Philadelphia merchant. His streak of luck continued. His wife's sister had married an even richer man, William Brigham. During the mid-1790s, Jackson worked closely with Brigham in a huge, somewhat dodgy land speculation scheme in which they tried to sell heavily forested acreage in far northern Maine to Europeans who wanted good arable land for farms. Predictably, the potential buyers lost interest when they realized that Jackson was offering rocky fields and pine trees in a very cold place, and the enterprise lost a lot of money. Jackson also served as a second for Hamilton in a duel with James Monroe, an event fortunately settled at the last minute through negotiation. But in 1789, no sign of such unpleasantness had yet appeared, and as he set off for New England, Jackson still dreamed of the opportunities that awaited him.

By eleven o'clock on this first day, the rain had stopped. The presidential cavalcade had reached Kingsbridge, now part of the Bronx. The cabinet members—Hamilton, Knox, and Jay—had already turned back to the city. According to Washington's diary, the party now included "Major Jackson, Mr. Lear and myself, with Six Servants." They dined "at the house of one [Caleb] Hoyatt" and then, even though the showers returned, the riders, wagon, and carriage pushed on several miles to Rye, New York. There they found a tavern known locally as the Square House, run by Mrs. Tamar Haviland. Washington described it "a very neat and decent Inn." [15] The Post Road to New Haven lay before them. So too did the stubbornly independent states that the president hoped to forge into a powerful union.

—II—

The idea of taking a journey to the people of the new nation had matured slowly in Washington's mind. The seeds of the enterprise seem to have been planted some months before he set off for New England. Of course, the exact moment when Washington discovered that he confronted an entirely new political climate, one that required a man elected by the people to engage with them in an ongoing conversation about the character of the republican experiment, cannot be dated with precision. Most likely the realization that he was operating in an unprecedented environment occurred during the trip from Mount Vernon for his inauguration as the president of the United States. The elaborate and enthusiastic celebrations he encountered on the road certainly alerted him to a new force in American politics: public opinion. In a republican form of government, the ordinary people could not be taken for granted. The journey to the nation's capital—a trip through the middle states of Maryland, Delaware, Pennsylvania, and New Jersey—brought home to Washington the possibility of an entirely new political theater in which he, as the lead player, would communicate to an adoring audience a powerful and compelling vision for the future of the new nation.

As Washington made clear before his election as president, when he was still enjoying a much-celebrated retirement from public life, he was extremely reluctant to take on the responsibilities of high office. He certainly did not welcome administrative routine. He informed everyone who would listen that he wanted to remain in Virginia, hunting with friends, experiencing the joys of family life, and developing new, more efficient forms of agriculture. He seems to have modeled himself on the virtuous Roman soldier Cincinnatus, who defended the republic on the field of battle and then returned to the simple pleasures of the farm.[16]

But tranquil retirement was not on offer. Whatever his misgivings about once again assuming a major national office, the pressure on Washington to accept once more the challenge of securing the future of the United States proved too great for him to reject. Although modesty prevented him from saying what was obvious to everyone else, Washington was the only person capable of leading the country at that precise historical moment. He alone seemed to stand above the regional jealousies and personal rivalries that threatened to destroy the federal order before the American people had a chance to discover its worth. Assurances that he would in fact serve as the first president of the United States convinced many critics of the Constitution to ratify the document, and it was no surprise that the Electoral College selected him unanimously for the presidency, an accomplishment never duplicated.

During his final days in Virginia as a private citizen, a flood of uncertainty overcame Washington. For all the enthusiastic expressions of support he had received, he worried privately that he might not be up to the task. He faced an entirely new challenge. He was now a political leader, an elected executive, and not a military commander who could give orders to junior officers and ordinary soldiers. The American people had minds of their own. Many had difficulty accepting authority of any kind. Because of their feisty independence, they expected their representatives to champion their interests against those of other highly independent Americans. It was a process that demanded patience and tact. However much Washington subscribed to the idea that republican government derived its powers from the people, he was not noted for his patience, and the prospect of endless bickering over governance must have struck him as potentially quite tedious.

And, of course, at age fifty-seven Washington was not the man he had been in 1775 when he took charge of the Continental Army. As he contemplated the presidency, he felt the burdens of age. He was a little frailer, more aware of his own mortality. It was in this reflective mood that Washington observed just after several key states had ratified the Constitution, "Although I shall not live to see but a small portion of the happy effects, which I am confident this system will produce for my Country; yet the precious idea of its prosperity . . . will tend to sooth the mind in the inevitable hour of separation from terrestrial objects."[17]

Even if he was fortunate to maintain good health, Washington harbored no illusions about the burden he had taken on. Neither his life nor that of his immediate family would be the same after he gave up the comforts of home. As he confessed in his diary on April 16, 1789, "About ten o'clock I bade adieu to Mount Vernon, to private life, and to domestic felicity; and with a mind oppressed with more anxious and painful sensations than I have words to express, set out for New York."[18] With Henry Knox, he was even more candid. Washington described himself at that moment much like "a culprit who is going to the place of his execution, so unwilling am I, in the evening of life, nearly consumed in public cares, to quit a peaceful abode for an Ocean of difficulties."[19]

Washington believed that the American people were engaged in a political experiment whose success was by no means guaranteed. They had endured a hard decade in which the national government—the government of the Confederation—had failed to fulfill the expectations of a Revolutionary generation. The states could barely bring themselves to cooperate. Congressmen often did not bother to appear for legislative sessions. Obtaining quorums was problematic. The very notion of a viable union seemed to have gone missing even before the British accepted defeat in 1783. More distressing for people such as Washington, the states not only refused to raise desperately needed revenue, but also adopted inflationary fiscal policies rewarding debtors and discouraging interstate commerce.[20]

—III—

Washington departed from Virginia for New York City on April 16. In addition to the usual complement of servants, two old friends accompanied the president-elect on this journey. Charles Thomson, the secretary of the Continental Congress, had rushed to Mount Vernon with news that Washington had in fact been elected president of the United States. Although everyone knew that the Electoral College had selected Washington, he waited in Virginia for the official announcement. Now there was no turning back. His task as messenger completed, Thomson returned to the capital with Washington.

David Humphreys, the other person sitting in the carriage, had served with Washington during the Revolution and enjoyed a relaxed intimacy with him that very few others ever achieved. At this time, Humphreys acted as one of Washington's secretaries, much the same position that Lear held. Humphreys had served in the Continental Army, always a positive attribute in Washington's judgment, and rose steadily through the military ranks until 1780 when he received an appointment as General Washington's aide-de-camp. Humphreys also spent a lot of time writing poetry. In his home state of Connecticut, he became a member of a small group of creative writers who aspired to provide the new nation with the literature they thought it deserved. Largely forgotten today, they were then known as the Connecticut Wits. Humphreys would go on to hold a number of important elective offices in

Connecticut, and during Washington's presidency, he performed ably as an American diplomat in Europe.

Although Colonel Humphreys played no part in Washington's subsequent trips to the eastern and southern states, he is of interest from our perspective largely for what he did not do. After the Revolution, he decided to write a full-length biography of Washington. Since he and Washington had developed a deep mutual trust, Washington offered Humphreys complete access to his huge personal collection of papers at Mount Vernon. Washington had warmed up to the project slowly, but once he made his decision to cooperate, he could hardly contain his enthusiasm. "I should be pleased indeed," Washington declared in 1785, "to see you undertake this business." He praised Humphreys's ability as a writer, his distinguished war record, his knowledge of the facts, and his impartial judgment. All of these splendid attributes combined to "fit you, when joined with the vigor of life, for this task." The burden of expectation was extraordinary, the certainty of success premature. Humphreys was no historian. A manuscript copy of several early chapters of "Life of General Washington" is all that has survived.[21] For the most part, the results were highly disappointing; the vast amount of archival material had overwhelmed the colonel.

One section of the work, however, provides valuable insight into Washington's state of mind as he was wrestling with the question not only whether to accept the presidency but also how a president in a republican government should interact with the people. Humphreys was then living at Mount Vernon, and the two men apparently discussed these issues almost daily. A surviving fragment reconstructs the conversation; at least, that was Humphreys's claim. The text of the exchange may strike modern readers as a little stiff, even contrived.

The colonel countered Washington's fears, point by point, and in the process he developed a powerful argument that the success of the new government depended almost entirely on Washington's acceptance of the executive office. During one exchange, Humphreys asserted, "I must avow, that in searching for arguments to justify you in declining appointment; I have been rather led to & confirmed in an opposite opinion." Was it not the case, he observed, that "it will be found that the very existence of the government will be much endangered, if the person placed at the Head of it should not possess the entire confidence of both its friends & adversaries." Popularity, of course, was not Washington's problem. "From all the treatment you have ever experienced from the people of this Continent you have a right to believe, that they entertain a good opinion of your abilities."

Humphreys urged Washington to stop focusing on negative possibilities. "You ought, at sometimes, Sir," stated the colonel, "to look upon the bright side of the picture; and not always to be pondering the objects you find on the Reverse. Nothing but clear common sense & good intentions, in our circumstances, will be necessary for conducting the affairs of the Commonwealth." It is hard to imagine anyone else addressing Washington so candidly and forcefully. But if Humphreys is to be believed, he softened Washington's resistance, and the fragment ends the account of the conversation with Washington grumbling, "If my appointment & acceptance be inevitable, I fear I must bid adieu to happiness, for I see nothing but clouds & darkness before me: and I call God to witness that the day which shall carry me again into public life, will be a more distressing one than any I have ever yet known."[22]

The trip north to New York from Mount Vernon should have allayed Washington's worst fears. The event was without precedent in American political experience. Spontaneous celebrations in town after town seem to have taken Washington by surprise. He may have anticipated a quiet journey. No doubt, he was a little naive to think that he could discourage the people from expressing their affection for the hero of the Revolution and the leader of the new constitutional government. The crowds numbered in the thousands, and while members of the local elite in some cities such as Baltimore and Philadelphia offered Washington official greetings, it was the ordinary men and women, many of whom could not vote, who made the deepest impression on the man who did not yet quite know what it meant to be the president of the United States.

Washington learned an important lesson on the way to his first inauguration. The political nation that he encountered contained distinct, though complementary, groups. Local leaders spoke for the people of their communities. They organized dinners in his honor; they drafted welcoming speeches; they called out the militia units that escorted Washington from place to place. But the ordinary people also participated, coming forward in huge numbers, representing what in Great Britain at the time was known as "politics out of doors." In the new republican government, both groups possessed real power, and the inability to vote—a condition that would seem to have deprived all women and many men without property of a political voice—did not in fact silence the people. The crowds, the fireworks, the special songs written for the occasion, the stunning illuminations: all these provided testimony to the fact that the people were telling Washington how he fit into their own story about the Revolution and republican government in the United States.

Witnessing from his carriage the repeated enthusiastic expressions of popular support, Washington may have sensed how much the character of political life had changed since the Revolution. His success as president would depend on both groups—local elites and ordinary people—and although it is tempting to interpret this journey as a kind of rehearsal for the later trips to New England and the South, there was a major difference. During the initial trip to New York City, Washington remained largely passive, accepting and praising the receptions along the road. But after he had become president, his journeys acquired more the character of a conversation. He had an appeal for a strong federal union to carry to the people; they had opinions about their own aspirations for the country to share with him.

Washington interpreted the enthusiastic receptions on the road as

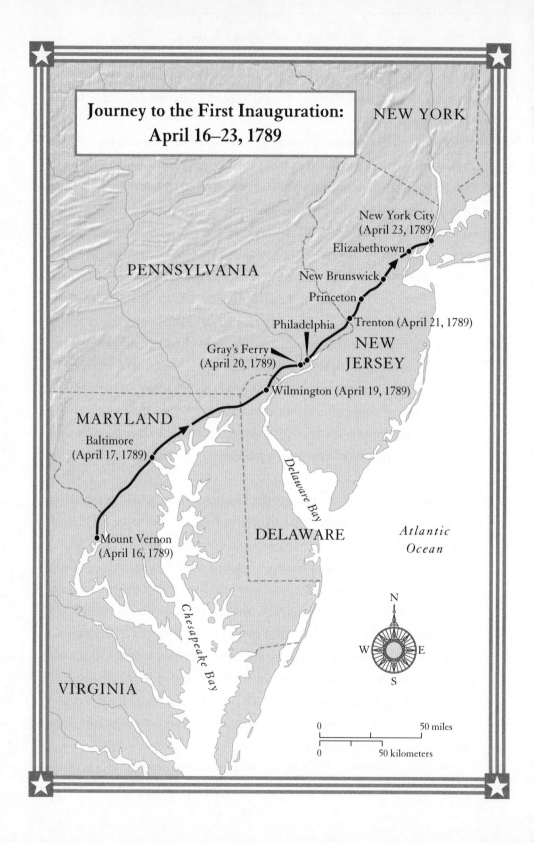

**Journey to the First Inauguration:
April 16–23, 1789**

NEW YORK

PENNSYLVANIA

New York City
(April 23, 1789)

Elizabethtown

New Brunswick

Princeton

Philadelphia

Trenton (April 21, 1789)

Gray's Ferry
(April 20, 1789)

NEW
JERSEY

Wilmington (April 19, 1789)

MARYLAND

Baltimore
(April 17, 1789)

Delaware Bay

DELAWARE

Atlantic
Ocean

Mount Vernon
(April 16, 1789)

Chesapeake Bay

VIRGINIA

N

W   E

S

0   50 miles

0   50 kilometers

an endorsement for the new federal government, a point of considerable importance. It is easy to overlook how much ordinary people—crowds of noisy supporters—reaffirmed Washington's faith in the republican experiment. Their cheers were as significant at this moment, as were the formal exchanges with the wealthy and well born who held local offices. No doubt, many Americans had strongly opposed ratification of the Constitution, but those people either stayed at home or separated their feelings for the president from their criticism of the national government. In Baltimore, for example, the members of a committee drew up a welcoming address that could not have been more to Washington's liking. The group proclaimed that it was celebrating a new political dawn for the United States. "We behold a new era springing out of our independence," the committee assured Washington, "and a field displayed where your talents for governing will not be obscured by the splendor of the greatest military exploits." The American people stood on the cutting edge of history. The representatives of Baltimore announced, "We behold, too, an extraordinary thing in the annals of mankind; a free and enlightened people, choosing, by a free election, without one dissenting voice, the late Commander-in-Chief of their armies, to watch over and guard their civil rights and privileges."

Caught up in the committee's buoyant vision, Washington matched its optimism. "It appears to me," the president-elect responded, "that little more than common sense and common honesty in the transactions of the community at large, would be necessary to make us a great and a happy nation." The Constitution was not the end of the national story. There was still a lot of work to be done in order to turn a constitutional blueprint for federal government into a palpable reality. "If the general government, lately adopted, shall be arranged and administered in such a manner as to acquire the full confidence of the American people, I sincerely believe they will have greater advantages from their natural, moral and political circumstances, for public felicity, than any other people ever possessed." [23] Of course, Washington's comment contained a sobering qualification, for only *if* the government satisfied the people would the people achieve the happiness that was within their grasp.

What happened next revealed how Washington almost intuitively sensed how to transform a simple, seemingly artless gesture into an expression of general principle—in this case, of humility and equality. Soon after his carriage had crossed into Pennsylvania, a large group of local militiamen greeted his party. The officers were distinguished gentlemen, many of them veterans of the Revolution. It was raining, and Washington felt awkward sitting in a coach, presumably protected from the moisture, while the troops escorting him to Philadelphia were clearly getting very wet. He insisted on riding with them in the open air. But there was a difficulty: he had not brought a special show horse from Mount Vernon, much less an impressive charger. The local officers quickly solved the problem, lending Washington a large white horse, a welcome move; once he was properly mounted, the people lining the road had a better, unobstructed view of the president.

Washington ordered the carriage to the rear of the parade and in the pouring rain took his place at the head of the assembly. The Philadelphia newspapers praised his thoughtfulness. In fact, this spontaneous act of generosity seemed to reflect the essence of republican government. The leader's humility at this moment justified the sacrifices of the war. One commentator explained, "How different is power when derived from its only just source, viz. THE PEOPLE, from that which is derived from conquest, or hereditary succession! The first magistrates of the nations of Europe assume the title of Gods, and treat their subjects like an inferior race of animals. Our beloved Magistrate delights to show, upon all occasions, that he is a man—and instead of assuming the pomp of master, acts as if he considered himself the father—the friend—and the servant of the People."[24]

Washington, of course, did not aspire to divinity. There were some Americans, however, who insisted on projecting the spirit of God onto the new president. One newspaper account of the horse story, for example, contained a curious aside—almost a footnote—for which it offered no explanation. The sudden appearance of the white horse apparently struck the editor as providential. It was certainly a sign. After observing that Washington now traveled "on a very elegant white Horse," the paper added from Revelation, chapter 6, verse 2: "And behold a white horse; and he that sat upon him had a bow, and a crown was given unto him, and he went forth conquering, and to conquer."[25] If the people wanted to invest Washington's progress with spiritual meaning, they were free to do so, but it is doubtful that Washington mistook the applause of ordinary American people that rainy day for the hosannas of the multitude.

The parade had not gone far when it encountered a scene that would have taxed the interpretive skills of a trained diviner. Washington's path led through a jumble of symbols thrown together in a great hurry by one of the country's most highly regarded artists, Charles Willson Peale. Washington trusted Peale, who had served in the army during the Revolution and some years earlier had painted Washington's portrait. The road crossed the Schuylkill near Philadelphia at Gray's Ferry Bridge, a structure owned by the brothers Gray. They commissioned "the ingenious Mr. Peale" to decorate the bridge in a manner appropriate for the occasion. The results certainly impressed people who came to witness the event. One hyperbolic viewer enthused that Peale accomplished something that "even the pencil of Raphael could not delineate." The American artist seems to have harvested all the available laurel plants in the neighborhood. A newspaper reported that the profusion of laurel "seemed to challenge even Nature herself for simplicity, ease and elegance." The ornamentation struck spectators as entirely appropriate in view of Washington's heroic past. They knew that in classical cultures such as Rome, garlands of laurel honored military victors.

After that, the symbolic agenda became more complex. On each of the four corners of the bridge, Peale placed a flag on which was emblazoned a painted image or relevant motto. The pennants addressed a common theme, proclaiming the importance of federal unity in promoting general economic prosperity. One flag depicted a "rising sun, more than half above the horizon." It carried a motto, "The Rising Empire." Another announced "The New Era." On a third corner, Peale placed on "a very high pole, the cap of liberty," and underneath this symbol of radical republicanism—one that appeared in the iconography of almost every late-eighteenth-century revolution—he added a rattlesnake and the words "Don't Tread on Me." Peale's fourth banner urged, "May Commerce Flourish." In addition, he included an American flag, and one for each of the eleven states that had already ratified the Constitution. North Carolina and Rhode Island had not yet joined the union.

Peale was not done. Over the bridge he "erected magnificent arches . . . emblematical of the ancient triumphal arches used by the Romans." He designed the structure so that Washington would have to ride under it to reach the other side of the river. It too was adorned with laurel. Just as Washington reached the midpoint of the span and was under an arch, out stepped a lovely young girl dressed entirely in white who just happened to be Peale's daughter, Angelica. Washington reined in his horse to greet her. That polite act triggered a bizarre series of events. A newspaper recounted, "As our beloved WASHINGTON passed the bridge, a lad, beautifully ornamented with sprigs of laurel, assisted by certain machinery, let drop, above the Hero's head, unperceived by him a civic crown of laurel." A very startled Washington seems to have brushed the crown aside, no doubt embarrassed that anyone who had just been elected head of a republic would accept a crown of any sort.[26]

The celebrations continued as Washington rode toward Philadelphia and then into New Jersey. Estimates of the size of the crowd along the way must be taken with grains of salt. One writer insisted that at least twenty thousand people "lined every fence, field and avenue between the bridge and the city." Even allowing for exaggeration, the turnout had no recent precedent in American history. The only person who may have drawn such large numbers was the Reverend George Whitefield, the famed evangelist who at midcentury attracted thousands of colonists to learn of the possibility of a new birth in Jesus. In Washington's case, commentators interpreted the immense crowds as evidence of popular support for a new, more inclusive political culture. After all, if only the members of the social elite had appeared to greet Washington, the crowd would not have reached more than several hundred. Although many Americans who rushed to view the president had no knowledge of the great crowds that came out to cheer George III, they assumed that their rejection of monarchy had invited fuller, more visible participation in the new political culture. "In short," wrote one person who had been at Gray's Ferry Bridge, "all classes and descriptions of citizens discovered (and they felt what they had discovered) the most undisguised attachment and unbounded zeal for their dear Chief, and I may add, under God, the Savior of their Country. —Not all the pomp of majesty, not even Imperial dignity itself, surrounded with its usual splendor and magnificence, could equal this interesting scene."[27]

At this early stage of Washington's journeys to the nation, he had not worked out how he wanted to present himself to the American people. The men and women along the road, however, were well on the way to inventing a new political culture that celebrated their independence from imperial rule as well as their commitment to a republican experiment. Washington reflected on the meaning of their behavior. The trip to New York was a key element in the process of learning how to present himself as president. What he discovered at Gray's Ferry Bridge was that ordinary men and women had already placed him in a political narrative of their own making. He was merely a prop in Peale's staging of the reception of a Revolutionary War hero. The laurel crown proclaiming Washington the American Caesar no doubt made him uncomfortable, but at that moment, it would have been extremely awkward for him to reject the dramatization on the grounds that it was insufficiently republican or overly militaristic.

A much more emotional welcome awaited Washington in Trenton, the community where twelve years earlier he had won a battle that saved his military career and perhaps even the Revolution itself. He remembered in vivid detail everything that had happened on January 2, 1777, when his Continental troops surprised British defenders who thought that no serious fighting would occur during the hard winter months. The victory had kept the hope of independence alive. The bridge over Assunpink Creek had been a focal point in the action. Riding an impressive horse and coming down a long hill, Washington suddenly saw in the distance a lot of activity on the bridge. One bizarre report claimed that at that moment, he encountered "a scene to which no description can do justice."

A group of extraordinary women had taken charge of the official greeting. Adopting a Roman theme, they constructed a large "triumphal arch," under which Washington had to pass. Giving Rhode Island and North Carolina the benefit of the doubt, they erected thirteen columns, which supported the laurel and evergreen arch. The structure reached twenty feet in height. Fortunately, on this occasion no mechanical device dropped a crown on Washington.

The focus of the entire reception at Trenton was the banners the women had placed on the arch. One carried a message made of "gilt" letters, "The Defender of the Mothers will also Defend the Daughters." The organizers had painted on the arch the dates of the Revolutionary battle. Even more poignant was the large artificial sunflower, which as a newspaper explained, "Always pointing to the sun, [it] was designed to express this sentiment or motto—'To you alone'—as emblematic of the affections and hopes of the people being directed by him, in the united suffrage of the millions of America." What brought Washington nearly to tears, however, was the group of little girls dressed in white, spreading flower petals in his path, and singing:

Welcome, mighty Chief! once more
Welcome to this grateful shore!
Now no mercenary foe
Aims again the fatal blow —
Aims at thee the fatal blow.[28]

One spectator offered special praise to "the ladies." After all, it was they "who formed and executed this design [and] have displayed a degree of taste, elegance and patriotism." [29] The word *patriotism* strikes an incongruous note. This attribute had long been associated with men like Cincinnatus who demonstrated their love of country by defending it with force of arms against all enemies. But in Trenton, at least for one remarkable day, the women of America proclaimed themselves patriots too.

—IV—

Washington's grand entry into New York City occurred on April 24. Between Trenton and Elizabeth Town, New Jersey, many communities had tried in their own separate ways to honor the first president, but the crossing of the Hudson River and the procession up from the wharves of New York to the house on Cherry Street where Washington would live sparked a public outpouring of support that he could not possibly have anticipated when he left Mount Vernon. The fullest account of this moment comes from Elias Boudinot, a congressman from New Jersey. In a touching letter to his wife, Boudinot captured the excitement surrounding Washington's arrival. Everywhere on the river, the president's party encountered a flotilla of vessels, some large, some small, and all brightly decorated. As Washington's barge neared the New York shore, "our train increased & the Huzzing and Shouts of Joy seemed to add Life to this lively Scene." Even the porpoises swimming nearby sensed the historical significance of the day. They "played amongst us, as if they had risen up to know what was the Cause of this Joy." Boudinot had never before encountered crowds of such size. There were thousands of "men, women & children." But then he immediately corrected himself. The number "may I venture to say, Tens of Thousands." He described the people as "Heads standing as thick as Ears of corn before the Harvest."

After Washington landed in the city, he joined a long procession of local dignitaries, including New York's governor, George Clinton. The group snaked its way from the harbor to Washington's house, a distance of only half a mile. The progress was slow. People pressed in on the president from all sides. Boudinot seemed a little unnerved by the confusion on the street. "It was with difficulty a Passage could be made by the Troops thro the pressing Crowds, who seemed to be incapable of being Satisfied by Gazing at this Man of the People," he told his wife. Faces of spectators filled every window. Although he did not speak with any of the women staring down at the president, Boudinot was certain that "innumerable Companies of Ladies" were vying "with each other to show their Joy on the Occasion."[30]

The cheering had a curious effect on Washington: he became increasingly apprehensive. He found that he could not fully share in either the enthusiasm of the people or the joy of the porpoises. To be sure, his entrance into the city had been a grand moment. The excitement of the masses, however, revived much of the uneasiness that Washington had originally felt when he left Virginia. Only now, after witnessing elaborate receptions in places such as Gray's Ferry Bridge and Trenton, the pressures on him to succeed seemed even greater.

His first journey to the new nation dramatically revealed that ordinary Americans—pushy, loud, excited, joyful, and demanding—could not be ignored. Indeed, the men, women, and children who lined the road to New York City spoke for a new open, participatory political culture. Reflecting on the day's events in a fragment of a diary, which no longer survives, Washington confessed, "The display of boats . . . the decorations of the ships, the roar of the cannon, and the loud acclamations of the people . . . filled my mind with sensations as painful . . . as they are pleasing." [31] The president-elect went to bed that night aware that if during the coming months in office he failed to perform the presidency as they expected, their joy could turn in an instant to criticism.

It is hard for us today to understand how a man who had demonstrated extraordinary leadership over a very long period could have experienced such anxiety about his ability to meet the challenge of the presidency. He certainly was not worried about enhancing his power. Indeed, political power had almost no appeal for Washington. If he had wanted to become the head of the new republic—a kind of American Oliver Cromwell—he could have easily done so, translating immense personal popularity into permanent national office. He repeatedly rejected that path.

Washington faced in 1789—on the eve of his inauguration—a situation that might best be compared with that which confronted modern revolutionary leaders such as Nelson Mandela or Mahatma Gandhi, revered figures who realized that postindependence rivalries could destroy the hopes of those who had sacrificed so much to liberate their countries from imperial rule. Like them, Washington championed a strong union. Localism and fragmentation threatened the Revolutionary heritage. The challenge for Washington was inventing a presidency that would encourage all the people he encountered on the roads of the new nation to expand their political horizons and share in the promise of a powerful new federal government.

CHAPTER II

Inventing a New Theater of Politics

From the perspective of more than two centuries, the widespread anxiety about how the president of the United States should present himself to the American people, indeed, to the entire world, may seem a little silly. Such a reaction would be a mistake. These issues acquired huge significance during George Washington's first term in office. Americans wondered how a president should dress. Should he hold dinner parties? Who would be invited? Should he bow to guests? Should the public have unlimited access to the president? And most important, what would be the appropriate title for the person elected to such a high office? At the time, commentators worried that if the president did not have a weighty title, European dignitaries would never give the struggling new nation the respect it deserved.

Washington was not a passive spectator to these debates. He brought impressively original insights to how best to create a republican theater of politics. On his own, he concluded that his audience must include the American people. If he failed to reach out to them—if he refused to make himself visible in the places where they lived—the new federal government could not possibly gain their full support. And therein lay an irony: it was a diffident, aging, extremely wealthy planter who decided to take the presidency to a national stage.

—I—

Throughout his long life, Washington often turned to the theater for entertainment and relaxation. Whenever the opportunity presented itself, he purchased blocks of tickets and invited friends to accompany him to productions, whether in Williamsburg or New York City. His tastes were eclectic. He thought every American—especially the officers of the Continental Army—should see Joseph Addison's *Cato*, a heroic account of resistance to tyranny. He also enjoyed Richard Sheridan's *The School for Scandal*, a spicy comedy involving sex and duplicity.

During his first months as president of the United States, Washington regularly attended performances, some of them no more than ephemeral productions. The quality of the plays, however, does not seem to have diminished his enthusiasm. Martha Washington's grandson remembered the president going to the theater "some five or six times in a season."[1] The actual number of outings was probably much higher. In his diary for November 24, 1789, for example, Washington noted that he "Went to the Play in the Evening. Sent Tickets to [several] Ladies and Gentlemen. & invited them to Seats in my Box." They sat through an obscure comedy entitled *The Toy; or a Trip to Hampton Court*. A few days later, he again recorded an evening at the theater. Washington "presented Tickets" to a group, which included the chief justice, the secretary of war, and the celebrated German drill instructor Major General Friedrich Wilhelm von Steuben. They were treated to a performance of *Cymon and Sylvia*, described in the newspapers simply as an "Opera or Dramatic Romance."[2]

Washington's enthusiasm for the theater had deep personal roots. Throughout his life, he showed an almost excessive concern for maintaining appearances. Perhaps his insistence that things look right—that he was always an actor onstage—reflected anxiety about his own modest social origins and lack of formal education. Whatever the causes, Washington struggled to make a proper impression on everyone he encountered. As a young man, he diligently copied the 110 *Rules of Civility and Decent Behavior in Company and Conversation*, a bizarre compendium of advice for proper etiquette in polite society. The rules included insights such as, "When in Company, put not your Hands to any Part of the Body, not usually Discovered" and "Cleanse not your teeth with the table cloth napkin, fork, or knife; but if others do it, let it be done without a peep to them."[3]

However ludicrous some of these rules of social interaction sound today, Washington seems to have taken the spirit of these recommendations to heart. He not only demanded a high standard of appearance from himself, but also from the people and objects that he felt reflected on his own judgment and character. He expected the soldiers he commanded during the American Revolution to be as well outfitted and professional as those in the British Army. Mount Vernon had to conform to his own sense of how the estate of a successful Virginia planter should appear. The same expectations applied to his horses and slaves, since they too mirrored his own exacting code of civility.[4]

Washington's fixation with appearances made him highly sensitive to the expectations of the different audiences that he encountered throughout his long career. In his attempt to craft the desired impression, he literally had to interpret the reactions of friends and strangers. Every social interaction raised new challenges concerning dress and manners, conversation and gesture. After all, if contemporaries did not find his performances as a general or as a planter persuasive—indeed, if he failed to understand the demands of the social script—then his attention to getting things right made no difference. For Washington, the task was never easy. Etiquette required him to respond quickly to those men and women in a position to judge whether he properly understood how a general or president was supposed to act.

The danger in managing these exchanges was excess. If Washington tried too hard to succeed in making the correct impression and thereby exposed the performance as merely a cover for ambition or ignorance, he was sure to come up short in dealings with people who knew the rules. Success required moderation, balance, and self-control. Long before he became president, Washington had worked hard to acquire these attributes. His reluctance to let down his guard in social situations, his formality even in the company of officers of the Continental Army and members of his own cabinet, reflected a fear that intimacy might somehow compromise the credibility of the performance.

Washington's concern for appearances complemented his assumption that the world was a stage and he an actor in the play. This notion was, of course, not original. In *As You Like It*, William Shakespeare drew on a long tradition when a character declares, "All the world's a stage, and all the men and women merely players." For Washington, the declaration made good sense. He conceived of life itself as a drama. His career as planter, general, and president involved different, though equally demanding, roles. It is not surprising, therefore, to discover that his correspondence frequently referred to "the stage of human action." In 1788, for example, Washington wrote to an English friend describing the public excitement surrounding the drafting of the Constitution in terms of a great and unprecedented theatrical production. "You will permit me to say," Washington wrote, "that a greater Drama is now acting on this Theater [the United States] than has heretofore been brought on the American Stage, or any other in the World." Here, on this extraordinary political stage, he witnessed the "astonishing Spectacle of a whole People deliberating calmly on what form of government will be most conducive to their happiness."[5] As Washington agonized over whether he should come out of retirement to accept the presidency in 1789, he spoke of the difficulties of coming "again on the Stage of public affairs."[6] He reluctantly accepted the burdens of the role of president, informing a group of well-wishers in Baltimore, "I have reconciled myself to the sacrifice of my fondest wishes, so far as to enter again upon the stage of Public life."[7]

No other public stage demanded more of Washington than did the presidency of the United States. As general of the Continental Army, he at least had a sense of how a general was supposed to act. History provided models of military leadership, some good, some bad, and when he assumed command of the American troops in 1775, he had an informed knowledge of how an officer should behave. But neither the chroniclers of ancient Rome nor the scholars who had written accounts of small Renaissance republics offered Washington much useful guidance in playing the part of president. Although he had no intention of imitating the court rituals of George III, he knew that many of his countrymen would inevitably view him as an elected king. It was not that they were nostalgic for the old aristocratic regime.[8] Rather, quite predictably, they drew on their experiences as colonial subjects of the British Crown.

The United States was a republic, however, not a monarchy. As the central figure in the new government, Washington was intensely aware that he represented the American people. How exactly the theoretical foundations of representative government translated into daily practice had to be worked out through trial and error. The challenge raised hard questions. How, for example, could he preserve the dignity of high elective office without thereby distancing himself too much from the very citizens who had chosen him president? How could he deny them access to his home or office without thereby seeming unsociable, even aristocratic, in his contempt for the people? What was he to wear? What sort of coach should he drive? Every detail counted.

In New York City, he found himself a character in a complex political drama with unclear stage directions. As Washington observed soon after his arrival in the capital, "Many things which appear of little importance in themselves and at the beginning, may have great and durable consequences from their having been established at the commencement of a new general Government."[9] He expressed similar sentiments to Madison. "As the first of everything in *our situation* will serve to establish a precedent," explained Washington, "it is devoutly wished on my part that these precedents may be fixed on true principles."[10] However worthy the goal, the challenge of devising a persuasive performance was made all the harder since Washington was in fact extremely reserved.

—II—

A marvelous analysis of Washington's theatrical abilities has survived from these early years. Although the two men were never close, John Adams praised Washington for successfully crafting the role of president. Adams observed in a letter sent in 1811 to Dr. Benjamin Rush, a gifted scientist and signer of the Declaration of Independence, that Washington had in fact mastered "the theatrical exhibitions of politics." Because of this extraordinary skill, Adams added, "we may say of him [Washington], if he was not the greatest President, he was the best actor of presidency we have ever had." He described Washington's political performances as "dramatical exhibitions."[11] Although the whole topic brought out Adams's truculence, he set out in this correspondence to examine in detail just how Washington had managed to play the part of president of the United States so convincingly. What exactly, Adams asked, were the secrets of his performance that had so spectacularly escaped Adams during his own ill-scripted presidency?

Reflecting on Washington's ability to play the part of president so convincingly, Adams listed ten elements that contributed to the man's amazing success. Adams claimed that Washington owed everything to a bundle of essential "talents." He did not use the word as most people would today. For example, he insisted that Washington's "handsome face" was a talent. Anticipating that Rush might challenge his choice of words, Adams insisted: "An handsome face. That this is a talent, I can prove by the authority of a thousand instances in all ages: and among the rest Madame du Barry, who said 'Le veritable royalty est la beauté.'"

Citing du Barry as an authority on political beauty was a stretch, as Adams surely must have known. The mistress of Louis XV, she had been one of the more celebrated courtesans of ancien regime France. In 1792 radical leaders of the Revolution accused her of crimes against the state, and during the Terror, she fell victim to the guillotine.

Adams also thought Washington's height had impressed the people. This too was a talent, for Washington was "like the Hebrew sovereign chosen because he was taller by the head than the other Jews." The inventory of talents included additional physical attributes—"An elegant form" and "graceful" movements—none of which the short, portly Adams enjoyed.

The grumpy Adams was just warming to the task. He argued that ordinary people had honored Washington not only because he was handsome, but also because he was extremely rich. At this point in his correspondence with Rush, Adams allowed jealousy to cloud better judgment. He connected Washington's success to "a large, imposing fortune consisting of a great landed estate left him by his father and brother, besides a large jointure with his lady, and the guardianship of the heirs of the great Custis estate, and in addition to all this, immense tracts of land of his own acquisition." Even in a republican society that proclaimed equality, there was no denying that in political affairs, the public regarded a "great fortune" as a sign of special ability and deep insight, a cynical piece of wisdom that seems as widely held today as it was during the 1790s. Adams appeared to be suggesting that Washington had a talent for choosing the right parents and a very rich wife.

More charitably, Adams conceded that even though Washington had amassed fabulous wealth, he had presented himself on the presidential stage as "disinterested." By that, Adams appears to have awarded Washington high marks for not playing favorites. He had a reputation for evenhandedness. Even on this point, the sullen Adams could not leave well enough alone. He immediately reminded Rush: "They gave him [Washington] more credit for disinterestedness than he deserved."

But perhaps Washington's most alarming talent—number six on Adams's list—was that he came from Virginia. For a New Englander, this identity was an almost unpardonable offense. It was "equivalent to five talents." Indeed, as Adams had learned from his edgy dealings with Washington, Jefferson, and Madison, "Virginian geese are all Swans." Although, as a New Englander, Adams found people from New York and Philadelphia unsavory, he concluded that they seemed "meek and modest" in comparison with the self-inflated Virginians.

Adams was not done. Washington, he asserted, had always enjoyed favorable publicity. Ordinary people were forever spreading stories about his heroic achievements. A positive reputation always went before him. He floated above normal criticism. And then, as he concluded his assessment of the talents, the loquacious Adams marveled that Washington "possessed the gift of silence. This I esteem as one of the most precious talents." And finally, Washington "had great self-command," and whenever he lost his temper, those around him concealed "his weakness from the world."[12] It was all too much for poor Adams to bear.

The curious thing about Adams's quirky inventory of theatrical talents is that it focused largely on external qualities of leadership such as good looks and inherited wealth. Adams argued that since Washington had been "Self-taught," he had been forced to develop superficial aspects of character. Any diligent person could acquire them, that is, if the person was lucky enough to have been born tall and rich in Virginia. The caustic appraisal, of course, revealed more about Adams's awareness of his own inadequacies than it did about the impressive accomplishments of the first president. Washington achieved something beyond the reach of Adams's largely intellectual abilities. As leader of the new nation, he figured out how to translate a concern for appearances and a love of the theater into a persuasive presentation of republican power. That was exactly what a country that had so recently threatened to dissolve into separate, hostile parts needed in 1789.

—III—

Washington was not alone in viewing the presidency as a role that had to be carefully crafted. The problem for him was that other formidable figures in the government who did not fully understand the issues at stake were eager to direct the performance. Even before Washington took the oath as president of the United States on April 30, Adams sparked a bizarre controversy over the staging of republican power that embarrassed both men.

Soon after arriving in New York City, Adams sounded the alarm. He announced in the Senate that the newly elected Congress faced a major crisis. The members of that body were surprised that he addressed them at all. As vice president, Adams served as the president of the Senate, and while the responsibilities of the position were still ill defined, they expected him primarily to maintain order and keep his opinions to himself.

Alas, Adams lacked Washington's talent of silence. He could not resist telling the senators exactly how he thought they should go about doing business. Only a week before Washington's inauguration, Adams pointed out that no one in the new government knew exactly how to address the president. From his perspective, this created a real crisis. How would the elected representatives welcome Washington when he appeared before Congress? Did they not realize the importance of titles in affirming Washington's dignity? After all, as Adams nervously reminded his colleagues, if they made a mistake—if they adopted an unworthy title—European rulers who knew the rules of political etiquette would surely ridicule the United States. Several senators suspected that the vice president had gone off the deep end. But most of them, at least during the early phase of the debate, understood that Adams had raised a serious issue about how they should present the president of the United States to the people.

Historians have generally treated Adams's campaign for titles as a kind of lighthearted Gilbert and Sullivan moment in American political history. One can imagine a chorus from the *Mikado* singing, "Behold his Elected Majesty, A personage of noble rank and title." But however misguided Adams's efforts may have seemed, we should appreciate that he did in fact offer a coherent theoretical justification for his insistence on giving the nation's central actor a proper title, one that Washington did not happen to share. For the subjects of eighteenth-century monarchies, however, Adams's position would have seemed unexceptional. Like them, the Vice President believed "in the efficacy of pageantry."[13] Labels mattered in political theater. They were even more important than character in commanding popular respect.

Adams argued—often for hours on end in the Senate—that seeking special social distinction was a basic element of human nature. Given that, it made sense to view high-sounding titles as a means to channel normal ambition in a positive direction. Providing incentives in the competition for recognition was just what the United States required to get off to a proper start. How else, Adams asked, could the new government hope to recruit the best and the brightest if it did not promise to reward them with external emblems of distinction? More to the point, awarding titles would ensure social stability in a constitutional republic, since the very individuals who might otherwise become dangerous critics of the new government would instead devote their energies to striving for titles.

About such matters, Adams was tone deaf. It does not seem to have occurred to him that his aggressive campaign for titles in a post-Revolutionary society smacked of monarchy and all the aristocratic orders that defined such regimes. He insisted repeatedly that he had no interest in restoring royalty to the United States. That was the truth. However, many colleagues in the Senate, not to mention the American people who followed the title debate in the newspapers, worried that Adams had lost his Revolutionary sense of equality. His problems were of his own making. In his writings, especially in *Discourses on Davila* published in 1790–1791, Adams insisted that despite the democratic intentions of the political society, a sort of natural aristocracy would inevitably emerge, a possibility that was apparently more objectionable at the dawn of the new constitutional order than it is today. According to Adams, political leadership should be the product not of inheritance but of "Education, Wealth, Strength, Beauty, Stature, Birth, Marriage, graceful Attributes and Motions, Gait, Air, Complexion, Physiognomy."[14]

On April 23 the Senate appointed a committee to resolve the controversy. Adams took the opportunity to make another passionate appeal for an exalted title for Washington, which the vice president insisted would guarantee public respect. In the staging of republican power, he may have also had in mind the grand title for himself as vice president. "A royal, or at least princely title," he lectured, "will be found indispensably necessary to maintain the reputation, authority, and dignity of the president."[15] Adams picked up several allies. Richard Henry Lee, a senator from Virginia, defended impressive artificial titles, since "a dignified Title would add greatly to the weight and authority of the Government both at home and abroad." Lee registered no objections with the thrust of Adams's plan because, as everyone knew, "all the world" used titles.[16] Although Adams was reluctant to push his own personal recommendation too aggressively in public, he apparently told friends privately that he favored "Majesty," as in "His Majesty George Washington."[17]

Adams met his match in the person of William Maclay, an outspoken senator from Pennsylvania who quite rightly saw the American Revolution as a rejection of aristocratic privilege. Although Adams dismissed the man as a second-rate politician, Maclay was no country bumpkin. Tench Coxe, a leading political figure from Pennsylvania, offered a more balanced appraisal. He reported, "Mr. Maclay, our Agricultural Senator is a decided federalist, of a neat clear landed property, with a law Education, a very straight head, of much more reading than the country Gentlemen in the middle states usually are, a man of fair character and great assiduity in Business."[18] Maclay came to the Senate a strong supporter of the Constitution, and he assured friends back home that he was fully prepared to back the new administration.

Once Maclay arrived in the capital, he quickly changed his mind. His colleagues in the Senate seemed determined to establish an American version of the British Parliament. But it was Adams who really got under Maclay's skin. Day after day he endured the vice president's ponderous interventions. In fact, contempt for Adams drove Maclay to keep an eccentric diary, a document that provides one of the very few surviving sources of information about political maneuvering in Congress during Washington's first term.

Often speaking on the floor of the Senate without notes, Maclay countered Adams's plea for lofty titles. On May 8, 1789, he gave a history lecture that reflected his own egalitarian interpretation of the Revolution. "The Subject of Government," he argued, had come a long way over the previous twenty years. He was certain that enlightened Americans knew more about "human affairs in General than for several Generations before." If nothing else, the progress in learning revealed that artificial and aristocratic titles made no sense. They reflected an earlier, more primitive stage of human development. Americans now knew better. Addressing Adams directly, Maclay insisted that "this light of Knowledge had diminished the veneration for Titles, and that Mankind now considered themselves as little bound to imitate the follies of civilized Nations, as the Brutality of Savages."[19]

In early May a joint committee of the House and Senate concluded that it was "not proper to annex any style or titles to [those] expressed in the Constitution."[20] The commonsense decision received enthusiastic endorsement from the House of Representatives, but the Senate refused to compromise. Once again Adams held forth. Unless Washington was awarded a weighty title, he insisted, no one in Europe would respect the new government of the United States. Maclay was nearly apoplectic. He blamed the Vice President for "this whole silly business."[21] From the floor of the Senate, he railed against artificial distinctions. They were the props of an aristocratic political theater. "At present," he said, "it was impossible to add to the respect entertained for General Washington; that if you [the senators] gave him the title of any foreign prince or potentate, a belief would follow that the manners of that prince and his modes of government would be adopted by the President."[22]

However much Adams and Maclay differed on the staging of republican government, they shared a kind of philosophic nominalism in which a title in itself had the power to determine how the president behaved in office. For them, names alone shaped perceptions of reality. If the Senate called Washington "prince" or "his majesty," then the president—whatever his personal beliefs—would be pulled irresistibly toward monarchy. He could not help himself. Finally, on May 14 a Senate committee announced its recommendation: Washington would be known throughout the world—in capital letters—as "HIS HIGHNESS THE PRESIDENT OF THE UNITED STATES OF AMERICA, AND PROTECTOR OF THEIR LIBERTIES."

This was too much for the House. Later that day, the Senate compromised, albeit with ill grace. Adams's supporters maintained to the end that they still believed that "it would be proper to annex a RESPECTABLE TITLE TO THE OFFICE OF PRESIDENT OF THE UNITED STATES." But out of a respect for harmony with the lower house, it accepted the wording of the Constitution; Washington would henceforth be addressed simply as "the President of the UNITED STATES."[23]

National leaders who had known Adams since the start of the Revolution, especially the famous flock of Virginia swans, found it hard to explain his behavior. They did not see his actions as the product of honest intellectual disagreement. Rather, it seemed to them that Adams's open flirtation with the trappings of monarchy indicated that the vice president had lost touch with his own culture. When Thomas Jefferson first heard of the protracted Senate debate, he exclaimed, "The most superlatively ridiculous thing I ever heard of."[24] Madison concurred. He claimed that Washington wanted no part of a campaign to "bedizen him with a superb but spurious title."[25]

Madison was correct. Washington wished that Adams had not raised the issue of artificial titles. As he often did when confronted with a hard problem, he sought advice from trusted friends. In this case, he received valuable counsel from David Stuart, who wrote candidly to the president about the state of local politics in Virginia. Stuart could afford to be frank, since he was not only a successful Alexandria physician, but also the man who had married the widow of Martha's son, Eleanor Calvert Custis. On July 14, Stuart alerted Washington to harmful rumors then circulating throughout Virginia. "Nothing," he reported, "could equal the ferment and disquietude, occasioned by the proposition respecting titles." People believed that the whole embarrassing campaign "originated from Mr. Adams & [Richard Henry] Lee." Stuart assured Washington that their efforts to create special distinctions "are not only unpopular to an extreme, but highly odious."

Of course, as Stuart confessed, it was possible that one might regard the entire controversy simply as a minor disagreement of no national significance. Historians have often taken that position. But that conclusion would be a mistake. According to Stuart, even apparently trivial matters—how to address the president of the United States—spilled over into other, more serious considerations. Minor differences over titles—over the performance of the Constitution—encouraged those who had recently opposed ratification to renew their attacks on the entire character of the new federal government. "The Opponents to the government affect to smile at it [the title debate in Congress]," explained Stuart, "and consider it as a verification of their prophecies about the tendency of the government. Mr. [Patrick] Henry's description of it, that it squinted toward monarchy, is in every mouth, and has established him in the general opinion, as a true Prophet."[26] As Stuart knew full well, Washington held Henry in low regard, and the discovery that Adams's actions had raised Henry's reputation in Virginia annoyed the president.

Stuart's letter was a key document shaping Washington's thinking about how best to present himself as a republican leader. He certainly studied the correspondence carefully. We know that he did so because of the detailed response he dispatched to the doctor only a few weeks later. In addition to warning Washington about Henry's boasting, Stuart had raised two crucial points about the shifting character of American political culture. First, there was the matter of public opinion. It is a topic to which we shall return, but here we should note that Stuart was not reporting to Washington only the reactions of elite planters and wealthy merchants. A larger audience, something he called the *public*, had registered its condemnation of artificial, potentially aristocratic titles. In this new political environment, what ordinary Virginians believed mattered not because they might vote the friends of government out of office, but because their support—expressed in churches, in courthouse gatherings, and in taverns—gave legitimacy to the federal government. In fact, Stuart was telling Washington that whether he liked it or not, the people would judge the credibility of his performance as president.

Second, and perhaps even more significant for Washington's thinking, the ordinary people would most likely rate the president's success on the political stage not on specific legislative policies or particular executive decisions, but on something much less precise—on emotions, impressions, and feelings. Stuart argued that appearance in itself was the key to effective leadership. He was not being cynical. Experience had taught Stuart that in the political forum, emotions counted for as much as reason. However ridiculous Adams's campaign for titles may have seemed to people knowledgeable in the affairs of government—to Jefferson and Madison, for example—impressions appear "to be more captivating to the generality, than matters of more importance—Indeed, I believe the great herd of mankind, form their judgments of characters, more from such slight occurrences, than [from] those of greater magnitude." After all, in politics as in other aspects of daily life, they listened to the intuitions of the heart. An error of political judgment,

Stuart concluded with remarkable prescience, "is more easily pardoned, than one of the heart."[27]

The positive news from Virginia was that criticism of the new government in no way reflected badly on Washington. Stuart awarded him high marks for acting like a proper president. Stuart expressed special pleasure on hearing "every part of your conduct [is] spoke of, with high approbation, and particularly your dispensing with ceremony occasionally, and walking the streets." Stuart was not suggesting that Washington had suddenly transformed himself into a backslapping politician. That was most certainly not how he expected the president to behave. But since one now had to take into account politics out of doors—in other words, the public—it was certainly a good idea to let the people see their president walking the streets.[28]

The contrast with Adams was instructive. According to Stuart, Virginians firmly believed that the vice president had arrogantly removed himself from the people's view and "is never seen but in his carriage & six."[29] The reference to the carriage and six was a gross exaggeration. In 1789 it is doubtful that anyone in the United States, even individuals of great wealth, drove coaches requiring six horses. Vehicles of that size were part of the monarchical world of George III and Louis XVI. And that, of course, was the thrust of the rumor. A person who held insufferably aristocratic views of the presidency would probably own a coach and six, and if he did not actually do so, then it was entirely plausible that he dreamed of acquiring one.

Stuart's letter provoked an uncharacteristically personal response from Washington. His answer revealed how seriously he was wrestling with the challenge of presenting the presidency to the American people in an appropriate manner. As he knew, failure in this role could jeopardize the entire union. First, Washington complained that Adams had acted entirely on his own. If he had bothered to consult with Washington, he would have learned that the process for establishing the conventions for performing the presidency required patience and experience, not bluster and confrontation. Unhappily for Washington, Adams and *"some others"* had launched the debate over titles before the president had even arrived in New York City, and in Washington's convoluted syntax, he insisted that it "has given me much uneasiness, lest it should be supposed by some (unacquainted with facts) that the object they had in view was not displeasing to me."

The truth was that Washington was greatly relieved that the Senate had refused to saddle him with a title more suitable for London or Paris than the capital of the United States. About Adams, Washington conceded one point. Stuart had been incorrect on the matter of the coach and six. The president noted in a backhanded way that Adams "has never, I believe, appeared with more than *two* horses in his Carriage."[30] Washington's observation did not, of course, address the growing suspicion among the swans of Virginia and throughout much of the rest of the South that on some level, Adams was really a six-horse kind of person.

The exchange with Stuart reminds us that early in his administration, Washington faced what we might describe today as essentially a postcolonial dilemma. Winning independence from a former imperial regime—in this case, Great Britain—represented only one stage in the difficult process of successful nation building. Like so many modern leaders of former colonies, Washington had to work out forms of ruling authority capable at once of commanding popular respect while at the same time avoiding the appearance of being too closely connected to the imperial customs and traditions that the people had just overthrown. As he explained, the legitimacy of the new central government depended in no small part on preserving "the dignity & respect which was due to the first Magistrate." But as Adams had failed to comprehend, artificial devices such as honorific titles could not—certainly not in a nation composed of former British provinces—be allowed to become "an ostentatious imitation, or mimicry of Royalty."[31] The pressure to get the script of the performance right was formidable. As he explained, "The eyes of

America—perhaps of the world—are turned to this Government; and many are watching the movements of all those who are concerned with its Administration."

At this moment, Washington hoped to discover from the forum of public opinion how he and the federal government were perceived. It was not praise he sought. He wanted reliable political intelligence, an accurate sense of how things were going. And therein lurked a danger. What if the people had been misinformed about what was happening in the nation's capital? "At a distance from the theater of action," Washington explained, "truth is not always related without embellishments, & sometimes is entirely perverted from misconceptions; or want of knowing the causes which have produced the conduct of which complaint is made." [32]

—IV—

The pressures of office made it hard for Washington to focus on the problem of crafting a persuasive political persona. He had not a moment to himself. He complained specifically that he had no time for reading, no time for correspondence. Strangers flooded into his home, some to express congratulations, some to satisfy curiosity, and some to lobby for personal projects. Of all the people who trooped into his quarters, usually without warning, the most annoying were the job seekers. They assumed that the creation of the new federal government would generate scores of new salaried positions. And, of course, every supplicant insisted on special treatment.

Washington was not alone in thinking that the situation was getting out of hand. Even the irascible Senator William Maclay of Pennsylvania agreed that something had to be done to manage better the president's contact with the public. The senator scribbled in his diary that Washington "stood on as difficult ground as he ever had done in his life: that to suffer himself to be run down, on the one hand, by a crowd of visitants so as to engross his time, would never do, as it would render the doing of business impracticable; but, on the other hand, for him to be seen only in public on stated times, like an Eastern Lama, would be equally offensive."[33]

It was a time for experimentation and invention. To shield himself from importuning strangers, Washington devised a plan that he thought would allow people access to him without thereby monopolizing too much of his time. It was a public relations disaster. The scheme involved organizing formal weekly receptions, which were regularly announced in the newspapers. These levees were scheduled for 3:00 p.m. on Tuesdays. They lasted one hour, and only men were welcome. On Fridays, his wife, Martha, hosted a tea, which was open to women as well as men, and Washington let it be known that he enjoyed these gatherings more than he did the Tuesday receptions.

In theory, these carefully scripted occasions addressed the challenge of how a president was supposed to converse with ordinary people who had no formal business to conduct. After all, as Washington observed in somewhat patronizing language, these functions encouraged "idle and ceremonious visits." At first, all seemed to go well. The president's secretary, Tobias Lear, reported that the scheme "allows two valuable ends—it allows a sufficient time for dispatching the business of the Office—and it gives a dignity to the President by not obliging him to expose himself every day to impertinent or curious intruders."[34]

It soon became painfully obvious to everyone, including Washington, that the receptions did not fulfill their intention; in fact, they alienated the very people they were supposed to charm. In large part, the problem was Washington himself. He made it clear to the visitors that he would have preferred to be almost anywhere else on the face of the earth than in a drawing room trying to make small talk with strangers. However much he may have wanted to avoid copying the rituals of European courts, that is exactly what he managed to achieve. Dressed in an impressive suit of black velvet and standing in front of the fireplace, he received each arrival without the slightest concession to cordiality. He never shook hands with the visitors, as if such a show of intimacy might somehow compromise his self-esteem. Washington offered instead a "dignified bow." The guests then drifted to the edge of the room, waiting for the privilege of exchanging a few words with the president. One surviving description of a typical levee captures its suffocating formality:

> As visitors came in, they formed a circle around the room. At a quarter past three, the door was closed, and the circle was formed for that day. He [Washington] then began on the right, and spoke to each visitor, calling him by name, and exchanging a few words with him. When he had completed his circuit, he resumed his first position, and visitors approached him in succession, bowed and retired. By four o'clock this ceremony was over.[35]

However much Washington claimed that he welcomed honest criticism, he had a very thin skin. He admitted that the levees had been a failure. But that confession did not keep him from reacting defensively when someone reported popular disapproval. Once again, Dr. Stuart served as the messenger of bad news. From him, Washington learned that people in Virginia such as Patrick Henry were saying that the president's receptions were far too formal for American politics. They were not sufficiently republican. Virginians assured one another that "there was more pomp" in evidence at Washington's levees "than at St. James's." The reference was, of course, to the Court of St. James, the palace of the reigning British monarch. Since not many Virginians could claim to have attended a royal reception, they had to take the accuracy of the comparison on faith. In other words, the story that George Washington was behaving like George III circulated as an ideological truth. So too did the complaint that Washington's "bows were more distant & stiff" than those encountered in Great Britain.[36]

George Mason, Washington's neighbor in Virginia and a leading spokesman in the fight against ratification of the Constitution, joined the chorus of detractors. It was reported that "Mason is generally condemning the Pomp & parade that is going on at New York, and tells of a number of useless ceremonies that is now in fashion." If it were not for Washington's strength of character, said Mason, "we should have the Devil to pay." Too many people around the president were playing at being aristocrats. It was only because of Washington's unquestioned integrity that it was "out of the power of those Damned Monarchical fellows with the Vice president, & the Women to ruin the Nation." Mason recommended a poem he had recently encountered in a Massachusetts newspaper:

> And lay that useless *etiquette* aside;
> The Unthinking laugh, but all the thinking hate
> Such vile, abortive mimickry of State;
> Those idle lackeys, saunt'ing at your door,
> But ill become *poor servants* of the POOR.[37]

Washington admitted that the receptions had not answered the central question he faced as the first president of the United States: he had not yet figured out how he could carry out his administrative responsibilities while at the same time preserving "the dignity & respect which was due to the first Magistrate."[38] He continued working on the problem—on his own. What he did not need was the ungenerous, ill-informed criticism of people who did not know what they were talking about.

Take the matter of bowing too stiffly. What, he asked a correspondent from Virginia, did Patrick Henry expect of an aging president? Instead of mocking Washington's awkward bows, "would it not have been better to have thrown the veil of charity over them, ascribing their stiffness to the effects of age, or to the unskillfulness of my teacher, than to pride and dignity of office, which God knows has no charms for me?" Detractors in Virginia were interpreting partisan tales for reality and then needlessly alarming the public about an alleged spread of dangerous monarchical beliefs. This was how conspiracy theories took root. And, of course, the complaint about the stiffness of his bows reminds us that for Washington, even minor details of his presentation as president mattered. In this sense, Adams touched a nerve: Washington did aspire to act like a republican leader; he just did not want others to define the role for him.

Although Washington had been in office for only a few months, he was already complaining of the burden of acting like a president. "I can truly say," he confessed, "I had rather be at Mount Vernon with a friend or two about me, than to be attended at the Seat of Government by the Officers of State and the Representatives of every Power in Europe." Escape was a dream. Even at this moment of despondency, he sensed that the solution to the problem of fashioning an appropriate public theater of politics is to be acquired "by observing a just medium between too much state and too great familiarity."[39]

— V —

While others argued over appropriate titles, Washington came up with an original solution to the presentation of the presidency: he would take the new federal government to the people; he would communicate to them directly, away from the partisan press and legions of job seekers. His decision, which evolved slowly over the first months in office, reflected a fundamental faith in the wisdom of the American people as well as his own political creativity. It was a difficult move. After all, he was a man of great personal reserve. He knew it. But however wanting in what might be called the common touch, he devised a plan that transformed permanently how subsequent presidents of the United States have presented the federal government to the public.

Washington's idea initially appeared in a remarkable letter circulated among the major figures of his administration. Among other things, the document demonstrates that the notion of taking a journey to the nation was Washington's; it was his alone, and not a suggestion first put forward by members of his cabinet. The only surviving copy of this memo was addressed to Vice President Adams on May 10, 1789. It took the form of a nine-part questionnaire. The majority of the queries related to official receptions and formal dinner parties at the president's home.

It was the eighth query that most fully revealed Washington's political insight. He had come to realize, perhaps as a result of the journey from Mount Vernon to New York City, that Americans needed to see their president in person. The opposite was also the case: the president felt compelled to escape the self-contained world known as capital society. Washington sensed the importance of interacting directly with the people. That was the whole point of a republican form of government in the United States. Moreover, his experiences during his first months in office convinced him that he had not only to dispel rumors about monarchical conspiracies in the capital—not to mention about bowing too stiffly—but also to gather reliable information about what issues were on the people's minds.

The notion that the president should make himself accessible to the nation seems commonplace today. Indeed, a president who never left the capital would be quickly labeled as arrogant and aloof—as somehow un-American. Washington understood the danger of isolating himself from the people who would ultimately judge the success of his presidency. It was from this expansive perspective that Washington solicited advice on "Whether, during the recess of Congress, it would not be advantageous to the interests of the Union for the President to make the tour of the United States, in order to become better acquainted with the principal Characters & internal Circumstances, as well as to be more accessible to numbers of well-informed persons, who might give him [the president] useful information and advices on political subjects?"[40]

Washington's initial goals may have seemed modest: he proposed talking with members of the local elites about current federal policies. But there was more to the plan than that. Driving the idea was a powerful although inchoate sense of the people. They were key to the new republican theater. The gentlemen who hosted dinner parties on the road were, after all, reporting to Washington what they had learned from friends and neighbors, ordinary Americans. And so, as Washington would soon discover on the tours of America, conversations of this sort had unintended consequences. They opened out unexpectedly and gave the people a chance to participate. Washington placed himself on a vastly expanded stage in which a noisy, demanding audience assumed it too had a role to play in defining the nation.

Once again Adams did not quite understand what was at stake. His answer to Washington's query about touring America lacked enthusiasm. If the president wanted to organize a journey, he could do so, of course, but before he departed, Adams urged him to remember all the problems in the capital that required Washington's personal attention. "A Tour might," wrote Adams, "no doubt be made, with great advantage to the Public, if the time can be spared." That seemed unlikely, since "foreign affairs arrive every day, and the Business of the executive and judicial departments require constant Attention." He recommended that "the President's Residence" would best "be confined to one Place."

No sooner had he responded to Washington, however, than Adams had second thoughts. Did the new administration really have an obligation to the public? What advantages could be gained by visiting the communities where ordinary men and women lived? Adams began to suspect that he, rather than Washington, might be out of step with a new set of political expectations. "My long Residence abroad," he admitted, "may have impressed me with a View of Things, incompatible with the present Temper or Feelings of our Fellow Citizens."[41]

Nothing Adams had to say deterred Washington. One suspects that the president had already made up his mind about the value of a tour to America. As he observed to Stuart, "seclusion would stop the avenues to useful information from the many, & make me dependent on the few." [42]

—VI—

At the very moment when Washington finally determined how he wanted to reach out in person to the American people—to act on a larger political stage—he almost died. The sudden emergency seldom receives much attention in the political histories of this period, and for an obvious reason: he recovered and lived for another full decade. He, of course, did not know that he would survive the illness. That is the point. The grave threat to Washington's health during the summer of 1789 helps us better understand his state of mind as he planned his first journey to the nation. The possibility of death added urgency to the trip.

The crisis caught Washington by surprise. Throughout the Revolutionary War, he had experienced remarkably robust health, and he insisted that his good fortune resulted in part from rigorous daily exercise, which for him usually involved long horse rides. But the more sedentary life in New York took a toll on Washington. In mid-June he began to run a high fever. The source of the infection turned out to be a large and painful cyst—he called it a tumor; one doctor termed it anthrax—on his left thigh. Someone in the Washington household summoned Dr. Samuel Bard, a leading physician in the city, who realized immediately that the president's life hung in the balance.

For days Bard refused to leave the president's bedside. On one occasion, Washington asked the doctor for "his candid opinion as to the probable termination of the disease." The report was not encouraging. City officials in New York ordered chains to be run across the street in front of the president's door to keep the noise of heavy wagon traffic from disturbing the patient. People suspected that Washington was in mortal peril, but because his staff wanted to keep the seriousness of his condition secret from the general public, it provided newspapers with vague stories that masked the real danger not only to the president but also to the United States at a time of great vulnerability.

About the political danger, his secretaries were correct: his death would have threatened the stability of the new federal government, which had been ratified only recently by the slenderest of margins. On June 27 the *Massachusetts Centinel* reported, "The publick anxiety has been conspicuously apparent, from some accounts received from New-York, which have mentioned the indisposition of our beloved PRESI-DENT." About the nature of this indisposition, the paper claimed to know very little. The article did not raise the possibility of death. "His Excellency," it explained, "was attacked by a slow fever, which continued on him for several days, and was at periods attended with some alarming symptoms."[43] Like other journals, the *Centinel* assured its readers of a swift recovery.

Optimism was premature. Assisted by his father, also a respected doctor, Bard concluded that the president required surgery, and on June 17, the team performed the operation. It was successful. Washington began slowly to show signs of improvement, but he remained weak. On July 15, a full three weeks after the fever had peaked, the president informed a correspondent in Baltimore, "My health is restored, but a feebleness still hangs upon me, and I am yet much incommoded by the incision which was made in a very large and painful tumor." At the time he wrote this letter, he could neither walk nor sit. Even in this condition, Washington insisted on getting out of the house. As he explained, "I am able to take exercise in my coach, by having it so contrived, as to extend myself the full length of it."[44]

Through it all, Washington never complained. From his stoic perspective, the threat of death seemed more an inconvenience than a genuine source of fear. His friend David Humphreys, the Revolutionary veteran who had accompanied him from Mount Vernon to New York, recorded an interview he had had with the president when it appeared that he might not recover. "When, in his dangerous sickness at New-York, soon after his election as President," Humphreys recounted, "he said to the Author [Humphreys]: 'I know it is doubtful whether I shall ever rise from this bed, & God knows it is perfectly indifferent to me whether I do or not.'" Such fatalism was not what Humphreys wanted to hear. The success of the new government continued to be uncertain, and Washington remained key to its survival. "If, Sir," Humphreys responded, "it is indifferent to you, it is far from being so to your friends and your Country. For they believe it has still great need of your services."[45]

Even after Washington had regained his health, he spoke of death. He seemed unsure how much time he had left to accomplish the goals he had set for himself. In September, for example, he told James Craik, a physician who lived in Virginia, "The want of regular exercise, with the cares of office, will, I have no doubt, hasten my departure for that country from whence no Traveller returns."[46]

It comes as no surprise that the president wanted to begin the first part of his journey to the nation as soon as possible. He waited impatiently for the end of the first session of Congress. As he told his sister, Betty Washington Lewis, he looked at the trip to the Eastern States as a "way of relaxation from business and reestablishment of my health after the long and tedious complaint with which I have been afflicted."[47] The near-fatal illness profoundly affected both the actor and his audience. Washington sensed that his tour of America could serve to bind scattered individuals and competing regions into a viable federal union. He had to move swiftly.

Ordinary men and women throughout the nation also felt the new sense of urgency. They wanted to see the general before he died. For Washington, his appearance in small communities from New Hampshire to Georgia, a series of trips taken over a period of several years, marked the beginning of a new political era; for many people on the road, it signified the conclusion of the Revolution. In either case, the president who survived illness found that more than ever before during a long public career, he had become the physical embodiment of the entire nation.

—VII—

As he slowly recovered during the summer of 1789, Washington focused his renewed energy on how best to present the presidency before an audience of so many strangers. At this point in our discussion, we are concerned primarily with how he devised general rules of conduct on the road. In later chapters dealing with New England and the South, we explore in greater detail specific incidents that occurred during his travel. But we should appreciate that even at the start of his journey to America, Washington concentrated on how he might control the performance, as would a general organizing a complex military campaign.

During the initial planning stage, Washington was adamant about escaping the long shadow of European monarchy. Perhaps because of the warnings from Virginians about the offensiveness of artificial titles, he insisted on avoiding even the possibility that Americans would interpret his travels as a kind of royal progress in which the king of the United States graciously acknowledged the cheers of adoring crowds and the groveling fealty of local leaders. Just a few days before Washington arrived in Boston, for example, local newspapers informed readers that the president "had expressed a wish that there might not be any parade on the occasion."[48] At about the same time, Washington instructed the governor of Massachusetts, "I am highly sensible of the honor intended me: But could my wish prevail, I should desire to visit your Metropolis without any parade, or extraordinary ceremony."[49]

Washington believed strongly that his journey to the nation should reflect fundamental republican values. It was a hard sell. Newspaper headlines closely followed the "PROGRESS OF THE PRESIDENT."[50] The word alone—*progress*—conjured up images of late medieval pageantry. Although Washington's journey could not avoid comparison with monarchical traditions dating back to Elizabethan times, Washington organized the trips on fundamental American principles. The fullest expression of republican ideology ran in the *Herald of Freedom*, a Boston paper, which strongly supported the new federal government:

> Not for the purposes of empty parade, or to acquire the applause of gaping multitudes—Not for the display of royal pageantry and courtly magnificence—Not to exact the homage of a depressed and impoverished people, or the blind adulation of a host of slaves—Not to interrupt the labors of the industrious in their several occupations, or to disturb the tranquility of domestic life, by being attended with a splendid mercenary guard—No. —Far other objects gave rise to the present excursion.
>
> Safe in the protection of heaven, and the affections of a grateful people, . . . he has no other guard; being attended only by his Secretaries, and a few servants; and though the spontaneous affectionate respects of an enlightened community are the richest reward of patriotism, yet we have every reason to suppose that the President will receive it as the highest evidence of attachment to his person for the people to dispense with every species of parade that may interfere with the prime object of his journey.[51]

As an elected leader, Washington felt obliged to make himself as visible as possible to the people. How exactly he hoped to accomplish this goal in the absence of large-scale parades was not clear, but intentions mattered more than execution. Because his constitutional authority derived from the people, he tried as much as possible to let them see their president. In the overwrought rhetoric of the time, one newspaper claimed that the success of his tour of America depended ultimately on "ocular demonstration."[52]

However much Washington discouraged intimacy with strangers, he fully appreciated that in this political show, he had become a republican prop. On this stage, just being visible argued that the president cared about the people enough to sacrifice his own comfort. Even when it was pouring rain, he never canceled the show. As one person commenting on the southern journey of 1791 explained, Washington's "object in coming, I suppose, is more to be seen and to gratify the Southern People in seeing him" than to gather detailed intelligence about the local economy.[53]

Although Washington did not wade into the crowds, shaking hands and signing autographs, he adopted certain theatrical gestures that ordinary men and women interpreted as signs of respect. He nodded to the people who lined the streets and saluted cheering supporters. As one person who witnessed Washington's behavior on such an occasion noted, the president "frequently bowed to the multitude, and took off his hat to the ladies at the windows."[54] There is no record that anyone on these occasions complained that his bowing was too stiff or formal for American sensitivities.

These small, seemingly self-conscious acts suggested that the formal man on horseback was actually a genuine human being. As one journal observed in 1791, "It is highly pleasing to a grateful and patriotic mind to reflect upon the happy consequences which will probably flow from the tour which the President is now performing. . . . The intelligent serenity of his countenance, the unaffected ease and dignity of his deportment, while they excite the most profound respect, naturally rivet the affections to him."[55]

Like an accomplished actor, Washington knew that his apparel would add to the success of the presentation. The appeal for the union depended on correct choices. His initial instincts seem to have been profoundly republican. From this political perspective, it was important to avoid ostentatious display. Since Washington was no longer commander of the Continental Army, he thought it prudent to appear in public in a plain although well-tailored suit. But once he was actually on the road — once he encountered crowds of admirers — he changed his mind.

When he first entered New England, newspapers informed readers that Washington wore a suit of "black velvet." A few days later, another journal reported, "To gratify the inhabitants [of Worcester, Massachusetts], he politely passed through town on horseback, dressed in a brown suit."[56] Soon after that event, however, the business suits began to figure less prominently in his performances. Since in almost every community, local officials asked him to review militia companies, Washington felt a need to change into his full military uniform on these occasions. By the time he reached Boston, the question about appropriate dress had been resolved. The *Connecticut Courant* explained that Washington rode into the city "dressed in his military uniform."[57] Even before leaving New York for New England, he may have sensed that the people wanted to see a Revolutionary general rather than a fellow citizen. In any case, the baggage wagon carried both military uniform and business suits. In the South, he appeared before the public as the aging military liberator.

Washington adopted an elaborate choreography before each public appearance. When he came within a few miles of a community, he ordered the little caravan to halt. He then exited his coach, went to the baggage wagon, and changed into his full uniform as commander of the Continental Army. He mounted a great white charger — in the South, it was usually Prescott — and rode impressively into town. His elaborately staged arrivals marked the high point in the histories of many small villages throughout America. Later chroniclers often recounted the moment that Washington came to town. The iconic image of General Washington astride a huge horse from this period was the product of carefully crafted political theater.

Washington also insisted that under no conditions would he ever stay in a private home. No doubt, he recognized the serious financial burden that a presidential visit could make on a private citizen. Queen Elizabeth and other English monarchs thought nothing of allowing dukes and earls to pay the bill for feeding more than a hundred guests. The contribution extorted from the nobility served to remind potentially rebellious subjects that it was the king or queen, not the local nobility, who actually ruled the nation. But Washington found demands of this sort unacceptable. Since he represented the federal government during his travels, he thought the government should cover the expenses. As Washington explained to one man who had begged the president to stay with him, he had made a firm determination not to make "my headquarters in private families." He saw no justification for the leader of the country "to become troublesome to them in any of these tours."[58]

Few Americans believed him, at least not at first. Powerful individuals from Boston to Charleston pleaded with Washington to accept their hospitality. His correspondence contains many heartfelt appeals. Could he not, the petitioners asked, make just one exception to the general rule? Could he not make their private homes his headquarters? But he always declined, even for distinguished Revolutionary veterans. Washington informed George Clinton, governor of New York, for example, that since he had accepted "a public *Station*, I shall make it a point to take hired lodgings, or Rooms in a Tavern." He resolved to do so "because it would be wrong, in my Judgment, to impose such a burden on any private family, as must unavoidably be occasioned by my company: and because I think it would be generally expected, that, being supported by the public at large, I should not be burdensome to Individuals."[59]

Washington's repeated protestations did little to discourage a flood of tiresome invitations. To cite the efforts of just one determined host, George Cabot of Beverly, Massachusetts, begged Washington to "take a little rest" at his house. Cabot pulled out all of the rhetorical stops. "I am fully aware that by indulging this hope," he informed Washington, "I expose myself to the imputation of vanity as well as ambition,

& therefore should hardly dare to have my conduct tried by the cool maxims of the head alone, but would rather refer it to the dictates of my heart."[60] Again Washington declined. He and his staff sought out public inns and taverns, accepting whatever food the proprietors brought to the table. They kept detailed accounts, knowing that the taxpayers of America, not a handful of privileged individuals, would pick up the tab.

Sometimes Washington found it hard to live up to his resolution to stay only in public inns. The problem was especially pressing in the South, where travel by land was much more difficult than it was in the northern and middle states. On one occasion, Washington spent a night in a house that he honestly believed was a proper inn, but in the morning, when he went to pay the bill, he learned that in fact he had slept in a private home. His host, Jeremiah Vareen, had fooled the president. As a contrite Washington noted in his diary, he had been directed to Vareen's house "as a Tavern, but the proprietor of it either did not keep one, or would not acknowledge it. We therefore were entertained & very kindly without being able to make compensation."[61] At another stop, between Charleston and Savannah, the president could not find a tavern or inn of any sort, and out of necessity, he accepted the hospitality of Thomas Heyward at White Hall plantation on Hazzard Creek, South Carolina. Washington apologized in his diary for the decision, "their [*sic*] being no public houses on the Road."[62] Still, considering the primitive travel conditions of the time, Washington compiled an impressive record of engaging public accommodations.

On one curious occasion, an innkeeper turned the president away. Washington was at the end of the New England trip and in a hurry to get back to New York City. One of his secretaries rode ahead of the president's party to reserve rooms at an establishment in the very small town of Uxbridge, Massachusetts. Washington later learned, "The House in Uxbridge had a good external appearance (for a Tavern) but the owner of it being away from home, and the wife sick, we could not gain admittance."[63] That was not the whole story, or so it seemed. Newspapers throughout New England claimed it was certainly true that Washington's agent had arrived at the Uxbridge tavern and inquired whether rooms were available for the president. According to the *Gazette of the United States*, "The Innkeeper was absent; the Landlady, supposing the messenger meant by '*the President*,' the President of Rhode Island college, for it was in the neighborhood of that State, and that of course he had his lady with him, and being herself unwell—she told the messenger she could not entertain '*the President*.'" Only after Washington's secretary had located another place to stay did the poor woman realize her mistake. It was reported that she exclaimed, " 'Bless me . . . the sight of him [Washington] would have cured me of my illness and the best of my house and in the town should have been at his service.'"[64]

The incident reopened the whole title debate. Some observers argued that if the woman had known that the president of the United States wanted a room, she would have been more cooperative. Her confusion revealed "that it is necessary the President of the United States should have some title, or address at least, to distinguish him from other great personages, who may have occasion to travel either in their own or other states."[65] If the secretary had announced that His Majesty was on the way, the poor woman would have opened the door. When another Boston journal heard this story, it cried foul. The entire episode, it claimed, was an insidious fabrication staged to restore monarchy to the United States. The Uxbridge tale was merely an excuse for some closet monarchists to call Washington "His Highness." In fact, if this kind of pressure kept up, "We will have the Head of our Nation known by the title of Majesty, and by the appellation of King."[66]

Washington took a measure of republican pride in his insistence on staying only in public inns, but in private, he told a different story. His diaries read like a travel guide aimed at people eager to learn which taverns to avoid. He was a tough critic. Everywhere from New Hampshire to Georgia, he chronicled how he had endured bad food, uncomfortable beds, and inadequate stables for his horses. On the road through eastern

Connecticut, he noted, "I stayed at Perkin's Tavern (which by the bye is not a good one) all day." A few days later, he lodged at Ozias Marvin's tavern "which is not a good House." In Spencer, Massachusetts, he reported that he "lodged at the House of one Jenks who keeps a pretty good Tavern." But at Watertown he had to stay "at the House of a Widow Coolidge near the Bridge, and a very indifferent one it is." [67]

Washington's complaints only increased in the southern states. Instead of comfort, he experienced martyrdom, at least in the smaller towns along the road. In April 1791 he crossed into North Carolina from Virginia hoping to find an inn where both he and the horses could recover from an unpleasant day of traveling in the rain. He had no luck. The single tavern open for business was so repellent that Washington could not bring himself to suffer a single night's stay. The inn, he explained in the diary, "having no stables in which the horses could be comfortable, & no Rooms or beds which appeared tolerable, & every thing else having a dirty appearance, I was compelled to keep on to Halifax." Tarboro, North Carolina, offered "a very indifferent house without stabling." There followed a series of "indifferent" inns, a description that in Washington's rating system apparently meant barely tolerable.

Just before returning to Mount Vernon from his long excursion through the South, Washington summarized in his diary all that he had suffered because of a republican resolution not to accept private hospitality. "The accommodations on the whole Road," Washington observed, ". . . we found extremely indifferent—the houses being small and badly provided either for man or horse." He had anticipated better. After all, he was the president, and in a curiously unrepublican lament, he complained that one would have expected "extra exertions when it was known I was coming." In a remarkable display of circular logic, he speculated that the problem with public houses was that they catered to the public. Without a hint of irony, Washington noted that southern inns appealed to "the kind of travellers which use them; which with a few exceptions . . . are no other than Waggoners & families removing; who, generally, take their provisions along with them."[68]

No evidence survives to indicate that anyone thought more highly of Washington because he suffered so many uncomfortable nights in the name of republican principles. But at the same time, it can be said that Washington, one of the wealthiest men in America, briefly experienced the world of ordinary Americans. He may not have enjoyed staying with wagon drivers and poor families in search of a better life, but unlike many modern political leaders who speak for the people, he knew firsthand how they lived.

Even the primitive roads of America played a part in Washington's performance as president. In a sense, their ill repair in itself affirmed that one of the richest figures in public life was somehow really a man of the people. That is certainly what European visitors would have concluded. Adopting an almost anthropological view of travel in the United States, one French traveler explained that on stagecoaches, "you meet people of all walks of life, one after the other." In comparison with his experiences in Europe, he found interaction on the roads of America open, less marked by class distinctions. "There is a special advantage of these stages," he reported, "they maintain the idea of equality. A member of Congress sits side by side with the shoemaker who elected him and fraternizes with him; they talk together on familiar terms."[69] No one—not even the president of the United States—traveled in substantially greater comfort than did ordinary citizens. His tribulations on the roads communicated to the public a willingness to suffer many of the same inconveniences as it did.

Certainly no one, including Washington, could have persuasively argued that half the fun of the trip was just getting there. At best, travel was slow, boring, and dirty. Washington constantly complained of the choking dust. Scores of admirers in each community insisted on meeting the president and then escorting him to his next destination. Their horses raised huge clouds of dust. At one point on his Southern Tour,

Washington could not stand these conditions a moment longer, and to escape the dust, he intentionally misled his hosts about the precise time of his departure from their town. On April 15, 1791, the man who allegedly could not tell a lie recorded in his diary, "Having suffered very much by the dust yesterday and finding that parties of Horse, & a number of other Gentlemen were intending to attend me part of the way today, I caused their enquiries respecting time of my setting out, to be answered that, I should endeavor to do it before eight O'clock; but I did it a little after five, by which I avoided the inconveniences above mentioned." [70] Perhaps even Parson Weems would have forgiven Washington for bending the truth on this occasion.

At worst, travel could be extremely dangerous. An Englishman who was on a trip through the South in 1786 almost canceled his plans when he heard a "dreadful account that a gentleman has given me who had lately traveled through North Carolina." [71] The encounter was not unusual. In taverns and inns along the road, travelers traded stories about the hazards they had been forced to overcome. They regularly complained of having to deal with poisonous snakes, annoying insects, rude companions, muddy roads in which coaches sank up to their axles, huge boulders and tree stumps that threatened to overturn vehicles, and steep hills that required everyone riding in coaches to get out and push. Mosquitoes presented an almost unbearable problem. "You would pity me if you knew how much I was last night tormented with bugs and mosquitoes," wrote one unhappy traveler. "It was in vain to seek repose." [72]

Even to obtain reliable directions from one town to another presented a daunting challenge. For a stranger, a simple request for information could end in humiliation. In 1799, for example, Isaac Weld Jr., a well-to-do Englishman, published an account of his journey through the northern states. "In the United States," Weld explained, ". . . the lower classes of people will return rude and impertinent answers to questions couched in the most civil terms, and will insult a person that bears the appearance of a gentleman, or propose to show how much they consider themselves upon an equality with him."[73] Weld was not alone. The marquis de Chastellux reported in his journal, "The difficulty of finding the road in many parts of America is not to be conceived."[74] Washington never had to endure such indignities, but even as an honored traveler, he was fully aware that a wrong turn or a sudden downpour could compromise the best-laid travel plans.

To be sure, a reliable map might have made the entire journey a lot easier. At the time, mapmakers in England and the United States offered for sale splendid maps of the entire continent east of the Mississippi River. Washington regularly consulted these materials, and he probably knew more about the course of the Ohio River than he did about the best route between Philadelphia and Charleston.[75] A few entrepreneurs attempted to provide travelers with up-to-date knowledge of local roads. None was more dogged than Christopher Colles, an extremely talented Irishman who came to America in 1771. He put forward several ambitious ideas for making a steam engine and improving water transportation, but nothing came of these schemes.

Colles was not easily discouraged. In 1789 he launched an even more demanding project: an intention to publish a road map under the title *Survey of the Roads of the United States of America*. The production consisted of a series of small strips "containing a delineation of near 12 miles of road upon a scale of about one inch and three quarters to the mile." This scale allowed Colles to specify "all the cross roads and streams of water which intersect it, the names of the most noted inhabitants of the houses contiguous to or in view of the road; the churches and other public buildings; the taverns, blacksmith's shops, mills, and every object which occurs to render it a useful and entertaining work." Although he guaranteed that no traveler following his map could possibly "miss his way," the sales of the atlas were disappointing.[76]

Washington seems to have owned a copy. It probably did not make much difference, however, for almost as soon as he left New York in 1789, he expressed surprise at the terrible condition of the roads, including the main post road to New Haven. "The Road," he noted in the diary, "for the greater part, indeed the whole way, was very rough and Stoney."[77] In any case, Colles did not have the resources to map the major highways south of Virginia. In planning that journey, Washington had to ask members of Congress who lived in the South how they managed to get home. Based on this informal information, Washington drafted his own crude map of the Carolinas.

—VIII—

Washington deserves high marks for his decision to take the presidency to the people. When he departed for New England, and later for the South, tours we will examine in greater detail in the following chapters, he did not know what we now take for granted about the history of our nation. He was not even sure that the Constitution would endure. For most Americans in 1789, the document was an abstraction, as was the national government housed in distant capitals. Washington understood that he had it in his power to nourish the emotional bonds, which were necessary to make the fragile new federal system a reality in the lives of ordinary men and women. In this sense, his contribution to state formation was as significant as were those of his more celebrated colleagues, Hamilton and Madison. On this point, Adams was correct: Washington was indeed a talented actor of the presidency.

Curiously, even the most celebrated man in America occasionally found himself playing to a skeptical audience. That is what happened one spring day in 1791 as Washington was returning to Philadelphia, then the nation's capital, from the long Southern Tour. Soon after crossing into North Carolina about six miles south of Salisbury, he came upon an isolated farm. The day was hot, and the president, who was riding a horse, decided to stop and ask for refreshment. He knocked on what appeared to be the front door. After some time, a twelve-year-old girl, later identified as Betsy Brandon, answered and explained that no one else was home. Indeed, she was in a sour mood, since everyone in her family had gone off to Salisbury to catch a glimpse of George Washington. To the stranger who was waiting for a cold glass of water, she exclaimed, "I do so wish I could see him." Washington was taken aback. Here he was, the president of the United States, and Betsy Brandon did not know who he was. "General Washington is now before you," he announced.[78] It is not known whether she believed him. Her reaction, of course, depended on how well he acted the part.

CHAPTER III

⇒•(●)•⇐

The Script:
Washington's Defense of the Union

The overriding sense of purpose that energized George Washington's journey to America derived from his uncompromising belief that the union must be preserved at all costs. That was the script of his performance, his message to the people at a critical moment. During the Revolution, he had become convinced that the security and prosperity of an independent republic depended on a strong central government. For the United States to succeed, it must be more than the sum of its parts. What changed over time — and defined his presidency — was a growing certainty that time was running out for the United States. As we shall discover, the whole point of Washington's attempt to reach out to the people was to alert them to the ever-present danger of fragmentation. If he sometimes seemed overly rigid in his judgments, a bit obsessive about creating a strong federal government, we should remember that for him, the stakes were very high.

—I—

The stimulus for Washington's message to the American people is perhaps best discovered in the maps that we know he consulted throughout his life. They spoke to him about exciting and expansive prospects for the nation. He was especially fond of the maps depicting the Ohio River

Valley. Long before the outbreak of the Revolution, he believed that the future of the American people was bound up with the development of the land and resources located west of the Appalachian Mountains.[1] What he made of representations of the original thirteen colonies is less clear. Washington certainly knew that their odd shapes and different sizes reflected decisions that British rulers had taken during a much earlier era. Many of them owed their strange configurations to European confusion and ignorance about New World geography.

However problematic their origins may have been, the colonies rapidly acquired distinct identities. Puritans and adventurers, Quakers and Catholics, great planters and small farmers took pride in having established discrete cultures in America, and within only a few years following the founding of the various colonies, there was no going back, no correcting mistakes based on new, more accurate geographic information. For almost two centuries, the colonies rarely cooperated, and when they did so, it was usually only out of temporary fears of a French attack along the frontier.

Even a widely celebrated figure such as Benjamin Franklin was unable to persuade colonial leaders to join together to address common problems. He intended his famous 1754 cartoon depicting a severed rattlesnake to generate greater unity, but the reptile failed spectacularly to achieve its purpose. Each colony continued to champion a different agenda. The snake reappeared on the eve of independence, yielding somewhat better, although short-term, results. The thirteen imperial provinces, of course, became states in 1776, but even then, unity remained elusive. Each state remained committed to preserving a large measure of sovereignty. And for Washington, that was the crucial problem. By the time he was elected president, he had come to regard the separate states as a serious threat to the stability of a fragile new republic.

Knowing how Washington reached this alarming conclusion not only helps to explain his decision as president to take the government to the people, but also challenges us to reassess exactly what we mean by "the American Revolution." It is a vexing problem. No doubt, it is true that most of us today assume the event ended with a peace treaty in 1783, which formally brought peace and recognition of the nation's independence. This perspective makes sense. After all, the date marks the moment the British went home, leaving the American people free to make their own history.

If we take a longer view—one in which achieving independence was only one stage in a continuing process of nation building—we realize that winning independence did not necessarily guarantee the success of the republican experiment. Other revolutions throughout the world have established national independence without being able to transform military success into a secure and stable state.[2] Because our nation has endured, spawning a robust economy and powerful military, we tend to take this transition for granted. As Washington realized, however, there was no guarantee that victory over an imperial power would yield a union of separate states capable of standing on their own.

Comparative studies in political science reveal that even in the best of circumstances, the road to national sovereignty is difficult. The list of dangers that impede the transition from revolutionary resistance to genuine state formation is daunting. Popular liberators such as Washington often turn into petty despots. Regional divisions—think of Spain, Sudan, Ukraine—can erode a meaningful sense of shared purpose. Appreciation of these many challenges provides insight into why Washington insisted during the 1780s that independence was not enough. For him, the major objective of the Revolution was the creation of a strong central government.[3]

—II—

The political crisis that persuaded President Washington to take his appeal directly to the American people first became manifest in the final days of the Revolution. It was during the early 1780s that Washington came to suspect that the original promise of independence was slipping away. In his opinion, the Articles of Confederation, also known awkwardly as the Articles of Confederation and Perpetual Union, could not meet the challenge. They certainly did very little to promote an effective sense of union.

Signs of trouble appeared quite quickly. The thirteen states did not get around to ratifying the Articles until 1781. Since the document, the country's first constitution, had been drafted some years earlier, the lack of enthusiasm for the new government served as a harbinger of future trouble. Eager to distance themselves from the kind of strong central authority that they understandably associated with the British monarchy, the members of the Continental Congress crafted a system of government that was intentionally loose. The states held the key elements of political power, and they jealously guarded their own sovereignty, so much so that the central government, which did not have the constitutional authority to raise taxes, had to beg the states for support even while the war was still in progress.[4] It is no wonder that the framers of the Confederation tellingly described the agreement as a "league of friendship," a virtual admission of the weakness of the structure. Local interests, especially in commercial and fiscal matters, always seemed to trump concerns that Washington regarded as key to the country's future.

Other Americans shared Washington's concerns about the impotence of the Confederation. Some of them, such as James Madison and Alexander Hamilton, ably addressed the challenge of nation building. Although Washington did not share their interest in the history of political thought, he aggressively allied himself with those who insisted that the United States had entered a period of severe crisis. More important, Washington brought his immense personal popularity to the cause. Even people who remained suspicious about the need to strengthen federal authority knew that they could not dismiss Washington's complaints out of hand. As Benjamin Lincoln, a respected Revolutionary officer, reminded Washington, "The share your Excellency holds in the affections of the people, and the unlimited confidence they place in your integrity and judgment, gives you an elevated stand among them which no other man can or probably ever will command."[5]

From Washington's perspective, the challenge facing the young republic was not simply protecting independence from imperial rivals, but keeping the states that had supported the common cause in 1776 from going their separate ways. After retiring from the Continental Army, he scoured the many newspapers delivered through the mail to Mount Vernon for information about local politics. What was the state of affairs in New England? In Pennsylvania? In South Carolina? What he read in the journals served to heighten his conviction that something was going terribly wrong.

Washington felt so passionately about the inability of the national government to control the independent-minded states that even a passing reference to the issue during a friendly conversation could cause him to become visibly upset. For a man who so studiously controlled his inner feelings, angry outbursts of this sort were themselves significant news. They demonstrated to skeptics that the most popular leader in America sincerely believed that there was a crisis. For example, when the French traveler Brissot de Warville visited Mount Vernon, he reported, "I saw him [Washington] lose his characteristic composure and become heated only when he talked about the present state of affairs in America. The schisms within his country torture his soul, and he feels the necessity of rallying all lovers of liberty around one central issue, the need to strengthen the government."[6] We should note in passing that Washington, unlike many modern critics, assumed that "liberty" depended on the strength of the central government.

By 1786, Washington had lost patience with the slow pace of reform, and he poured out his frustration to anyone who would listen. In a letter reviewing the nation's recent political history sent to his fellow Virginian Henry Lee, Washington recalled, "In our endeavors to establish a new general government, the contest nationally considered, seems not to have been so much for glory, as existence. It was for a long time doubtful whether we were to survive as an independent Republic, or decline from our federal dignity into insignificant and wretched Fragments of Empire."[7] Independence had been achieved, and yet federal dignity remained elusive.

During this trying period Washington seemed uncertain about whether the country was heading for *"Anarchy or Despotism."*[8] For him, both possibilities were real, and both led inevitably to the destruction of republican government, that is, a collapse of a government deriving its power from the people. At times, he expressed anxiety that the threat of the breakdown of the social contract would tempt ordinary Americans to accept some form of authoritarian control, a not uncommon phenomenon in elective governments when fear overrules trust.

It was not that Washington feared a creeping nostalgia for monarchy, although in fact some Americans of conservative temperament thought precisely along these lines.[9] Rather, he lamented what he viewed as the breakdown of "equal laws and equal protection," the very elements that most of us regard today as the essence of a civil society.[10] As he gathered news from around the country, Washington wondered whether his fellow Americans had lost their ability to work together for the common good. They certainly seemed unable to appreciate what had gone wrong under the Confederation. Selfish ambition had created debilitating paralysis. "To be fearful of vesting Congress," he explained to John Jay, ". . . with ample authorities for national purposes, appears to me the very climax of popular absurdity and madness."[11]

Like-minded people from other sections of the country knew exactly what kinds of reports were most likely to provoke Washington. Whether they consciously engaged in hyperbole is impossible to discern. Perhaps they really believed that the social order was in peril. But whatever their intentions may have been, they filled their letters with dark predictions of impending doom. Since Washington trusted many of these correspondents and since their observations generally confirmed his own misgivings, he tended to take the reports at face value. Accurate or not, they added to his sense of urgency. Each disturbing account made the next one all the more plausible.

One hopes that Washington greeted Dr. Benjamin Rush's dramatic assessment of the national malaise with a smile. At the time, Rush was a highly regarded scientist in a society that as yet had not produced very many. In an essay published soon after Washington became president and entitled "Influence of the AMERICAN REVOLUTION upon the HUMAN BODY," Rush recounted the outbreak during the late 1780s of a dangerous political disease, which he named *"Anarchia."* Rush argued that the Revolution had not in fact ended with the signing of a peace treaty. Rather, liberation from British rule had introduced a kind of mass craze. His research revealed "the excess of the passion for liberty, inflamed by the successful issue of the war, produced in many people, opinions and conduct which could not be removed by reason, nor restrained by government." The dangers posed by Anarchia were terrifying. Rush warned specifically that "the extensive influence which these opinions had upon the understandings, passions, and morals of many of the citizens of the United States constituted a species of insanity." [12]

John Jay adopted an even more ominous tone. Indeed, few American Cassandras could match New York's John Jay, future justice on the Supreme Court, for dispensing bad news. However Washington harshly diagnosed the country's troubles, Jay told him the situation was actually much worse. He replaced the threat of "Anarchy or Despotism" with his own inventory of national "Evils and Calamities." Whatever the descriptive language one employed, the outlook for the United States was much the same. Freedom from imperial rule seemed to have yielded a frenetic culture of public greed. Everyone appeared bent on pursuing private advantage. According to Jay, the real danger posed by the recent explosion of selfishness was that it might persuade respectable citizens—those who had understood and fought for the true values of the Revolution—to give up on the whole republican experiment. Tyranny by another, perhaps more acceptable name might be deemed preferable to chaotic liberty. "What I most fear," Jay confessed, "is that the better kind of People—(by which I mean the People who are orderly and industrious, who are content with their situations, and not uneasy in their Circumstances) will be led by the Insecurity of Property, the Loss of Confidence in their Rulers, & the Want of public Faith & Rectitude, to consider the Charms of Liberty as imaginary and delusive." [13] Another correspondent who worried about what might happen if the people lost trust in their government informed Washington, "I have now twice heard . . . [that] some principal men of that State [Massachusetts] begin to talk of wishing one general *Head* to the Union, in the room of Congress!" [14]

Comments of this sort suggest the possibility that an American Julius Caesar or Oliver Cromwell was about to establish a military dictatorship. Washington certainly entertained such fears. But we need not share his anxieties. In fact, we might observe in passing that the rich and well born—people such as Jay—often confused the desire of ordinary men and women to achieve a better material life with grubby and vulgar striving. For these people, it was quite possible that Anarchia was not a dreaded political disease but a healthy sign of mobility brought on by freedom and social equality. Because Washington valued the good judgment of his Revolutionary friends in these matters, however, he never stopped to consider whether less fortunate Americans trembled at the thought of anarchy. [15] For him, the union was at stake.

Washington expressed not the slightest doubt about where to locate the root cause of the nation's weakness: the states were to blame. In another letter to Henry Lee, he launched a blistering attack on the narrow-minded representatives who sat in the Confederation Congress. Faced with serious problems affecting the entire nation, they refused to contemplate even the slightest diminution of state sovereignty. How could one explain such obstructive behavior? "My opinion is," thundered Washington in 1786, "that there is more wickedness than ignorance in the conduct of the States, or in other words, in the conduct of those who have too much influence in the fabrication of our Laws."

Washington wanted to expose the representatives' parochial agenda to public scrutiny. If Americans could just learn what the men they had elected to the Continental Congress were actually doing—or, in this case, not doing—the people might demand reform. "Till the curtain is withdrawn, and the private views, & selfish principles upon which these men act, are exposed to public notice & resentment," Washington declared, "I have little hopes of amendment; without another convulsion."[16]

The reference to another convulsion coming only three years after the conclusion of the Revolution was chilling. Such extreme rhetoric, rare in Washington's correspondence, spoke to his growing exasperation with a Congress paralyzed by the intransigence of the representatives who claimed to speak for the states. Letters sent to Mount Vernon by friends around the country provided ever more evidence of the nation's impending collapse. From Massachusetts, Henry Knox sent Washington a brief, unsettling political history of the United States. "Our political machine constituted of thirteen independent sovereignties, have been constantly operating against each other, and against the federal head, ever since peace." The negative results were now clear. "The human mind in the local legislatures seems to be exerted," exclaimed Knox, "to prevent the federal constitution from having any beneficial effect."[17]

When he reviewed the situation in the states during the 1780s, Washington gave the worst grades for irresponsibility to Rhode Island and Massachusetts. For Rhode Island, the problem was useless money. The state legislature had adopted fiscal policies that made a mockery of legal contracts. The local government printed so much unsecured paper money that it quickly became worthless in the marketplace. Debtors reportedly chased creditors through the streets of Rhode Island with piles of inflated currency. "There is no State or description of men but would blush to be involved in a connection with the Paper-Money Junto of that Anarchy [Rhode Island]," Washington concluded. "God grant that the honest men may acquire an ascendancy before irrevocable ruin shall confound the innocent with the guilty."[18]

For those who genuinely feared anarchy, a small rising of impoverished farmers in Massachusetts seemed to suggest that the end was near. Daniel Shays, a Revolutionary veteran, had fallen on hard times, as had many of his struggling rural neighbors, and during summer 1786, they staged an armed protest against the hard money policies of the state that had burdened them with intolerable debt. Although these desperate men had a point, Washington's correspondents made it sound as if Shays threatened the very foundations of civilization. He did nothing of the sort. For men already worried about the nation's future, fear was contagious. In October, Henry Lee told Washington, "In a word, my dear General we are all in dire apprehension that a beginning of anarchy with all its calamities has approached, and have no means to stop the dreadful work."[19] For his part, Knox warned of "insurgents," whom he characterized as "desperate & unprincipled men."[20] Knox ignored the irony in the situation. At the start of the Revolution, the British had described the American rebels in precisely the same terms.[21] The political environment had changed. The problem with Shays was that he and his followers threatened the viability of the union. A federal government that tolerated local insurgencies because it lacked the power to crush them was no government at all.

However querulous Washington may have sounded at times during this period, we should note that he never lost faith in the people. To be sure, they could be misled. One only had to look at Rhode Island to see what harm they could do. But at the end of the day, Washington believed that if they had full knowledge of the true state of political affairs, they could be trusted to cleanse the Augean Stables.[22] Moreover, it would be a mistake to cast Washington simply as an American Jeremiah who confused normal social change for a betrayal of fundamental republican goals. Over the last several centuries, not a few revolutionary leaders have lost touch with their followers, infatuated with their own power. For Washington, however, this was never a possibility. Behind his unstinting criticism of the Confederation lay a positive vision of what the United States could become if it only brought forth a strong federal union. For him, this aspiration marked the fulfillment, not the betrayal, of the Revolution.

—III—

What would become the core of Washington's appeal to the nation contained three fundamental elements. First, he argued, the fragmentation of political authority—each state looking out for its own interests—had served only to compromise the prosperity of all Americans. Commerce was properly a national concern. The unencumbered flow of goods linked merchants and farmers; it strengthened the bonds between the new western settlements and the eastern ports. By condoning destructive competition among the states, the Confederation retarded robust economic development.[23] In a word, trade was too important to allow the individual states to control it.

Second, an impotent government—one incapable or unwilling to raise adequate revenue—could not possibly defend the American people against predatory imperial powers. As the maps in his own study revealed, the great European powers still ruled most of the New World—Great Britain to the north and Spain to the south—and it did not require much imagination to appreciate that they would welcome any opportunity to obstruct the interests of the United States.[24] The British occupied western posts around the Great Lakes even though they had promised in the peace treaty of 1783 to leave. The Confederation Congress accepted this diplomatic humiliation largely because it had no alternatives. It was too poor and too weak to confront America's former rulers.

Washington's third justification for a strong central government deserves closer analysis, since it addresses the protection of basic human rights. As he recognized, rights claims without secure guarantees are meaningless. If during the ordinary course of political affairs, local groups can trample the rights of other citizens with impunity—if they have the power to constrain freedom of speech or religion, for example—then rights talk becomes no more than a rhetorical move incapable of securing lasting social justice.

As Washington understood, the preservation of the rights for which American Revolutionaries had fought depended ultimately on strong central authority. Unless people living in the separate states, or in sections of the states, could count on an external arbiter possessing sufficient power to enforce its decisions, minorities could never feel safe from potentially intolerant or violent neighbors. Over the long course of our nation's history, many people—some of them passionate liberals—have missed this basic point. They have celebrated the rich and intimate social exchanges allegedly found in small communities. That is generally a mistake. Minority rights assume the existence of a government able to defend them. Or, stated another way, localism almost always puts the universal rights that Americans cherish in jeopardy.

This fundamental insight was precisely what Washington was getting at in a sharply worded letter to Jay. "Experience has taught us," he wrote in 1786, "that men will not adopt & carry into execution, measures best calculated for their own good without the intervention of a coercive power. I do not conceive we can exist long as a nation, without having lodged somewhere a power which will pervade the whole Union in as energetic a manner, as the authority of the different state governments extends over the several States." [25]

Washington discovered on his journey to the nation an unsettling example of what could happen to rights when no coercive power was able or willing to enforce them. Returning from the South in 1791, he reflected on a disturbing situation in Georgia. A group of large-scale land speculators in that state seemed intent on pushing the Native Americans aside in the name of quick profit. These self-serving citizens not only criticized the new federal government but also were determined to cheat the Creek Indians out of rights to land they had obtained through a treaty with the United States. It was clear to Washington what had gone wrong: the Georgia authorities had fallen under the spell of "some demagogue, or speculating character." As a result of the federal government's inability to intervene effectively, the Indians stood no chance. They were the victims of "Land Jobbers, who, Maugre [in spite of] every principle of Justice to the Indians & policy to their Country would, for their own immediate emolument, strip the Indians of all their territory." Alexander Martin, governor of North Carolina, echoed the president's concern—at least, that is what he told Washington in June 1791. The governor, Washington noted in his diary, "seems to condemn the Speculators in Lands and the purchase from the State of Georgia, & thinks as every sensible & disinterested man must, that schemes of that sort must involve the Country in trouble—perhaps in blood." The only hope for the beleaguered Creek Indians was that "the good sense of the State [Georgia] will set its face against such diabolical attempts."[26] It was but a hope. If the federal government could not protect the rights of its citizens from a state, then rights counted for nothing at all.

—IV—

Washington supported the call early in 1787 for a Constitutional Convention, which he regarded as the last best chance to curb the power of the states. But during the planning stages, he did his best to downplay his enthusiasm. In letters to friends, he expressed a curious ambivalence about actually taking part in the great debate. Historians of this period have made a lot of Washington's vacillation at this key moment. There is no question that he expressed uneasiness about participating in the

Philadelphia gathering. He seemed genuinely worried about the propriety of appearing at the meeting when he had already promised the
Society of the Cincinnati, an honorary association of military officers
who had served during the Revolution, that he would attend its convention scheduled for the same time. Pulling out at the last moment
and thereby disappointing his fellow officers of the Continental Army
struck Washington as possibly dishonorable. And so, as Madison and
Hamilton were preparing for the convention, Washington fretted about
the appearance of honor.

As Washington soon discovered, however, saving the nation at
a moment of severe crisis counted for more than disappointing the
Cincinnati. His correspondence during the run-up to the convention
suggests that the business with a prior commitment to the Society of
the Cincinnati was only a passing distraction.[27] His heart was with the
group of men determined to strengthen the federal government. Washington's guarded response to questions about his possible participation in the meeting probably reflected his entirely justified fear that
the Constitutional Convention might fail. It seemed almost as if he
worried that by voicing too much excitement, he would tempt fate.
Public enthusiasm courted opposition and disappointment and a threat
to his reputation.

And so, as his allies made plans to travel to the meeting, Washington
was still asking whether the American people were really prepared to accept far-reaching government reform. Perhaps they were not ready for
a radical change. Perhaps they had to feel a little more pain—experience
additional outbreaks of anarchy—before they genuinely saw the need
to check the independence of the states. As Washington told Jay, "My
opinion is that this Country [must] . . . *feel* and *see* a little more before
it [a major reform] can be accomplished." Quite predictably, he laid the
blame on the states and the narrow-minded politicians who endorsed
state sovereignty. "A thirst for power," he continued, "and the bantling
[bastard]—I had liked to have said monster—sovereignty, which have

taken such fast hold of the States individually, will . . . form a strong phalanx against it [the Constitution]."²⁸

Even before the Philadelphia meeting opened, Washington sensed that he and his friends would be forced to compromise on the issue of state power. It was a matter of pragmatism. However irrational their sizes and shapes may have been, the states could not now be erased from the political maps. Washington was working against history and tradition. In a key letter drafted on the eve of the convention, Madison candidly laid out the prospects. He described two extreme and opposing possibilities, neither of which stood the slightest chance of becoming part of the new constitution. On the one hand, he explained, "An individual independence of the States is utterly irreconcilable with their aggregate sovereignty." But on the other hand, "a consolidation of the whole into one simple republic would be as inexpedient as it is unattainable."

This was the situation in a nutshell. People of Washington's persuasion had to find a way to curtail state sovereignty while at the same time conceding that the states would still play some part in a reconstituted federal system. The tension between state and nation compelled Madison to seek "some middle ground, which may at once support a due supremacy of the national authority, and not exclude the local authorities wherever they can be *subordinately* useful."²⁹

Since Washington respected Madison's political instincts, he must have invested high expectations in the word *subordinately*. He knew that Madison shared his views on state sovereignty. They traveled to Philadelphia intent on advancing a plan in which a greatly strengthened federal government would possess an absolute veto over all state legislation. This was, of course, an extremely radical proposal. One wonders how Madison thought that it could ever win sufficient delegate support to become part of the new constitutional order.

But on this point, Madison was determined. In an April 1787 letter to Washington, Madison insisted that "a negative *in all cases whatsoever* on the legislative acts of the States, as heretofore exercised by the Kingly prerogative, appears to me absolutely necessary." One can imagine Madison's embarrassment had the reference to *kingly* prerogative been later broadcast to the public. This was a very different Madison from the man who during Adams's administration joined with Thomas Jefferson in defending states' rights and who became a leading spokesman for the Republican Party. But the Madison of the Constitutional Convention spoke words that Washington welcomed. They agreed at that moment that "national supremacy" depended on finding "some disinterested & dispassionate umpire in disputes between different passions & interests in the State."[30]

Washington accepted the position as president of the convention. Day after day, he monitored the debates, seldom speaking, always listening. At some point it became apparent that Madison's scheme for a federal veto of state legislation was a nonstarter. The ability of the states to resist substantial reform annoyed Madison; in part because of this setback, the chief architect of the Constitution left the Philadelphia meeting with a sense of disappointment. He soon rallied, however, and in a brilliant effort to sell the final document to the American people, he joined Jay and Hamilton in writing the *Federalist Papers*. Washington tried to put a good face on the results of the convention. The states remained a problem, to be sure, but his experiences under the Confederation had convinced him that "there is no alternative between the adoption of it [the Constitution] and anarchy." Of course, the battle to save the nation from disintegration had just started. Some months after having returned to Mount Vernon, Washington still believed that the "General Government is now suspended by a thread." And then, in the same letter, he revised that statement. No, what he really intended to say was that meaningful national authority "is really at an end."[31]

Like Madison, Washington soon overcame his initial disappointment. Selling the Constitution to the American people presented him with an entirely new challenge. The contest with the Antifederalists brought out Washington's competitive spirit. This was a battle he intended to win. He mustered his allies and encouraged writers to take up the pen to counter the arguments of the Antifederalists. Some critics rejected the Constitution out of hand. Others accepted the need for reform but thought that the Philadelphia document had gone too far. They insisted on amendments, most of them having to do with the protection of various natural rights. But whatever the character of their complaint, Washington saw the Antifederalists as opponents who threatened his vision for the United States.

Like modern political figures on election night, Washington followed the results of the state conventions for ratification with intense personal interest. The early returns were encouraging. In January 1789 he informed his close friend Lafayette that "the federal sentiments seem to be growing with uncommon rapidity." Not surprisingly, he interpreted the results as evidence of "the good sense of the Americans."[32] Whether he was correct about the nation's reservoir of good sense depended, of course, on one's ideological perspective.[33] The Antifederalists mounted a spirited campaign to defeat the Constitution, and although we today tend to take ratification for granted, the final tabulations in the various states were very close. A shift of a few votes would have put an end to the efforts of Washington and his friends to bring greater *"energy & stability"* to the government.[34]

Each state joining the new government represented a victory for meaningful reform or, as Washington declared, an advance for "the Federal interest and the glory of the American Nation."[35] Defeat was unthinkable. The country had already witnessed the fragmentation of authority, and if the people did not now come forward, they would soon witness the final collapse of the republic. There would be thirteen Rhode Islands or, at the very least, several independent regions. In the *Federalist Papers*, number 5, Jay described what would happen if the people did not support a powerful union of the states. "Instead of their being joined in affection and free from all apprehension of different interests," Jay warned, "envy and jealousy would soon extinguish confidence and affection, and the partial interests of each confederacy, instead of the general interests of all America, would be the only objects of their policy and pursuits."[36]

Before it was clear that a sufficient number of states would ratify the Constitution, Madison warned his allies against premature optimism. He had heard rumors that opponents were considering a call for a second constitutional convention charged with addressing alleged deficiencies found in the document that he and the other delegates had just drafted in Philadelphia. Like Washington, Madison regarded this as a terrible idea. As many countries have discovered over the past two centuries, revising a constitution is a kind of slippery slope. After all, too many revisions make a mockery of fundamental principles. Writing to Jefferson, Madison described the hazards the advocates of a new convention posed, a warning of enduring relevance in our society. "The great danger in the present crisis," he explained, "is that if another Convention should be soon assembled it would terminate in discord, or in alterations of the federal system which would throw back *essential* powers into the State Legislatures."[37]

Madison had hoped, as had Washington, that the Antifederalists who championed state sovereignty would see the light. But dissenters in several states, including Rhode Island and North Carolina, rejected the arguments for a strong central government. Madison had no sympathy for their scruples. "It is truly mortifying," he told Washington, "that the onset of the new Government should be immediately preceded by such a display of localism."[38] To be sure, the critics had scored some points. Even fervent supporters of the Constitution admitted that the plan contained flaws, but at this moment in the country's history, perfection was not the goal. The agreement worked out in Philadelphia—considering that several southern states threatened to leave the convention if the delegates tampered with slavery—was as good as the Federalists could expect. Madison did not get a federal veto of state legislation. And so, one might well ask, with all the compromises, why did he and Washington fight so hard for its adoption? To this question, Madison responded, "I thought it safe to the liberties of the people and the best that could be obtained from the jarring interests of the States, and the miscellaneous opinions of Politicians."[39]

Documenting Washington's growing hostility to the defenders of state sovereignty is key to understanding why he decided as president to take the government to the American people. Another element that was shaping his thinking is easily overlooked. The process of ratifying the Constitution dramatically transformed the character of American political culture. Before the convention delegates decided to send the document for approval by specially elected state conventions, the people had not had a significant voice in political affairs. It is true that during colonial times, mobs of ordinary men and women occasionally took to the streets to protest British policies, but interventions of this sort were rare. Revolutionary leaders were not inclined to take the major issues of the day to the people for approval.

The process of ratifying the Constitution radically changed previous practices and assumptions. Winning support for the Federalist cause required making direct appeals to the people through newspapers and pamphlets. Significantly, the audience in the contest consisted of more than just the propertied white males who enjoyed the right to vote. Ratification opened the door to public opinion, to politics out of doors, and to conversations with ordinary Americans about the future of government.[40]

What Washington learned was that the great mass of white citizens could not be ignored—controlled, perhaps, occasionally manipulated, but never again treated as irrelevant. In an age before sophisticated opinion polls, it was hard to determine what was on the people's minds, but however fuzzy the calculations, ratification brought home the responsibility of elected leaders such as Washington to interpret the will of the people, women and men. As a Boston newspaper declared in language that would have made sense only in theory before this moment in American history, "We rejoice in a government, supported by the force of public opinion, grounded upon the honor and interests of all the people, without the aid of halters, axes or standing armies. The united sentiments of a wise and virtuous people, maintain a free government."[41]

—V—

Washington fully appreciated that securing the Revolution required establishing enduring emotional ties between the people and their new federal government. In 1789 these bonds were extremely tenuous. Although the state contests over ratification had generated fierce partisan rhetoric the likes of which the country had never before witnessed, ordinary people still identified with the states in which they lived.[42] As the *Gazette of the United States*, a New York newspaper that celebrated the new constitutional order, observed, "We have been accustomed to distinct, independent governments: We have not been used to think nationally—to consider ourselves as an indivisible whole."[43]

It is easy to mistake what Washington was trying to achieve when he spoke of a strong central government. His goal was not to encourage the spirit of nationalism, at least not in the way that term is ordinarily used. The country had already demonstrated an ability to support a common cause during the Revolution.[44] The people had cooperated in defeating the British. The problem facing leaders such as Washington during the late 1780s was finding how best to encourage the development of what might be termed *federal nationalism*. The concept was the product of pragmatic compromise. However much Washington wanted to reduce the power of the states, he knew that they were not about to disappear, and no matter how he performed as president, the people would still identify primarily with states such as South Carolina or Massachusetts.[45]

Federal nationalism invited Americans to overlay those local identities with a larger one that promised benefits that no single state could provide: a strong defense against imperial predators, a robust national marketplace, and a reliable protector of civil rights. It was a matter of balance. The states reinforced the bonds of local loyalty through their own histories and shared traditions. For the Constitution to represent more that a paper agreement, Washington had to convince Americans to take on another level of political identity, one able to coexist with strong feelings about the states while simultaneously putting forward powerful symbols of union, of which Washington himself was the most visible. It is testimony to his political genius that he comprehended so early and so fully the emotional dynamics of federal nationalism.

Even after being sworn in as president, Washington remained on the alert for indications that the old troubles that had plagued the Confederation had returned. Although it would be unfair to describe his uneasiness about the nation's future as the product of conspiratorial thinking, he did in fact continuously search the political landscape for hints of fragmentation. He worried that the Antifederalists might be staging a renewed assault on the Constitution. How many members of Congress, he wondered, did not support a strong central government? Why were Rhode Island and North Carolina taking so long to join the union? What we encounter during the early months of his first term is an uneasiness that dissent might at any moment give birth to full-scale faction, and for Washington, faction posed a grave threat to the security of the union.

Later, a year or two after he had completed his journeys to the people, Washington's concerns about the growth of formal opposition to his policies increased, and during his second term, they served to justify his suspicion that former friends such as Jefferson and Madison had become political adversaries. But even during his first days as president, Washington was on guard for any hint of faction. Organized dissent, he believed, would most certainly lead to a breakdown of union—and possibly domestic violence. At the time, most political theorists would have agreed with Washington. As a newspaper that supported his policies proclaimed, "FACTION; properly speaking, is the offspring of disappointment, pride, inordinate ambitions, and the whole train of the malevolent passions: Its object is in the first place the promotion of its own individual advantage, without any regard to that of the community at large."[46]

What today we would regard as serious partisan rivalry lay in the future, since in 1789 no real political parties existed—no Federalists, no Republicans. And yet even during a year or two of relative tranquility and cooperation, Washington still nervously scanned the political news that reached his desk for indications that the demons of state sovereignty were at work in the countryside. He not only wanted to promote federal nationalism but also to gauge for himself popular support for the new government.

When he received negative reports—when he learned of possible discontent with his administration—Washington offered a convenient although somewhat circular explanation. Since his own decisions as president reflected the fundamental values of the Revolution and since people possessing accurate knowledge of what their government was doing would surely support him, dissent could only be the result of purposeful misinformation, of the dissemination of self-serving lies.

When asked who would behave so irresponsibly, Washington had two ready responses. First, on the state level, narrow-minded demagogues posed the greatest challenge to the new federal government. These figures—Washington had self-promoting men such as John Hancock and Patrick Henry in mind—advanced their own standing with constituents by exploiting the rhetoric of state sovereignty.

Washington gave little credit to such arguments. He had an explanation for why anyone would work so hard to pervert the truth. According to Washington, the troublemakers were often people who dreamed of acquiring influence on the national stage but who, because of poor character or limited talents, had failed to fulfill their own career aspirations. Such ambitious men then returned to the states, angry, disappointed, and eager to get a measure of revenge on those who had thwarted their political desires. In 1790, Washington explained to his Virginia friend

David Stuart that the most annoying opponents ofconstitutional order—meaning, of course, critics of a strong central government—were "men who go from hence [the nation's capital] without *feeling* themselves of so much consequence as they wished to be considered—disappointed expectants and malignant designing characters."

When the small-timers returned home, they filled the heads of the local people with distorted stories about a grasping federal government, poisoning the very possibility of building a strong union. The agitators, Washington exclaimed, "miss no opportunity to aim a blow at the Constitution, [and] paint highly on one side without bringing into view the arguments which are offered on the other."[47] In another letter, Washington condemned the whole lot as "political Mountebanks"—in other words, as charlatans.[48] Some potential enemies were more contemptible than others, and for Washington, the greatest villains were unscrupulous speculators, especially the greedy agents who jeopardized peace on the frontier for their own profit.[49] Calling the critics of the new government malignant and disingenuous may seem overly harsh, even grossly exaggerated, considering that Washington himself hoped to make money selling land in the Ohio Valley, but again, we should take into account that like other leaders of the Revolutionary generation, Washington sometimes confused disapproval of his administration with calculated dishonesty. He was certainly not alone in failing to appreciate how his own financial agenda might be part of the problem.

The second danger to the creation of a stronger union was the rise of what Washington might have called sensationalist journalism. His hostility toward newspapers comes as a surprise, since he regularly examined as many of them as he could obtain. But once he became president, his attitude toward the press soured. Although he did not advocate censorship, he concluded that some editors—and at the time, there were no reporters—recounted what was happening in the nation's capital in such a biased and inaccurate manner that ordinary American citizens had no means to discover for themselves what the new administration was really doing. Like the mountebanks who told the people lies in order to advance their own careers, the editors stood between a well-meaning president and the American people.

In a perfect society, of course, newspapers would have provided not only reliable political information but also a vital forum where readers discussed plans for the country's future.[50] While he was traveling through South Carolina, Washington explained to an admirer, "To endeavor to diffuse a knowledge of the *true* interests of our Country in a commercial or political view is certainly a meritorious attempt, and in this age of free inquiry every one has a right to submit to the consideration of his fellow citizens such sentiments or information as he thinks may conduce to their interest or happiness."[51]

The giveaway in this letter was the word *true*. Washington, perhaps naively, believed that newspapers should be transparent, so that someone in Georgia reading about events in New York City would know what national leaders were doing as well as why they were doing it. But the process never seemed to operate as he imagined it should. "It is to be lamented," he observed in 1790, "that the Editors of the several Gazettes of the Union do not more generally & more connectedly publish the debates in Congress on all the National questions." What did they do instead? They stuffed "their papers with scurrility & malignant declamation, which few would read if they were apprised of the contents." It was no wonder that people living far from the capital thought that Washington bowed a little too stiffly or that he secretly aspired to be crowned king of the United States. They just did not know the truth.

The blustering demagogues and sensationalist editors challenged Washington to find how to get around the self-appointed gatekeepers of public opinion. The obvious answer was to go directly to the people and by so doing remove the veil of misinformation. He had a coherent, honest message to offer, and he believed that if they listened to him—if they saw him in person—they might realize more fully that their political identities were not tied solely to the states.

Washington explained his goals for the nation most movingly in a statement sent to the Pennsylvania legislature in September 1789. His prose seldom achieved the rhetorical heights associated with Lincoln or Jefferson, but at this particular moment his words possessed power and beauty. They summoned the people to a higher destiny: "It should be the highest ambition of every American to extend his views beyond himself, and to bear in mind that his conduct will not only affect himself, his country, and his immediate posterity; but that its influence may be co-extensive with the world, and stamp potential happiness or misery on ages yet unborn." For this end, "the *union* of the States is absolutely necessary."[52] A few weeks after he sent this declaration to Pennsylvania, he launched the first journey to the nation.

—VI—

Washington had a "marvelous talent"—to borrow Adams's vocabulary—to translate a complex vision about the future of America into a set of highly visible symbols that every citizen could understand. Indeed, his actions as president revealed that his special political ability lay in making abstract political ideas concrete, in turning principles into actions. Almost intuitively, he saw that if he was going to strengthen the union—successfully promoting federal nationalism—he needed to put forward an unmistakably American story. To that end, Washington seized on the Revolution, and in town after town, he turned memories of the shared sacrifice of the American people against Great Britain into a powerful tool to counter the emotional attraction of local identities. It was an inspired strategy. By taking control of the country's past, he advanced a positive message about its future. And more, his upbeat approach to the problem of unity freed him from the burden of having to attack the states, at least in his public pronouncements.

Within this interpretive framework, the Revolutionary battles that had taken place in South Carolina or Massachusetts were not South Carolina or Massachusetts battles. During his travels, he treated them as chapters of a larger shared history of the United States. As must have been obvious even to the dimmest spectator, Washington visited America to remind the people that since they had cooperated so effectively during the war, they could certainly do so again. A strong union was their Revolutionary heritage.

In communities throughout the nation, ordinary people watched as their president visited the places where Americans had fought and died for independence, sites of national sacrifice. In Savannah, for example, he walked the land where a fierce engagement had taken place. In his diary, Washington noted how difficult it had already become to locate the lines of defense that the troops had constructed. "To form an opinion of the attack at this distance of time, and the change which has taken place in the appearance of the ground by the cutting away of the woods," he wrote in 1791, "is hardly to be done with justice to the subject." But such details did not matter. Washington described the assault as a joint action "under the combined forces of France and the United States." His appearance at the site of combat honored the entire nation's resistance to imperial rule.[53] Newspapers recounted the president's tour, and thus, by communicating a local event to a broader national audience, they situated the defense of Savannah in a national chronicle of shared sacrifice.[54]

Soon after, Washington again dramatically linked the history of the Revolution to his own appeal to the American people. In Camden, South Carolina, he visited the grave of Baron de Kalb, a German officer who had achieved a distinguished record as a major general in the Continental Army. The two men had suffered together at Valley Forge. Later in the war, de Kalb served in the South under the command of General Nathanael Greene, and during an attack on enemy positions in Camden, had a horse shot from under him. As he lay on the field, British troops repeatedly bayoneted de Kalb. General Cornwallis reportedly offered de Kalb medical assistance, to which the German responded, "I thank you sir for your generous sympathy, but I die the death I always prayed for: the death of a soldier fighting for the rights of man."[55] Again, the newspapers throughout the nation reported how Washington had honored his dead comrade. The *Maryland Gazette*, for example, reprinted the report from Camden describing how the president "viewed the places where the British redoubts had been erected, and after pausing a few minutes at the grave of Baron de Kalb, he set out from our village.—On his way, he viewed, in a very particular manner, the ground on which General Greene, was attacked by the British troops."[56]

People from all parts of the country watched—through the newspapers—how Washington reexperienced the Revolution. It did not take much imagination to know how he felt when he paused for a few moments at a soldier's grave. The public knew that he had visited the defenses of Charleston, spent time with General Greene's widow, and explored the battlefield at Augusta. In several cities, he received effusive welcoming speeches from the members of the Society of the Cincinnati, the officers of the Continental Army. Veterans of all ranks came out to pay their respects to their commander.

On the road to the nation, Washington's memories merged with America's memories. No one mentioned that the states had in fact only reluctantly sent money and supplies to support the Continental Army. The troops at Valley Forge had nearly starved. But in the name of securing the union and the Constitution on which it now depended, the Revolution acquired the nobility of a common cause. In particular, Washington's stop at Lexington in 1789 had special meaning for the entire nation. In his diary he noted only that he had spent a few private moments at the place where the "first blood was spilt."[57] The blood was America's blood, not the blood of a few stubborn militiamen from the state of Massachusetts.

CHAPTER IV

━━◦◉◦━━

Voices of the People

As George Washington became the main actor in a political theater of the
new republic, the American people were his audience. They were a demanding body—noisy, pushy, and ready to pass judgment on what they
saw. These were the children of the Revolution. And yet, surprisingly,
it is these very men and women who often go missing from the political
narratives of the period, shunted aside to make room for tales of ambition and intrigue among a small group of famous leaders.

The people cannot be silenced so easily. As Washington discovered
during his several journeys, ordinary Americans had come to assume
by 1789 that they deserved a voice in shaping the new republican culture. They realized, as perhaps we no longer appreciate today, just how
revolutionary the American Revolution had been. It achieved far more
than national independence. The break with Great Britain overturned
the fundamental conventions of an aristocratic world. It is true that we
still treat the current members of the royal family as celebrities—as if we
had not centuries ago rejected the pageantry of monarchy—but bless-
edly, we no longer award people special privileges in our society solely
because they happen to be the sons or daughters of nobility. Americans of Washington's generation had freed themselves from the tyranny
of inherited titles. As a result, they—largely white men of European
background—imagined themselves to be social equals.

This wonderfully expansive vision of a republican society recently born of revolution provided the social and political context for Washington's journeys to the new nation. Everywhere he traveled, he encountered crowds of Americans, most of them young and optimistic about their futures. For these people, the Revolution had presented personal opportunities unimagined under the old colonial regime. Despite Washington's fear of anarchy, the 1780s were in fact a wonderful time for most Americans to be alive. The future held promise. Everyone seemed to have a scheme to make money. Some plans were ill conceived—canals funded by investors who had no knowledge of how to build locks and machines that never quite worked—but failure never discouraged eager entrepreneurs. These newly independent Americans were ambitious, commercial, and, by the standards of contemporary Great Britain, a little vulgar.

The president's journey to the nation sparked a marvelously inventive conversation about exactly what kind of political culture the American people had created. The challenge was great. Ordinary men and women had to discover on their own—and within a short time—how properly to honor Washington. In this uncertain landscape, they invented republican rituals of greeting and honor; they also devised ways to project meanings of their own onto the face of power. The forms they created may strike us today as unexceptional—endless toasts, huge parades, formal exchanges of welcome, long receptions, and elaborate entertainments—but as we should appreciate, for Americans of the founding generation, these public celebrations were new and exciting.[1]

By weaving two political narratives together, the local and the national, Washington's visits achieved something that the debates over the drafting and ratification of the Constitution seldom did: they transformed theoretical generalizations about political systems into an emotional reality for ordinary Americans and provided the social glue required for the success of the new government. We should remember that the development of a strongly felt sense of solidarity was key to transforming the Constitution from a bold experiment into a stable and enduring system, a transition that during this period was still very much in doubt.

The forging of a persuasive link between a new federal system and local experience was fundamental to the process of strengthening the effective bonds of union. Top-down models of political history focusing largely on the activities of a few privileged leaders tend to ignore the fact that the legitimization of power in a republic is a process of negotiation. It assumes an open, ongoing exchange between the people and their elected officials. At the same time that Washington advanced his own appeal for a strong federal union, the people sought to situate the president persuasively within local stories reflecting their own separate histories. For them, he was a revered Revolutionary figure, to be sure, but he was also a political leader who in their lives achieved special and enduring significance as the Washington of Charleston, or Boston, or Newport, or scores of small communities that greeted him so enthusiastically.

—I—

The story of one of the more famous surviving portraits of George Washington reveals how local and national perspectives complemented each other in surprising ways. The president visited Charleston, South Carolina, early in May 1791. The extravagant welcoming ceremony exceeded others he had experienced during his long journey through the South, a trip that we examine in greater detail in another chapter. In Charleston, an elaborately decorated barge transported him across the harbor. Other boats carried musicians; the people honored him with song. And at the moment when he landed in the city proper, a huge artillery salute announced his arrival. Over the next several days, his hosts treated him to feasts. He met with members of the Society of the Cincinnati; he examined Revolutionary battle sites. In every respect, the event was a great success. When he departed, Washington went out of his way "in the most affectionate manner . . . [to] communicate to all the citizens of Charleston his best thanks, for the very polite and great affection to him during his stay in this city."[2]

Everyone was so pleased with Washington's visit that it seemed quite reasonable that the people of Charleston should devise a way to commemorate the historic moment. The members of the city council decided that what they most wanted was a formal portrait of the president that they could display in a place where the public would readily see it. On May 7 the council announced its unanimous resolution, proclaimed significantly in the name of "their constituents," that Washington would "when it was convenient to him . . . permit his portrait to be taken by Colonel Trumbull, in order that it may be placed in the city hall, as the most lasting testimony of their attachment to his person, to commemorate his arrival in the metropolis of this state, and to hand down to posterity the resemblance of the Man, to whom they are so much indebted for the blessings of PEACE, LIBERTY, and INDEPENDENCE."[3]

Since Washington had in fact thoroughly enjoyed his stay in Charleston, he graciously consented. The nomination of John Trumbull was an inspired act. Trumbull not only had established a reputation throughout the country as an outstanding painter, but also had developed over several decades a close personal relationship with the president. Trumbull owed his professional acclaim to natural talent as well as social standing. His father had been a highly respected governor of Connecticut, and the son enjoyed the best education that the country could provide. An accident had deprived John of the sight in one eye, a misfortune that critics thought accounted for the flatness of some of his works.

The mishap did not hold him back. Trumbull trained in Great Britain with Benjamin West, an American émigré from Pennsylvania who would later become the president of the Royal Academy in London.

1

The Washington Oak, Hampton Plantation, McClellanville, South Carolina.

2

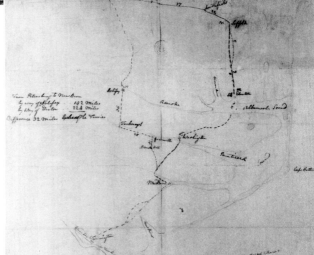

George Washington's itinerary for the Southern Tour, 1791.

3

An East View of Gray's Ferry, on the River Schuylkill (woodcut attributed to Charles Willson Peale).

4

View of the triumphal arch at Trenton, April 2, 1789.

Benjamin Franklin cartoon, "Join, or Die" (1754).

6

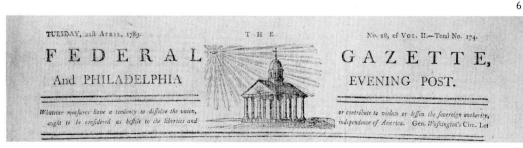

Federal Gazette.

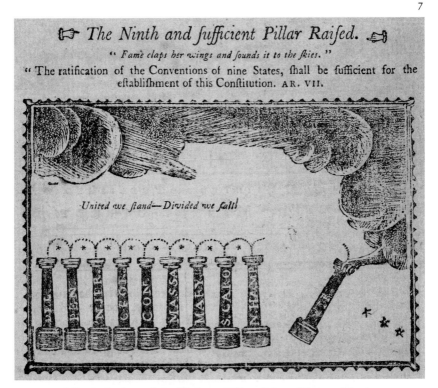

☞ *The Ninth and sufficient Pillar Raised.* ☞

" *Fame claps her wings and sounds it to the skies.* "

" The ratification of the Conventions of nine States, shall be sufficient for the establishment of this Constitution. AR. VII.

United we stand—Divided we fall

The Ninth and Sufficient Pillar (New Hampshire).

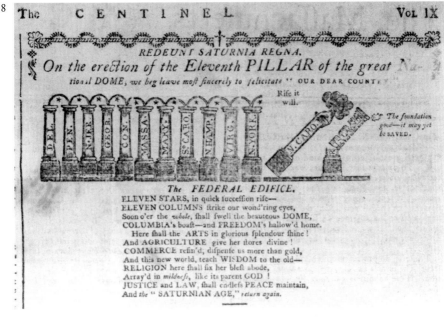

The CENTINEL. VOL IX

REDEUNT SATURNIA REGNA.

On the erection of the Eleventh PILLAR *of the great Na-tional* DOME, *we beg leave most sincerely to felicitate* " OUR DEAR COUNTRY."

Rise it will.

The foundation good—it may yet be SAVED.

The FEDERAL EDIFICE.

ELEVEN STARS, in quick succession rise—
ELEVEN COLUMNS strike our wond'ring eyes,
Soon o'er the *whole*, shall swell the beauteous DOME,
COLUMBIA's boast—and FREEDOM's hallow'd home.
   Here shall the ARTS in glorious splendour shine!
And AGRICULTURE give her stores divine!
COMMERCE refin'd, dispense us more than gold,
And this new world, teach WISDOM to the old—
RELIGION here shall fix her blest abode,
Array'd in *mildness*, like its parent GOD!
JUSTICE and LAW, shall endless PEACE maintain,
And the " SATURNIAN AGE," *return again.*

The Eleventh Pillar (New York).

9

General George Washington at Trenton, 1792 (John Trumbull).

10

George Washington at Charleston, 1792 (John Trumbull).

View of the triumphal arch and colonnade at Boston 1789.

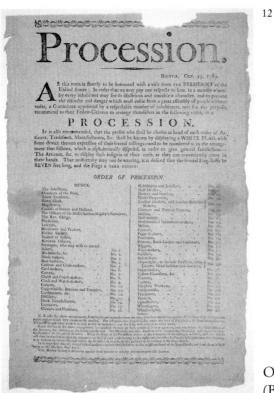

Order of Procession
(Boston, 1789).

13

Touro Synagogue (Newport, Rhode Island, external view).

14

Touro Synagogue (internal view).

Portrait of George Washington's Cook (Hercules) (attributed to Gilbert Stuart).

15

The West Front of Mount Vernon, c. 1792 (attributed to Edward Savage).

Detail of Savage's *The West Front of Mount Vernon*.

POWEL COACH, AS EXHIBITED AT CENTENNIAL EXPOSITION, PHILADELPHIA, 1876; IN COACH-HOUSE AT MOUNT VERNON SINCE 1901.

Powel Coach, as exhibited at the Centennial Exposition, Philadelphia, 1876.

Powel Coach in the stables at Mount Vernon.

Coach on display at Mount Vernon.

West urged Trumbull to devote himself to large historical canvases that captured the nobility of the leaders of the American Revolution. Trumbull followed the advice, and his celebrated *Declaration of Independence* hangs today in the rotunda of the United States Capitol.

Washington did not require West's endorsement. The president admired Trumbull's careful realism. Indeed, the painter traveled hundreds of miles throughout America to make sketches of Revolutionary survivors so that his huge paintings would reflect as accurately as possible the faces of the great men who had shaped the nation's history. And for a veteran such as Washington, it helped a lot that Trumbull had seen active military service during the Revolution.

When the president returned to Philadelphia, he sat for the promised portrait. Trumbull welcomed the Charleston commission, since among other benefits it carried a handsome fee and he needed the money. As he acknowledged, "The commission was unlimited."[4] His labors resulted in a painting that many viewers over the centuries have come to regard as his best work. Known as *General Washington at the Battle of Trenton,* it gives dramatic expression to the leader's state of mind at a crucial turning point in the conflict with Great Britain. In the portrait, Washington surveys the scene of the coming struggle. He realizes that the odds of victory are long, and yet he faces the challenge with unflinching courage. Beside the general stands a wild-eyed charger. The animal seems to sense the historical significance of the event.

In his autobiography, Trumbull explained that he aimed to capture Washington's "military character, in the most sublime moment of its exertion." How better to do this than render the man when he confronted "the vast superiority of his approaching enemy, and the impossibility of again crossing the Delaware, or retreating down the river." At this decisive point, Trumbull's "Washington conceives the plan of returning by a night march into the country from which he had just been driven, thus cutting off the enemy's communication, and destroying his depot of stores and provisions at Brunswick."[5]

When Trumbull completed the work, he showed it to William Loughton Smith, then a member of Congress from South Carolina. If the artist expected praise, he was in for a disappointment. Smith muttered polite words of appreciation, but it was clear that he did not regard the painting as acceptable, at least not to the people of his home state. As Trumbull reported, Smith was "personally pleased, but he thought the city would be better satisfied with a more matter-of-fact likeness, such as they had recently seen him—calm, tranquil, peaceful."[6]

Rejection placed the artist in a difficult situation. He wanted the generous commission, but he was understandably reluctant to ask a busy president to sit for a second portrait. Finally, Trumbull gathered his courage. He explained to Washington "Mr. Smith's objection, and he [the president] cheerfully submitted to a second penance, adding 'Keep the [first] picture for yourself, Mr. Trumbull, and finish it to your own taste.'" In the new work, the painter tried to accommodate the concerns of the Charleston committee. He delivered a placid Washington with "a view of the city in the background, a horse, with scenery, and plants of the climate."[7]

Although he managed to produce an acceptable picture, Trumbull remained in an irascible mood. The new horse carried the message. Unlike the Trenton painting in which Washington's charger seems to face the oncoming contest with as much determination as did its master, the Charleston horse exposes a good portion of its backside to the viewer. Moreover, the horse's tail seems suspiciously rigid, as if the animal might be contemplating activities other than heroic Revolutionary battle. To make matters even more alarming, the tail appears poised over the skyline of the city.

Whatever Trumbull's intention may have been, the members of the Charleston committee expressed pleasure with the second rendering of Washington. A year later, the president responded to a letter praising the new portrait from South Carolina's Revolutionary hero William Moultrie. Whether Washington was being sarcastic is difficult to discern, but he informed Moultrie, "I am much pleased to hear, that the picture by Colonel Trumbull gives so much satisfaction. The merit of this artist cannot fail to give much pleasure to those of his countrymen who possess a taste for the fine arts; and I know of no part of the United States, where it would be put to a stronger test than in South Carolina."[8]

The protracted negotiations over Trumbull's painting provide a particularly well-documented example of the kind of conversations generated by Washington's journey to the nation. The Charleston committee did indeed obtain the picture that it desired for its constituents. The local people found a way to honor their own Washington—the Washington of Charleston, the man who had spent a pleasant week in their city. And by hanging the work in a prominent place, the members of the committee established a lasting public reminder—at least, during the early years of the new republic before talk of secession sullied the political landscape—that the president standing among familiar plants and with the Charleston skyline at his back had once visited South Carolina to affirm the importance of a strong federal union.

—II—

Wherever Washington traveled, Americans flocked in large numbers to honor him. One Connecticut newspaper reported, "In every place through which he [Washington] passed, people of all ranks, ages and sexes, have testified their joy, at the opportunity to behold the political savior of their country."[9] As we shall discover later in this chapter, in some of the larger cities such as Boston and Charleston, they organized elaborate festivals and parades, receptions and feasts. But the journey also profoundly touched the people as individuals. From Hartford to Augusta, they regularly encountered the president in less structured, more personal situations. And on such occasions ordinary men and women suddenly found themselves caught up in a transcendent event that for many of them became a defining moment in their lives. In more modern times, we recognize this as a common experience. People generally remember, often in amazing detail, what they were doing when they first learned of some major disaster or encountered a celebrity. At such moments, they find themselves thrust into a larger story; the experience becomes special.

A kiss could do the trick. As a child, Hannah Gowen of Weston, Massachusetts, received one from the president, and when she looked back at the moment as an adult, she explained, "It was a matter of great pride and glory as long as [I] lived."[10] Another young woman helped serve dinner to Washington when he visited Exeter, New Hampshire. It was reported that Washington "saw at once that she was no menial servant, and calling her to him, addressed a few pleasant words and kissed her. She lived to attain a good old age, and was the friend of some of the most distinguished men of a subsequent generation, but probably no incident of her life made so lasting an impression upon her memory as the kiss of Washington."[11]

Even Americans who experienced no physical contact with the president still struggled to discover how to behave in his presence. Just what sort of man were they meeting? A newspaper account written during Washington's tour of New England reflected the widespread uncertainty about greeting him in an appropriate manner. "The President hath visited us," the journal reported, "[and] all his steps were dignity and love — It was glorious at once to embrace our Friend and Brother — Fellow Citizen — General — Supreme Magistrate — Political Father — Head of our Nation — and Representative of the Majesty of the United States."[12]

In a profoundly religious society, it was not surprising that some spectators associated Washington with divinity. For them, if he was not a god himself, then at least he enjoyed a special relation with Providence that radically separated him from the world of ordinary people. However enthusiastic the vice president had been for high-sounding titles, he never tried to associate Washington with the Lord. But others did.

One modestly gifted poet, for example, insisted that God had given the president preternatural abilities. It seemed to this local author, "As if the *very* DEITY *who guides him* were crept into his human powers to give him grace and honor!"[13] A few people even marked the moment by composing what might be described as secular prayers for Washington. A person writing for a Connecticut newspaper drafted a kind of spiritual address that he claimed had been inspired by seeing Washington: "ILLUSTRIOUS PATRIOT—our obligations to thee are infinite—but you have a recompense in the reflection that your country has approved your conduct, and that you reign in the hearts of every individual of your fellow citizens."[14]

Far more common was the assumption that Americans should honor Washington not simply as the president, but rather as the central figure in the American Revolution. There was no question that the aging hero deserved universal praise for liberating the nation from British oppression. As Washington learned during his journey to the nation, he would always be General Washington to those who remembered his personal sacrifice for independence. Militia units greeted him in almost every town, and he patiently reviewed the local troops. Aging veterans walked miles to pay their respect to their former commander.

But few pushed the military aspect too far. After all, it was one thing to honor Washington for his service during the Revolution and quite another to proclaim the leader of the new republic an American Caesar. A leading newspaper at the time specifically warned readers that they should not confuse Washington's tour with "the triumphal entries of the Roman conquerors." They should remember that Roman emperors were tyrants who had once tortured ordinary people merely for entertainment. "Can it be possible that a people who took delight in such spectacles of barbarity, ever felt a sentiment of generous freedom?" The answer to the rhetorical question was obvious. All Americans should understand that Rome's "boasted freedom, and love of liberty, consisted in a power and disposition to humble and enslave all the world beside. With what propriety then are their example cited . . . for the rule and enlightened citizens of the American Republic?"[15] And so Americans learned to honor Washington as a great soldier of memory, as a genuine Revolutionary hero, as the father of independence, but as they have had to relearn after almost every major war in the country's long history, they were ill advised to substitute past military achievement for that "respect which is due to the ruler of a free people."[16]

If most Americans saw the danger of addressing Washington as their American Caesar—he had absolutely no interest in becoming emperor—they nevertheless found it surprisingly appealing to depict him as a king, as in King George I of the United States. Their extremely unrepublican behavior when they encountered him on the road probably drew on their recent colonial past. While Americans had just ratified a republican form of government, which among other things abolished monarchs and aristocrats, many of them almost reflexively imagined Washington as a kind of elected monarch. It seemed quite unexceptional, therefore, for them to call Washington "His Excellency."[17] But however strong the force of habit, he was not a king, and any suggestion that he wielded authority as a monarch rather than as the elected representative of the people was bound to be viewed as a betrayal of the Revolution.

From time to time, however, Washington had to be reminded that his extreme formality signaled to sensitive republicans that he secretly harbored monarchical intentions. When crowds of ordinary people in city after city belted out the song, "He Comes! He Comes! The Hero Comes. Sound, sound your trumpets. Beat your drums," it certainly seemed as if they were imitating spectacles organized for English kings and queens during a royal progress. Ironically, the song itself had been written some sixty years earlier to welcome George II in towns throughout Great Britain. Such fawning court behavior disturbed Lucy Cranch, Abigail Adams's niece, who had witnessed with growing uneasiness the grand Boston reception for Washington in 1789. "Was there ever any people who acted so inconsistently as some of ours do," she asked rhetorically, "to clamor and rave if there is a shadow of power given their rulers and at the same time pay them homage in the manner that would disgrace the subjects of the Grand Turk?"[18]

Some Americans adopted a completely different strategy, one that had a solid foundation in common sense. They concluded that Washington deserved their approval not because he was a god, a king, or an emperor, but rather because he happened to be an extraordinary human being. This view stressed the president's exceptional character. Brave, honest, and modest, Washington possessed innate goodness. Perhaps the people who spoke in these terms simply wanted to humanize a figure who seemed even in the flesh a little distant and intimidating. According to one account of Washington's visit to Savannah, for example, "a company of nearly 200 citizens and strangers" experienced the joy of paying their respects "to the merit of a man who is, if possible more beloved for his goodness than admired for his greatness."[19]

It is highly questionable that anyone at the time really discounted Washington's greatness, but by focusing on the man's virtues, people of highly developed republican sensitivity could explain why Washington required no special titles. In the United States, men gained respect as men, not as officeholders. And this was as it should be. "Let it [Washington's sterling character] teach rulers hereafter to be MEN, if they wish to be treated in like manner," advised the *General Advertiser*. "*Titles*, like . . . bishops in the female dress, or like large cravats and high collars in the dress of gentlemen, were introduced only to supply the absence of real beauties, or to cover some existing defects. When the United States, or any single State shall have the misfortune to be governed by a *Tyger*, an *Ass*, or a *He Goat*, then let titles be applied to supply the absence of *majesty, serenity, wisdom* or *excellency*. In the present state of our country such substitutions for real merit are not generally necessary."[20]

A wonderful letter written by an obscure young woman known only as N. Fisher reflects how one person tried to humanize Washington without thereby undermining his special place in American society. We do not know her full name. But whoever she may have been, she penned an excited note to her brother describing her reaction to the president when he visited Salem, Massachusetts, during the fall of 1789. She recounted local gossip among friends about the details of a grand party held in his honor. The group hotly interrogated a lucky girl who happened to have been seated near the president. " 'Well, Nancy what did he say to you? Why he said So and so.' 'Well what else? And she, good girl, did not, I believe forget a word.' "

The account then took a more serious turn. The writer read deep emotion in the president's countenance. When he appeared before the people of Salem, "every muscle of his face appeared agitated, and he was frequently observed to pass, not 'the back of his hand,' but his handkerchief across his eyes." A tear, a suggestion that he was on the verge of losing his composure, made the man a better man in her eyes. "After all," she observed, "some wise people will tell you as the boy [who] walked thirty miles to see the President told him; 'you are a man, you are nothing but a man.' " In her estimation, that was the correct judgment, for if Washington had in fact been "an angel," he would have had nothing to do with ordinary men and women. "But he is a man and we feel proud of it." And then this remarkable young woman added a striking opinion. The only thing better than discovering that Washington was a man, a particularly good man, would have been to find that he "were a woman."[21] At the very least, her letter reveals that even at this early date, it was possible to imagine a broader, more inclusive political culture.

From New Hampshire to Georgia, other people much like N. Fisher experimented with names to call the president. Most of these had a very short life (for which we should be grateful), but they reflected the need to situate Washington in an American political narrative. A survey of terms of greeting gathered from contemporary newspapers reveals amazing diversity. Some titles were cumbersome, others unintentionally humorous. The *Massachusetts Spy*, a newspaper that had enthusiastically supported resistance to Great Britain during the Revolution, welcomed Washington as "his Highness the President general," an all-purpose phrase that combined several categories of popular description.

Without the slightest sense of irony, others were content to call him "His Majesty the President." Quite a few people focused attention on Washington's leadership during the Revolution. For them, he was the "Great Deliverer of our Country" or "the great and glorious Avenger of the violated rights of humanity." Americans everywhere proclaimed him "Hero." Some adopted a more personal vocabulary. Washington became the "beloved Father of the great American Family," "the political father and savior of his country," "great father of the people," "dearest friend," "Columbia's favorite son," and even "chieftain." Political salutations were also common. In many places, Washington was hailed as the "Illustrious President," "Head of the combined American Republic," or "First Magistrate of the Union." In New York City, the Washington who had just completed a tour of the nation was honored awkwardly as the "Illustrious visitant." More generic addresses included "the chief treasure of America" and the "Delight of Human Kind."[22]

One occasionally encounters in all this confusion about titles evidence of the true heritage of the Revolution. The ordinary people of Boston dealt with the challenge of addressing Washington in the same manner as they had solved other problems for almost two centuries: they took the matter to a public town meeting. It was a crowded gathering. The members of a special committee charged with drafting a welcoming speech for Washington had just finished their work. The only detail that remained was filling in the blank space where an appropriate title for the visitor would appear. If John Adams and other Bostonians who favored grand titles for national leaders expected a heated exchange, they were in for a surprise. At the start of the debate, a man described in the newspapers only as "a citizen" proposed that Washington "be addressed as the PRESIDENT of the United States, simply, without any addition." No one disagreed. The motion quickly received "a unanimous vote, no person appearing to advocate any title whatsoever."[23]

Soon after Washington departed Boston, an anonymous essayist writing for the *Massachusetts Magazine* explained the egalitarian assumptions that had energized the town meeting. "Let me remark," the author stated, "without giving offence, that titles of distinction, preeminence, and ceremonies, both religious and civil, have generally denoted the enslaved condition of the mass of the people where they have most prevailed." He continued, insisting that "the more free the constitution of any country, the less we see of pageant, titles and ceremonies, and consequently less of that demonstration of the inferiority of various classes of men in the presence of their superiors in rank."[24]

— III —

When they actually confronted the president on the road, many Americans suddenly discovered that they had lost the capacity for speech. No doubt, meeting such a celebrated figure made them extremely nervous. At the time, however, no one explained the loss of speech in psychological terms. They argued instead that silence indicated a profound sense of awe. At such a sublime moment of seeing the president for the first time, it seemed quite reasonable that ordinary men and women would fumble for words.

In any case, it was the inadequacies of the language, not of the people, that created the phenomenon. Nothing that such people could possibly say to the president could add to his stature. There were no words in the ordinary vocabulary capable of expressing the emotions felt by dazed Americans who imagined Washington to be a person existing on a much higher plane of experience. "If the weak powers of language could add to his worth," noted a writer for a popular newspaper, "or futile attempts to aggrandize his fame, by titular adjectives, give him one moment's pleasure, we should not be found wanting in the scale of praise. But our ideas of the transcendent merit of the best of men, cannot be expressed in words." [25]

Charles Caldwell, who during the early nineteenth century became a leading physician and founder of a medical school, recounted his own humiliating loss of speech as a young man when he tried to greet Washington on the border between South and North Carolina in spring 1791. In an autobiography published in 1855, Caldwell recaptured the excited preparations for the visit. The members of the local honors guard, called cadets, selected Caldwell to deliver a short address to the general as soon as he appeared on the road running north to Charlotte. He worked hard on his presentation. "In a short time," he recounted, "my address was mentally composed, not indeed to paper, but to my memory." Like an actor practicing for a leading role, he repeated the words. Indeed, Caldwell thought "of little else, either by day or night, except the strict discipline and soldier-like appearance of my little band." The grand moment finally arrived. Everything was in order; the cadets were in place. "Each man, his cap and plume adjusted, seated firmly and horse-man like in his saddle, and our swords drawn and in rest, the sheen of their blades as bright and dazzling as the beams of a southern sun could render it."

And then the entire plan came undone. For Caldwell, the sight of Washington approaching the honor guard created emotional turmoil. "As the figure advanced, in the symmetry and grace of an equestrian statue of the highest order, it reminded me of Brahma's descent from the skies." When the president reached Caldwell, the young man lost all composure. The speech he had memorized came out as incoherent babble. He confessed, "I was now unmanned. Not only did I forget my oft-repeated address, but I became positively unable to articulate a word." What could he do? Mounted on a stunning white charger before him was Washington, "a man so far above the rank of ordinary mortals, as to be approximated to that of the gods of fable."

The situation quickly spun further out of control. "I became actually giddy," Caldwell confessed, and "for an instant my vision grew indistinct." Washington may have witnessed such embarrassing scenes on other occasions. Whatever his experience with stumbling speech, he certainly showed the young man extraordinary understanding and generosity. The president invited Caldwell to ride with him, and this opportunity gave the embarrassed cadet a chance slowly to regain the ability to speak. Later in the day, the president went out of his way publicly to praise Caldwell, and when it came time for Washington to continue his journey, "he bowed in his saddle, and extended to me his hand." According to Caldwell, everyone who witnessed the farewell exchange broke down in tears.[26]

Caldwell need not have experienced such embarrassment. Other Americans could have told him that silence was actually a sign of virtue. Drawing perhaps on a new "sentimental project" in the United States and Great Britain known as sensibility, they insisted that the inability to speak in Washington's presence communicated profound meaning. The appeal of sensibility, at least for many late-eighteenth-century novelists and poets, was that it sanctioned an exaggerated display of emotion.[27] In this case, the inability to speak in Washington's presence revealed a depth of feeling, a genuine sincerity that could best be expressed without words.

An account of the president's tour through Connecticut, for example, noted that people of all sorts, "old and young—men and women," came forward to pay tribute to the president. And like Caldwell, they discovered that "language has been found inadequate to express [their] joy." To be sure, they tried to put their thoughts on paper, preparing short speeches of welcome, but these efforts proved inadequate for the purpose. As a newspaper concluded, "They have been necessitated to own, that *'expressive silence'* alone can sing his worth." [28] Eager greeters in Richmond ran into the same problem. They wanted to praise Washington, but their words fell flat. They apologized to the president, since "they cannot approach you without emotions of veneration too big for utterance." [29]

Americans quickly discovered how to tell whether expressive silence was sincere. After all, one supposes that the lack of words might possibly indicate boredom or diffidence. Real sensibility was different. Speechless emotion relied on gestures, heartfelt gazes, and tension in facial muscles, for example. It was as if the honesty of the heart's performance could be graded simply by looking at the faces of the ordinary people who came out to greet the president. Someone who witnessed Washington's reception in Boston reported, "Everything was conducted with the greatest possible order and regularity, each countenance beamed with lively joy—sorrow was banished far away, and each heart beat grateful to the name of WASHINGTON." [30]

Since we know that it was in fact a cold and rainy day when the president arrived in Boston, we might wonder at the evidence of so much lively joy. But others insisted that the visit unleashed a flood of wordless feeling. Another account from Boston insisted that the "joy which palpitated in the breasts of all the Citizens glowed in their cheeks and sparkled in their eyes." These external signs of political sensitivity provided "a stronger proof of the gratitude of our townsmen than can be expressed by the pomp of processions or the parade of regular addresses." [31]

Washington's actual presence was almost guaranteed to trigger genuine public displays of expressive silence. Pictures of the president were a poor substitute for the actual man. When he finally arrived in a community—a real person riding a great white horse—people reported not only that they were speechless, but also that they were able to read profound meaning in the man's face. Without the benefit of everyday language, they could see—even feel—for themselves the most inspiring aspects of the president's character. It was all a matter of gestures and facial muscles.

The organizers of a huge reception for Washington in Savannah understood the importance of personal contact in promoting wordless political feelings. "It is only by personal interviews that a just idea can be acquired of the amiableness of his temper and his engaging manners," they observed. "The intelligent serenity of his countenance, the affected ease and dignity of his deportment, while they excite the most profound respect, naturally rivet the affections to him."

To encourage wordless exchange, the Savannah planners centered the event in a broad, open space. The decision allowed a larger group of people to share a transcendent experience. "The principal advantage," claimed a Savannah commentator, "was the opportunity which it afforded to a great body of people to have a distinct and uninterrupted view of the object to which all eyes and hearts appear to be attracted."[32] The heart spoke to New Englanders as well. A young woman from Massachusetts described experiencing a kind of political epiphany when Washington visited her community. "You must know," she informed a relative, "that I have had the happiness (which I suppose you have enjoyed in a much higher degree) of seeing this incomparable *President*. You may laugh, but he has a most *beautiful* face. Did you ever see a countenance a thousandth part so expressive of that goodness, benevolence, sensibility, and modesty which characterize him?"[33]

Today it is hard to gauge whether such moments made a lasting political impact on the public, especially on how ordinary Americans perceived the new federal government, but contemporaries had no reservations on this matter. They thought that people who read so much into a brief sighting of the president were bound to transfer their emotional ties to the union. After all, the people claimed to have perceived the country's founding values etched on Washington's aging face. They looked at the man, seeing all that was good in the new republic and, perhaps, all that was good in themselves. As one newspaper exclaimed, "As the most unlimited confidence is reposed in [Washington's] prudence, abilities, and patriotism, this effect must have essential influence in giving energy to that government in the administration of which he has so considerable a part."[34] And that, of course, had been the president's original goal in touring America.

—IV—

Public spectacles organized to honor Washington during his journeys were complex, raucous affairs. They engaged the imagination and sparked unprecedented levels of participation. Indeed, a modern anthropologist would relish the challenge of interpreting these elaborate events. Of course, the people who planned these spectacles did not see their parades and festivities as necessarily carrying deeper meanings about the culture of the new republic. They simply wanted to honor the president and have a good time in the process. Nevertheless, with hindsight, we can appreciate that the elaborate displays were a way in which Americans told themselves political stories about how they fit into the new republican order.

In this highly charged post-Revolutionary environment, public displays invited Americans to reinvent themselves. It was an exciting prospect. No longer subjects of the Crown, they prided themselves on being republican citizens. Their creativity was impressive. After almost two centuries of monarchical rule, the citizens of the United States crafted a way of staging a persuasive political performance that we take for granted today. Much the same process occurred in other Revolutionary societies. As historian Mona Ozouf explained about the character of huge political celebrations following the overthrow of the French monarchy, popular political festivals communicated a "new social bond." Everything about these events held special significance. Details mattered. The spectacles helped transform "the huge crowd of isolated individuals into an organized community."[35] And so it was in the United States.

Washington did not quite know what to make of these massive celebrations. At the start of his journeys, he attempted to discourage effusive welcoming ceremonies, expressively wordless or not. Whether he really thought that he could contain the popular outpouring of emotion is impossible to discern. He may have worried that too much enthusiasm might spark public disorder, which would fuel criticism from those who claimed that republican government was inherently unstable. But however serious his attempts to control the people's excitement may have been, he had absolutely no influence on what actually happened. As the president set off for New England in 1789, the *Boston Gazette* announced that he "had it in view to travel without that temporary parade which his dignified station might justly claim." No one listened. Wherever he traveled, "his merits were already known, and the people with heart-felt joy, and high approbation of his virtues, saluted him as the *Defender* of their *Freedom* and *Independence*."[36]

Another newspaper explained that nothing in the president's power could possibly alter how the people received him in their communities. During the journey from Salem, Massachusetts, to Portsmouth, New Hampshire, Washington "was heard repeatedly to solicit, that the crowds who attended him, and lined the roads as he passed, would not follow him, but would return to their homes and their employ, as he could not be convinced but that it must be inconvenient to them." The report concluded with obvious relief that Washington's "solicitations were fruitless," and with a rhetorical flourish, the paper exclaimed, "The ball as it rolled on, [the celebration] . . . rapidly increased—even rivers and other natural obstacles neither impeding its progress, nor diminishing its size."[37]

Surviving records do not provide much insight into how smaller American towns and villages organized Washington's reception. Many communities seem to have formed special committees charged with overseeing the details of his visit. But this practice, especially when we turn our attention to the larger cities, only begs the question of how the members of the committees knew what a political spectacle of this sort was supposed to look like. After all, no one had had much experience in organizing the kind of huge public displays that greeted the president in places such as Boston and Newburyport. We know that people constructed impressive floats, painted special flags, and prepared fulsome speeches. But in many cases, the instructions for how the people were to behave were surprisingly vague. A committee in one Massachusetts town, for example, advised residents that "in the course of a few days the illustrious PRESIDENT of the UNITED STATES is expected to visit this town; the inhabitants of which will undoubtedly feel the most exquisite pleasure from such an event, and testify the same by showing their DELIVERER every mark of respect in their power." [38]

What we do know is that large-scale events like those that Washington encountered in Charleston and Boston could not claim long histories. During the colonial period, Americans had marked the arrival of new royal governors with solemn processions, which usually ended in the statehouse, where he read a formal statement. The obvious model for popular political celebrations was in fact of much more recent invention. In 1788 several major American cities held large parades to celebrate ratification of the Constitution. Although Europeans regularly organized elaborate spectacles for their monarchs, there was no domestic experience on which ordinary Americans could draw. [39]

The fullest account of one of these events comes from Boston. It occurred only months before Washington arrived in the city on his first tour of the nation. After a Massachusetts convention officially voted to ratify the new national government in 1788—the tally had been extremely close—a "Committee of Tradesmen" invited the city's "mechanicks and artisans" to put together a "Grand Procession." In response, each group of tradesmen—bakers and blacksmiths, tailors and cabinetmakers—came forward with special displays and marched under their separate banners. "The hardy sons of Neptune," for example, constructed a boat, which they fixed to the runners of a sled, and as they dragged the contraption through the snow-covered streets, the crowds cheered wildly.

Another boat, also mounted on a sled, bore the title "a Long-Boat call'd the OLD CONFEDERATION," a direct reference to the previous ineffectual government that had driven Washington and his friends to distraction. This political vessel sailed through the icy Boston neighborhoods, ending up in the evening at "the Commons, where, being deem'd unfit for further service, was ordered burnt, which was accordingly done, accompanied by the repeated huzzas of the people." City laborers, anticipating that the Constitution would stimulate Boston's depressed commerce, were obviously taunting the defeated Antifederalists. The revelers seized the memory of the Revolution to legitimize their support for the new federal government. One curious float, which would have flunked the basic requirements of modern risk management, promoted violence against symbols of the British Empire. According to a newspaper account, "In a cart, drawn by five horses, the British flag was displayed, and insulted by numbers [of men] placed in the cart, armed with muskets, who repeatedly discharged the contents of them through the tattered remnant, in contempt of that faithless nation."[40] Amazingly, there were no reports of children or pets accidentally gunned down in Boston's first major political parade.

Although the people of New Hampshire did not encourage firing muskets in crowded streets, they organized an impressive parade to mark the state's ratification of the Constitution. The final vote in the convention had been fifty-seven for and forty-six against, hardly compelling evidence of broad popular support, but the citizens of Portsmouth were not in the least discouraged. Like the Boston event, New Hampshire's featured a large ship bearing the name *The Union*, which was "completely rigged, armed & mann'd under an easy sail with colors flying, elevated on a carriage, drawn by nine horses, a tenth (emblematical of Virginia) completely harnessed, led and ready to join the rest." The organizers correctly reasoned that if a key state such as Virginia rejected the Constitution, the new government had little chance. Groups of artisans followed the great vessel through town. According to the local newspaper, "Every profession was distinguished by some insignia or badge, peculiar to it: The procession moved on thro' all the principal streets of the town, the band playing and singing the Federal Song, 'It comes! It comes!'" (After Washington became president in 1789, the lyrics changed to, "He comes! He comes!") After a dinner to which everyone was invited, the band continued to perform, and various individuals offered toasts to the new nation—for example, "May America be as conspicuous for Justice, as she has been successful in her struggles for Liberty" and "May America become the nurse of manufactures, arts and sciences, and the asylum of the oppressed in every part of the world." The whole scene astonished the writer for the Portsmouth journal, who confessed that "language is too poor to describe the universal joy that glowed in every countenance."[41]

When South Carolina joined the union in May 1788, Charleston held what it termed a "Federal Procession." City organizers grouped the local workers alphabetically by calling. A "Marshal of the Procession" instructed the marchers to follow the ship *Federalist*, which was drawn through the city "by eight white Horses, representing the eight States who have adopted the *Constitution*; each Horse having the name of his respective State on his forehead." The members of the various professions had prepared "decorated emblems" representing their different crafts. The town's butchers distinguished themselves by providing "a fine Ox," which when roasted provided dinner for all participants "without distinction." The *Columbian Herald* praised "a joyful spirit of *Republicanism* [that] seemed to pervade every breast." One man who watched the entire parade "from a convenient stand" claimed to have counted twenty-eight hundred people marching.[42] For a city whose population was barely sixteen thousand people, this was a large number, especially when we consider that women, children, and African Americans could not take part in the grand procession.

For larger cities, the ratification celebrations offered a useful template for how the nation would greet Washington only a few months later. It was fortunate that they had this experience to guide them, for neither the president nor his secretaries provided communities along the travel route with much advance information about the precise time of arrival. In Boston and Charleston, Washington's staff made certain that he had an appropriate house to rent during the visit, and since he refused to stay in private homes, the local arrangements committees had to find convenient public quarters for the president.

These were relatively minor matters. Much more demanding was organizing a large body of men and women to welcome a traveling celebrity. The recent ratification displays helped a lot at these moments. Although the earlier parades were not conceived as pilots for how to receive a president, they provided a useful blueprint for the tour. We will examine the grand Boston parade in another section, which recounts in more detail Washington's triumphal tour of New England, but here we can confidently state that the Washington celebrations were more elaborate—much larger in scale and less spontaneous—than were the ratification events. But whatever their character, these public displays dramatically revealed the nation's creative ability to stage a new republican political culture that owed its existence to a recent revolution.

—V—

How Americans living in different parts of the nation so quickly devised common rituals for greeting a president is a remarkable story of communication. However these ideas may have been transmitted over huge distances, by 1789 a set of shared ceremonies marked all of Washington's visits. It is a story of invention rapidly becoming custom, with experiment yielding tradition. Whether one lived in Boston or Charleston, Portsmouth or Savannah, one came to expect a formal military escort, an official welcoming statement and a response from the president, several huge dinners where the guests toasted the visitor long into the evening, and an illumination of the entire city at night.

The first people to welcome the president were usually members of local military units. Most troops served in state militias. They provided a kind of self-appointed honor guard that met Washington at the boundary of a state or community and then escorted him through the town or to the tavern where he planned to stay for the night. In more populous regions of the country, the number of soldiers participating in the initial greeting was large, often several hundred men, and since they were frequently under the command of officers who had fought in the Revolution, Washington felt obliged to treat them with respect. However, the routine that was repeated in every city and village tried his patience. The review of the troops took valuable time that he would rather have spent traveling to his next destination. Moreover, the men and horses raised annoying clouds of dust.

There was no escape. The troops became key actors in a routine that at once honored the general's military record and demonstrated that even though the country was young and weak, it was nevertheless capable of defending itself against imagined enemies. In Savannah, for example, Washington met a light infantry company and an artillery company. In South and North Carolina, the story was much the same. New Hampshire called out the entire state militia. The governor of Massachusetts, a person Washington grew to dislike, "ordered two troops of Middlesex Horse to escort him [Washington] thro' the Country, and permitted General Brooks to exhibit to the President on Cambridge Common, as he passed, a fine body of militia of the 3rd division, consisting of about a 1000 men, all in complete uniform and equipment." The entire body then saluted Washington "as he passed them."

Colonel Tyler's "Corps of Horse" soon replaced Brooks's men, and it was Tyler's mounted troops who "introduced him [Washington] to the Capital of the Commonwealth."[43] Wherever he traveled, the military was present—local soldiers who were not members of the US Army but were, rather, the defenders of states, who now mustered to affirm support for a strong union.

Americans came to regard an artillery salute as a necessary part of the show. Cannon began blasting as soon as the President appeared on the horizon. The gunners of Worcester were not to be outdone. As a newspaper reported, "On notice being given that his Highness was approaching, five cannon were fired, for the five New England States: three for the three in the union—one for Vermont, which will speedily be admitted—and one as a call to Rhode Island to be ready before it is too late." When the president reached the meetinghouse, another "eleven cannon were fired."[44] Although Washington claimed not to expect large demonstrations of respect, he was clearly surprised by the salvo he witnessed in Tarboro, North Carolina. He confided to his diary, "We were received at this place by as good a salute as could be given with one piece of artillery."[45]

The next phase in the rituals of arrival had no precedent in American politics. Indeed, Washington's actual entry into the center of a community, a main square or more densely populated street, was a moment of high theatricality. The details of the passage varied from place to place, but in many cities, especially in the South, the initial expression of public welcome focused on a celebration of the number thirteen. The political symbolism was not subtle; the local participants wanted to show the president that they too took pride in a strong union of states. But even if the message they intended to convey was clear, the scripts that the actors followed must have struck even Washington as a little bizarre. When he traveled down a short stretch of a river to reach Savannah, he sat on a small boat rowed by thirteen ship captains, never ordinary members of a crew, "who were dressed in light blue silk jackets, black satin breeches, white silk stockings, and round hats with black ribbons having the words 'Long live the President' in gold letters." Other boats carried spectators who bellowed out songs of welcome.[46] Washington's grand reception at Charleston also involved thirteen colorfully dressed ship captains who propelled him across Cooper River. A flotilla of private vessels surrounded the president's barge, each containing a group of eager singers. Washington received a less elaborate but equally curious greeting in Wilmington, North Carolina. At a river landing, he met thirteen young women wearing white dresses, and as he walked up a street from the dock, the girls scattered flower petals in his path.[47]

Soon after Washington entered a community, a group of city leaders would appear bearing a carefully crafted formal statement of welcome. The routine had several variations. Sometimes the city fathers would wait for a special dinner before delivering their address. Occasionally the Masons, the members of the local chapter of the Society of the Cincinnati, or president of a local college would also offer words of welcome. In New Haven, Connecticut, the president received addresses from the city's Congregational ministers and the members of the state legislature, but generally a local committee prepared the documents. Since the prose was usually stilted, it is easy to treat the performances—and Washington's responses—as an interesting but ultimately quite uninspiring part of his journey to a new nation, something expected for the occasion that did not generate much passion.

That would be a misreading of the evidence. Slighting these welcoming statements would miss their significance, particularly for the people of the towns or cities receiving a presidential visit. The formal exchange of greetings between a visiting national ruler and a local community had a long history in Western Europe. In England, for example, borough officials used these opportunities to bring their special concerns to the attention of the monarch and affirm whatever privileges they had acquired over the centuries. The ritual of official welcome was a means of marking the boundaries of overlapping spheres of authority. Unlike the major towns of Great Britain, most American cities did not trace their rights and privileges to special charters issued by the Crown. They certainly could not claim to be sovereign entities, but the towns and cities along Washington's route had customs and traditions that commanded respect. Moreover, the welcoming speeches communicated to Washington what was on the minds of a people who had only recently accepted the new constitution.

As soon as city organizers learned that the president would appear, they appointed a drafting committee usually made up of respected, well-educated citizens. John Quincy Adams, for example, helped write the welcome for Salem, Massachusetts. Many of these statements were later published in newspapers throughout the country, and so however grandiloquent they may strike us today, they clearly spoke to a country in the process of defining the proper spheres of local and federal authority. No doubt, Washington listened politely as a designated speaker read the welcoming document explaining why his city was especially honored to receive a visit from the first president. And then, in equally ponderous prose, often drafted by Major Jackson, Washington thanked the representatives of the community for their generous welcome.

Scores of these documents have survived. For the most part, they praise Washington in such inflated language that it would seem that the goal in part was to show that the citizens of a new republic could outdo the subjects of long-established monarchies in praising their leader. A New Hampshire observer insisted, for example, that the addresses to the president "were such as the crowned heads of other countries would part with their diadems to receive—They contained the grateful incense of honest hearts—where soul met soul together:—Indeed, the great and good man appeared sometimes to be almost overwhelmed."[48]

Petersburg, Virginia, offers a well-documented example of the formal exchange of greetings. A committee composed of the mayor, recorder, aldermen, and members of the Common Council drew up an address, which was read to the president on April 14, 1791. They had an impressive audience. One person who witnessed the event reported, "So great was the desire of the people to see him [Washington] that by the time of his arrival, there were not less than several thousands after him."[49] The turnout was impressive. Washington estimated the city's entire population to be no more than "3000 Souls."[50] The statement opened with predictably flattering rhetoric: "We avail ourselves of the earliest opportunity that your presence has afforded us, to offer you our sincere and affectionate respects." They then added an observation, which in the context of the times—the aftermath of a bitter fight over the ratification of the Constitution—had significant political meaning. The committee described Washington to the people of Petersburg as "the father of your country," and it expressed the hope, "May you long continue at the head of our government."[51]

Whatever issues had previously divided the state and however much the followers of Patrick Henry had insisted that the new federal system would destroy the freedom and liberty of all Virginians, the elected leaders of Petersburg communicated to Washington and their own constituents their willingness to give the Constitution and his presidency a chance.[52] That was precisely what he wanted to hear. In his response, he reminded the people of Petersburg, "The government of the United States, originating in the wisdom, supported by the virtue, and having no other object than the happiness of the people, reposes not on the exertions of an individual."[53] This was a gentle way of stating that the success of the republican experiment in the United States did not—could not—depend on the actions of a single man, no matter how famous. Long after he had left office, the Constitution would endure.

Washington received two very different welcoming speeches in Boston—one from the governor of Massachusetts and his council, the other from a group identified simply as "the Inhabitants of Boston." Both documents and the president's responses were published in all the major New England newspapers. As one might expect, the governor's words were cordial. He invoked a shared memory of sacrifice for national independence. The Revolution, he observed, may have started in Massachusetts, but the struggle against imperial control belonged to the entire country. "We can never forget the *time* when in the earliest stage of the war, and the day of *our* greatest calamity, we saw you at the head of the army of the United States." Even then, Washington had arrived as a national figure who represented the American cause. And in 1789, he returned. "We now have the pleasure of seeing you in a still more exalted station to which you have been elected by the unanimous suffrages of a free, virtuous and grateful country."

In response, Washington declared that the governor's praise had rendered him almost speechless. The need to properly thank his hosts "requires a force of expression beyond that which I possess." But if we read the president's words closely, we realize that he viewed the brief exchange as an opportunity to remind the leaders of the state government that he had come to Massachusetts as the head of a new federal structure. He was pleased for the expression of "remembrance of my military services," but at this moment, he was much more determined that the men greeting him not be disappointed by "my civil administration." Washington took care to note the professionalism of the state militia units that had escorted him from town to town, but in this conversation, he cleverly subsumed the local troops under the national banner, since, as he informed the governor, even independent soldiers on the state level "present the fairest prospect of support to the invaluable objects of *national* safety and peace."

A second "Address" delivered to Washington in the name of the "Inhabitants of Boston" was a much more complex and interesting statement. The prose was less guarded; the content blended specific concerns about the economy with philosophical issues that went to the heart of what it meant to be an American in 1789. They insisted that the Revolution had been about basic political rights. Washington had commanded an army for the sole purpose of preserving those rights from British tyranny. "As men," the townspeople explained, "we have long since considered you, under God, as the great and glorious Avenger of the violated rights of humanity." And now that America had secured its independence, even the most obscure among them took pride in being a "citizen," a term that in a new republican society implied equality. These people, no longer obliged to bow to pretentious aristocrats, "have observed with peculiar satisfaction, that you have invariably respected those liberties, which you have so successfully defended." The ordinary people, newly empowered in a republican government, were politely but forcefully reminding the president that whatever his own agenda may have been, they wanted him to defend their rights and liberties. There was no point in having a strong federal government if it could not meet this fundamental expectation.

In what was in fact a kind of formal conversation, the inhabitants of Boston also used the occasion to remind Washington that "as inhabitants," they hoped the new government would promote commercial prosperity. They assured the president that they regarded him as a capable leader, known for "the conspicuous and unaffected piety of your heart." What, then, was the promise of America? In words that remain relevant to this day, the people's committee announced:

> To the future we look for those virtues which adorn the man and mark the wise and accomplished legislator. We anticipate from your discernment the happy union of liberty and law, lenity and vigor, mercy and justice: The enlightened policy of a mind calm amidst the influence of power, and uncorrupted by the fascinating allurements of avarice or ambition.

The values that had called forth such sacrifice from ordinary Americans during the Revolution could not be taken for granted. Sustaining the original goals of that contest demanded vigilance. The inhabitants of Boston knew that they could trust Washington, but after he had departed the scene, the threat of corruption, avarice, and ambition would always remain.

In Washington's response, probably written by Jackson or Lear, he again raised the topic of military strength. But instead of talking about national security, he took a different tack. He expressed sincere pleasure in learning that in the inhabitants' eyes "my military commission has contributed to vindicate the rights of humanity, and to secure the freedom and happiness of my country." They had once come forward to fight imperial tyranny, and now they had an obligation—as great as the president's—to preserve the values that had brought forth a new nation. "Your love of liberty—your respect for the laws—your habits of industry, and your practice of the moral and religious obligations, are the strongest claims to national and individual happiness."[54] That was the message in a nutshell: a strong and honest federal government and a citizenry committed to the preservation of human rights and liberty were required to make the republic work.

—VI—

A much more enjoyable ritual occurred at almost every stop during Washington's journeys from New Hampshire to Georgia. Like other aspects of the president's trips to America, the practice of toasting is easy for us to take for granted. Today it provides those who attend weddings and retirements with an opportunity to say something fulsome about the person being honored. But during the late eighteenth century, toasts carried more cultural weight. Before the development of sophisticated polling, the declarations offered up at dinners or large receptions afforded a rough measure of what was on people's minds in different regions of the country. Ceremonial toasts allowed them—at least those of high social standing in the communities—to voice aspirations and beliefs that might not have been deemed appropriate in conversation with the president. And what is more, like the formal exchanges of greetings between Washington and town fathers, the precise wording of the toasts was published in newspapers throughout the United States. Americans did not interpret the toasts as mere examples of polite rhetoric, but as an index of support for the goals of the new administration. As with the other elements of his interaction with the people, the toasts were a form of public conversation—highly stylized, to be sure, but an effective means of giving and receiving messages about core concerns of an evolving political culture.

Even if he had wanted to do so, Washington could not have escaped the ritual of toasting. After a demanding day of visiting Revolutionary battle sites or reviewing parades, the local organizers—in most communities, wealthy and influential men, many of whom had served in the war or had recently supported the ratification of the Constitution at state conventions—invited the president to dinner. Often these meals drew more than a hundred people, men as well as women, and after everyone had finished dining, it was expected that the entire assembly would participate in an extensive and exhausting round of toasts. By doing so, they partook in an ancient tradition. Raising the glass in honor of some cause or dignitary had a long history in early modern Europe. Those occasions had provided a formal means of communicating local concerns as well as uncompromising loyalty to monarchs and other leaders who happened to be traveling through the countryside.

During Washington's tours, local organizers often offered as many as fifteen separate toasts. It was a wonder that the entire dinner party was not completely drunk at the end of these sessions, but in fact, the participants probably either watered down the wine or politely sipped it as person after person rose to pay tribute to yet another worthy subject. Although the choice of topics differed from community to community—something that sophisticated newspaper readers would have noted—the structure of the ritual itself followed set rules. The toasting opened with Washington offering words of esteem for the state or city in which he was staying. He would stand to recognize the State of South Carolina or Commonwealth of Massachusetts, for example, usually without going into any detail. In New Bern, North Carolina, he toasted the state, an act that we are told received "stentorian cheers."[55] Then various individuals would follow Washington, observing in a pithy phrase a shared memory or common civic goal that deserved special recognition.

Although one could note exceptions, these toasts generally fell into five categories: declarations of support for the new government and the noble principles it represented, expressions of hope that peace would continue and commerce flourish, statements backing America's former French allies during a time of great upheaval in Paris, tributes to the Revolutionary officers and soldiers who had sacrificed so much for independence, and finally, words of praise for the "fair" women who graced these events but were not expected to offer toasts of their own. After the dinner guests had worked their way down the list and seemed to have grown weary of the exercise, Washington rose from the table and departed. As soon as he was out of the room, the remaining men and women toasted the president of the United States. Some communities took the toasting extremely seriously. In Savannah, for example, each declaration, no matter what the subject, was "succeeded by discharges from the fieldpieces of the artillery company."[56]

Of the many accounts of ritual toasting that have survived, Savannah's may be the most detailed. For three consecutive evenings, Washington attended large dinner parties in that city. The first two events were held in Brown's Coffee House, probably the largest public space then available. The initial "entertainment," as it was called, included an impressive body of local gentlemen: judges, clergymen, legislators, military officers, and city officials. After the formal meal, they drank fifteen toasts. They began by honoring "The United States," a good opening, since Washington was visiting in part to strengthen the union.

The president then proposed a toast to "the State of Georgia; May she increase in population and wealth." The group made its way down a roster of largely predictable topics, including Louis XVI and the French Assembly, the Congress of the United States, the "Sons of Freedom in every part of the globe," Lafayette and General Nathanael Greene, "agriculture and commerce," and, at number eleven, the "Fair daughters of America."

The members of the Georgia Chapter of the Society of the Cincinnati organized the next night's reception. They too offered fifteen toasts. As might have been expected, their list placed greater emphasis on military subjects. The memory of General Greene appeared as number two, up some twelve places from the previous dinner. "The American Fair" dropped three slots. Two declarations remind us how much people of the time viewed the American Revolution as an ideological event that had the capacity to transform other nations. The Cincinnati declared, "May the virtues which inspired the Revolution continue to support the present establishment," and, "May the principles of a free government be universally disseminated."

On the third occasion, which seems to have been more open to the ordinary people of Savannah, Washington began by toasting the city. "The Fair of America" had jumped to number two on the toasting list. The other declarations echoed the sentiments of the earlier entertainments. The Savannah assembly agreed that it was important to support "the friends to free and equal government throughout the globe." And curiously, at number eleven on a list of twelve toasts, we encounter an expression of hope: "May religion and philosophy always triumph over superstition and prejudice in America."[57] At the time, no one bothered to record what Washington made of this statement. It is likely, however, that he thought that the man who proposed this toast had a good point.

Other cities crafted similar lists. At a gathering in Columbia, South Carolina, described in the newspapers as a "farmers' dinner," the president learned that local men and women wished well for the "National Assembly of France" and desired "a happy termination to their manly revolution." They also declared, "May our mild laws, and the happy administration of them, render America an asylum for the oppressed." They recommended to the new government "sufficient means and speedy measures for opening the inland navigation of America." And they felt it would be a good idea to improve the country's educational institutions.[58]

At a "sumptuous and elegant dinner" in Boston, attended by some 150 men and women, the people proposed eleven toasts. They used the occasion to express positive thoughts about the king of France, the president, and the independence of the United States. The sixth toast surely pleased Washington. The Bostonians called for "the completion and cement of the Union."[59] At an entertainment in Charleston, South Carolina, where "the wines [were] excellent and in great variety," an assembly offered seventeen toasts, many of which praised the new constitutional government and the members of Congress. Louis XVI remained a favorite, as did "the Fair Daughters of America." The guests also praised "the Defenders of the Rights and Liberties of the People throughout the world." And like other communities anticipating a more prosperous future as part of a revived union, the celebrants at the Charleston dinner sipped excellent wine in praise of "the Navigation of the United States, protected by the strong arm of the Federal Government, may it increase and flourish." Martha Washington, who was not present at the dinner, received the final toast of the evening.[60]

The toasting rituals were constrained by the rules of etiquette. No doubt the dinner guests wanted to be polite. It would have been awkward for someone formally to propose a toast to the opponents of the Constitution. Hospitable dinner guests also surely knew what Washington wanted to hear about strengthening the union. Nevertheless, at the time, toasting was an important vehicle for political communication, linking local groups to the head of the new federal government. What the people told the president on his journeys was that they believed that the United States had a revolutionary obligation to promote rights and liberties throughout the world. They revealed in toast after toast that the horizons of their political imagination extended beyond the states in which they happened to live. They anticipated commercial expansion on a national scale. They welcomed a future in which merchants and farmers would work together to advance the entire country's prosperity. Washington did not put such thoughts into their heads, but his appearance in their communities encouraged people to affirm a vision for the United States that he enthusiastically shared.

At the end of the day, after all the toasts had been made and Washington returned to his room, the people illuminated their towns and cities. The denial of darkness became a key element in the choreography of Washington's travels. Thousands of candles lighted the windows of private homes and public buildings. In Boston and Charleston, the ships in the harbors sparkled with special lanterns. The desire to turn back the night had a rich European history. Monarchs called for massive illuminations to signal their power. One account of these extraordinary displays describes them as "essential tools of government."[61] But as we have seen with other traditional forms of projecting power in the republican United States, the illuminations dropped their association with elite privilege. During Washington's tours of America, these nocturnal entertainments came to mark the support of ordinary men and women for his administration.

The practice of general illumination became so common that some people worried that if they failed to light their windows, they would be subject to discrimination or, worse, violence. When Washington traveled from Mount Vernon to New York City for his first inauguration, he received a plaintiff letter from a Philadelphia Quaker, William Hartshorne. The writer reminded the president that after the announcement of the American victory over the British at Yorktown, patriotic groups had roamed the streets of Philadelphia looking for homes without celebratory candles. If the mob saw no light, they broke the windows. As a Quaker, Hartshorne did not condone such artificial decoration, and he did not want to endure similar attacks on his property if a crowd insisted on illumination to honor Washington. The request caught Washington by surprise. He was just learning how difficult it was for a popularly elected leader to control his own enthusiastic supporters. "I must prepare myself," he informed Hartshorne, "to meet with many occurrences which will be painful and embarrassing." He hoped the welcoming ceremony would be peaceful. "But, situated as I am at present, and knowing nothing of the intentions of the people respecting my passing through the several towns . . . I do not see how I can, with any degree of propriety or delicacy, interfere, at this moment, to prevent the ill effects which are feared from an illumination of the City of Philadelphia."[62]

Communities located along Washington's route wanted their light displays to be as impressive as possible. When organizers in Boston were planning for the president's visit, they realized that since candles were expensive, the poor people of the city might not be able to illuminate their humble windows. Concern about a disappointing display of light sparked charity. A newspaper advertisement announced: "At a time when our ILLUSTRIOUS PRESIDENT intends to visit this metropolis, a correspondent would urge the propriety of a general illumination, as a testimonial of the joy that will undoubtedly be felt upon this occasion, and would propose a public subscription for the purpose of supplying those persons with candles, whose circumstances will not permit of such an expense, as undoubtedly their feelings, upon this occasion will be equal to any of the first citizens of this Commonwealth [Massachusetts]."[63]

If the Boston planners appealed for more light, leaders in other parts of the country experienced the opposite challenge: they feared that popular eagerness for large-scale illuminations could accidentally cause the destruction of entire towns. Petersburg, Virginia, had to cancel its display when it became apparent that the dread of fire was a greater concern than defying the darkness. Charleston faced the same challenge. Local officials published a request that "citizens will not, on the approaching occasion exhibit any fire works or illuminations, within the city, as from the long dry weather, the shingles and wooden buildings are rendered highly inflammable."[64] The huge fireworks displays that brightened the night skies in Washington's honor do not seem to have posed the same hazard as did several thousand burning candles.

—VII—

Of the many exchanges that Washington had with the American people during his journeys, the most difficult to interpret were those with women. That women appear at all in the story is worthy of comment. In scholarly discussions of the political culture of the Early Republic, they are often nearly invisible, figures in the background of government affairs. Politics therefore is little more than a narrative of elite men making decisions about the character of civil society. In recent years, historians have invited women back into the chronicles of power, but only in a supportive role. We learn that even though women could not vote or hold public office, they advanced the general welfare of the nation as "republican mothers." The point seems to be that while women did not have a real voice in politics, they still managed to earn respect, presumably from the men of their communities, as highly principled mothers determined to raise their sons to be men of honor and virtue.[65]

American women may in fact have taken pride in nurturing future male leaders of the United States. The problem for us is that such women were not those who appeared repeatedly during Washington's trips. He did not spend time with women who presented themselves as passive mothers, nor did the women who flocked to participate in his visits disappear quietly into the background of these events. In town after town, from New England to the South, American women refused to be excluded from the celebration of Washington's journeys.

The president's diaries, our main source in such matters, rivet our attention on the issue. Wherever Washington traveled, he made special note of the women he saw. It is tempting, of course, to put forward a prurient explanation for these frequent observations—about the beauty of the women, how many of them came out to greet him, even their hair color. In Portsmouth, New Hampshire, for example, he described an evening assembly "where there were about 75 well dressed, and many of them very handsome, Ladies—among whom (as was also the case at the Salem & Boston Assemblies) were a greater proportion with much blacker hair than are usually seen in the Southern States." [66]

His appraisals of American women were not restricted to those of the upper class. When he met a group of young female textile workers in Boston, they completely distracted his attention away from the display of advanced looms. One reporter who witnessed Washington's delight at this moment claimed that the president "made himself merry on this occasion, telling the overseer he believed he had collected the prettiest girls in Boston." There were other encounters. Later that night, Washington attended a dinner where he met "upwards of 100 ladies. Their appearance was elegant and many of them were very handsome." [67]

Apparently the president found the women of Charleston even more impressive. According to a newspaper, at the corporation ball he was introduced to "nearly 250 ladies, elegantly dressed." In his diaries he raised the number to 256. After he had entered the reception hall, it was reported that "joy sparkled in every countenance; but more so when, after being seated a few minutes, he rose, went around the room and bowed to every lady—this gave particular satisfaction, as every one was anxious to have a good view of him." [68] He could not get these Charleston ladies out of his mind. Several months later, Washington wrote to his friend from the Revolution, William Moultrie, thanking Moultrie and his "fair compatriots, [who are] upon every occasion, to be remembered with grateful respect." [69] Then, almost a year later, Washington urged Moultrie to go to "the trouble of presenting me to the recollection of the Ladies in the circle in which you move." [70]

The reason for his fascination with women may seem obvious. Washington was certainly an attractive man, tall and athletic. Even in middle age, he possessed an appeal often associated with power. But this analysis holds no water. Not a shred of evidence survives to suggest that Washington's interest in women translated into the kinds of sexual behavior that embarrassed Jefferson and Hamilton. The fact of the matter was that Washington simply liked talking with women. He relaxed in their company. According to Isaac Weld, an English visitor to the United States, Washington was "much more open and free in his behavior . . . in the company of ladies . . . than when solely with men." [71] Moreover, the president loved to dance. On several occasions after the long sessions of toasting had concluded and he had departed for his rooms, Washington would reappear at the reception so that he could dance with as many of the local women as possible.

Still, even if he indulged in mild flirtations, there is no denying that Washington paid close attention to the numbers. His diaries occasionally read like stock market quotations. Each community during his travels brought forward scores of women. Precise counts mattered. The impression that the town made—not only to Washington but also to its own citizens—depended in some fundamental way on the visibility and enthusiastic participation of its females. They figured centrally in how the community presented itself to the outside world. By coming forward, local women provided an index of culture, even of civilization. Reports from Savannah were quite candid about this phenomenon. The local organizers selected a large room for a reception, one "which had been lately handsomely fitted up, and was well lighted, [and which] afforded the President an excellent opportunity of viewing the fair sex of our city and vicinity." [72]

Washington's sensitivity to the number of women who came out to see him first became evident during his tour of the Eastern States. In Boston, he encountered "upwards of 100 Ladies." In Salem, there were "at least an hundred handsome and well dressed Ladies." Portsmouth mustered only seventy-five "well dressed" women, but their lower turnout could be forgiven, since "many of them [were] very handsome ladies."[73]

The accounting continued during the Southern Tour. Here, we have not only the diaries but also contemporary newspaper reports. The journals shared Washington's assumption that the success of a visit depended in part on the number of women who participated. New Bern produced "about 70 ladies." At Wilmington the count was 62. As we have seen, at Charleston the number rose initially to over 250, and at a second reception, the figure topped "at least 400 ladies." This performance overwhelmed the president. He confessed that "the Number & appearance . . . [of the Charleston women] exceeded any thing of the kind I had ever seen." The smaller Savannah could hardly compete with Charleston, but it managed to record a respectable "100 well dressed & handsome Ladies." Although Augusta did not do so well in terms of total numbers—only "60 & 70 well dressed ladies"—a local newspaper defended the showing, since the tally did in fact represent "the largest number of Ladies ever collected in this place." Another journal reported that in Columbia, South Carolina, Washington "was conducted to the room of the representatives in the statehouse, where were assembled sixty-seven ladies, who upon his entering the room, arose and made an elegant appearance, to whom he was individually introduced."[74] Even Salisbury, North Carolina, which Washington described as unimpressive, was able to organize a tea party with "about 20 ladies, who had been assembled for the occasion."[75]

Whatever Washington intended when he recorded the numbers of American women he encountered, we should recognize that his perspective on their participation was not the only one that mattered. He and other elite males may have interpreted the well-dressed women as an index of the growing sophistication of republican culture—perhaps they measured such things in comparison with an English society from which they had so recently rebelled—but the women were not simply props carted out for the pleasure of the president. They wanted to be present, to see him and be seen. And in political terms, they had greater access to Washington than did their husbands, who would have been fortunate to exchange a few formal words with him. The women danced with him for hours. What they talked about during these moments is not known, but it would be perverse not to appreciate how conscious the women were of having a significant voice in the new political culture of the United States. Their presence at the parades, the receptions, the balls, the dinners, and the tea parties reminds us of how women could be political in an age before suffrage.[76]

Perhaps the reason that women have frequently gone missing from the political narratives of this period is that they publicly transmitted their beliefs largely without words. In city after city, American women employed special devices and ornaments to communicate their enthusiasm for Washington and the new federal union. One newspaper clearly documented how physical appearance, the body politic, became an effective way for women to broadcast a strong political message. Commenting on the president's visit to New Hampshire, the journal observed that "the testimonials of respect" paid the president were "not confined to the Male creation." The women of the state had been particularly creative in developing wordless forms of expression. "The Ladies have invented sashes, on which the bald Eagle of the Union, and G. W. hold conspicuous places." One woman attending a concert in Washington's honor "exhibited on the bandeau of her hat, the G. W. and the Eagle set in brilliants, on a black velvet ground."[77]

Women throughout the United States fashioned themselves in similar ways. They probably learned how other women greeted the president from reading accounts in the major journals. In any case, the specially designed sashes appeared in almost every major city. From

Boston, for example, it was reported that "THE LADIES in honor of THE PRESIDENT, have agreed . . . to wear the following DEVICE in a sash—a broad white ribbon, with G. W. in gold letters (or spangles) encircled with a laurel wreath in front—on one end of the sash to be painted the American Eagle, and on the other a fleur-de-lis."[78] William H. Sumner, a distinguished antebellum military figure in Massachusetts who lived until 1861, remembered how, when he was a young boy, his mother prepared to meet the president. He was especially impressed by "the large gold letters, 'G. W.,' which my mother wore on her black velvet belt, when she went to the Washington Ball."[79] In the South, women quickly picked up the new political fashions. Washington spent an enjoyable evening with ninety-six Savannah women, "some of whom displayed infinite taste in the emblems, and devices on their sashes and head dresses."[80]

Although their husbands—members of the local elites—probably shared the political sentiments exhibited in their wives' dress, there is no evidence to suggest that they coerced the women to communicate with Washington through emblems and devices. As the president discovered, their performance was indeed a rough gauge of public opinion in the era before women were allowed to vote. The women adored Washington, and by doing so publicly, they also generated support for a strong federal government.

Marvelous testimony of the political performance of American women—it is probably the fullest report as well—comes by chance from Georgetown, South Carolina, where Washington arrived in May 1791. A commentator insisted that the entire visit was a success, but what he stressed was that "upon the whole of this occasion, nothing was more conspicuous than the patriotism of the ladies." They dominated the moment. They even competed among themselves "in showing him marks of the highest respect." The women "waited upon him in the morning," and during an afternoon tea party, they appeared in "sashes highly beautified with the arms of the United States." Others

"wore head-dresses ornamented with bandeaus, upon which were written, in letters of gold, either 'Long Life to the President,' or 'Welcome
the Hero.'" Washington responded positively to such attention. In
the evening, the organizers of an entertainment placed a special chair
in the center of the assembly, "handsomely decorated with arches and
festoons of laurel, interwoven with flowers." But instead of taking the
seat of honor, Washington declared that he would not follow the anticipated script. "He declined the formality of being placed in a manner
unsocial, [and] after being introduced to all the ladies present, he seated
and entertained several of them, in succession, in the chair intended for
himself."[81]

—VIII—

When Washington first appeared in their communities, men and women
bellowed out their conviction that even people of modest means had
as much right to participate in the celebration of republican values as
did their wealthier and more powerful neighbors. This conviction was
entirely sincere. The festivities were an honest expression of the popular
belief that ordinary people—women as well as men—in this country had
managed to escape the aristocratic constraints of European monarchies.
That had been the point of the war against Great Britain. Washington's
tours provided a catalyst for a shared realization that the Revolution had
in fact succeeded. It produced a new society.

What we must appreciate is that the conversations and rituals associated with Washington's trips invited Americans to view one another from
a fresh perspective. During the exchanges on the road, differences that
divided the people seemed to melt away temporarily. The old tensions—
between loyalists and patriots, Federalists and Antifederalists—did not
dissolve, of course, and some strains such as those related to slavery
would lead to serious violence in the future. But when Washington

appeared, it was possible for one inspiring moment to imagine that a political union composed of so many ambitious, independent-minded people would flourish.

Although one commentator in 1789 may have exaggerated, he announced a significant change in what it meant to be an American. "A happy revolution of sentiment is observed to have taken place throughout the United States," he exclaimed. "Local views, and narrow prejudices are universally reprobated—a generous, national spirit, pervades the whole Union." He even thought that ethnicity meant less than it had in earlier times. "Formerly we used to call ourselves Englishmen, Germans, Irishmen, Scotchmen, &c. according to the Country from whence we respectively originated—but NOW, even the distinctions of States are scarcely heard—and like other Great Nations, who have risen to Fame and Empire, we are proud to be distinguished by the name of the Country we inhabit, AMERICANS."[82]

Washington's journeys of discovery took him to two quite different regions of the new nation. His reception in New England and then later in the South reveals something significant about the president's ability to communicate effectively his vision for the union as well as something about the tensions that were pulling the country apart even as he appealed for solidarity. The tour through New England in 1789, with a short separate trip to Rhode Island, was a personal triumph for the president, and his appearances allowed him to promote key themes. He stressed the need for expanded manufacturing to create greater economic self-sufficiency. He also had an opportunity to register his contempt publicly for the inflated claims for states' rights made by some critics of the new federal government. And he provided moving support before a small Jewish congregation for religious toleration in the new republic. The Southern Tour, however, was more ambitious—and more sobering. Although Washington called on the American people to incorporate quickly the new settlements west of the Appalachians into one great federal union, he encountered signs during his travels of resistance to his vision for the republic. He discovered on the southern roads that the deeply divisive practice of slavery could not be ignored, and while he urged his most trusted political colleagues to avoid faction, they did in fact turn on one another, championing party agendas over the unity that Washington had espoused.

CHAPTER V

The New England Tour: Triumphant Moments

George Washington's tour of New England in the fall of 1789 was a personal triumph. The president brilliantly used the opportunity to reach out to the American people, performing on a new political stage, to rivet public attention on themes about which he cared deeply. In Hartford, he drew attention to a struggling woolen mill, declaring that this was precisely the type of industrial enterprise that would help the new nation achieve full economic independence from Great Britain. Later, in Boston, he confronted John Hancock, then the governor of Massachusetts. An incident that began as a quarrel over etiquette—Did the governor of a state outrank the president of the United States?—sparked a contentious debate over state sovereignty. Washington's victory in this contest allowed him to champion a strong federal union. And finally, as we follow Washington's travels, we reconstruct the president's visit to a Rhode Island synagogue. On this occasion, he delivered a speech that explained in moving terms the meaning of religious toleration in the United States. We might say of these events—the factory appearance, the besting of Governor Hancock, and the defense of Jewish worship in Newport—that these were the president's finest hours.

—I—

When Washington set out on his journey to the Eastern States, he projected an unmistakable sense of well-being. As we have seen, he was happy to have recovered from a serious illness, and he was certainly pleased to have escaped the demanding social life of the nation's capital. But what raised his spirits even more was the conviction that the United States had gotten off to a very good start. After almost a decade of worrying about the future of the union—about the threat of anarchy—Washington concluded that his cabinet and the First Congress had made splendid progress in turning the Constitution into an effective working government.

The challenge of setting up a working government had demanded his full attention. During their first session, the members of Congress had wrestled with a number of hard issues, such as where exactly to locate the nation's permanent capital, but however divisive these questions, the legislative debates had largely been open and constructive. Everyone wanted the republican experiment to succeed. It is true that profound ideological differences and intransigent localism would plague Washington's second term, but for the moment, the domestic problems facing the United States seemed solvable.

It was harder to make sense of the international situation. Early reports from Paris were confusing and incomplete. There was no doubt, however, that some news from France was genuinely disturbing. On October 14, Washington wrote to Lafayette, observing, "The revolution, which has taken place with you, is of such magnitude and of so momentous a nature that we hardly yet dare to form a conjecture about it."[1] Washington was inclined to believe that the king and trusted French friends from the time of the American Revolution would somehow weather the political storm. At this moment, however, no one in the United States could have anticipated the Terror.

The president's confidence in the ability of the American people to cooperate for the common good helps to explain the upbeat tone of his correspondence. Just before leaving New York City for the Eastern States, Washington informed Gouverneur Morris, a longtime friend and able diplomat, "It may not . . . be unpleasing to you to hear in one word that the national government is organized, and, as far as my information goes, to the satisfaction of all parties."[2]

The president's optimistic assessment of the nation's health echoed in the press. On the eve of Washington's departure, one popular journal proclaimed in the hyperbolic rhetoric of the day, "The present year [1789] is the most remarkable that the annals of the time have produced. No other period of equal extent is marked with such efforts of the human mind to increase and perpetuate human happiness." Of course, there had been skeptics who predicted that the nation would come unraveled. This did not happen. "All has terminated well. The government is organized, and the people are happy."[3]

At the time, Americans sincerely believed that they were on the cutting edge of history. They viewed their achievement in the name of universal rights and liberties as a model for oppressed men and women throughout the world. For modern Americans, who view distant insurgency as a threat to their security, it is hard to imagine a time when our own revolution seemed a harbinger of liberation from tyranny. But in 1789, this was surely how people situated the United States in world affairs.

Washington planned this journey not only to gather intelligence about local affairs but also to remind Americans that the success of the new government was their success. His trip, which carried him over "very rough and Stoney" roads, followed a long looping route that took him to scores of New England communities, the largest being New Haven, Hartford, Worcester, Boston, Salem, and Portsmouth.[4] During his initial tour, he carefully avoided setting foot in Rhode Island, since that state had not yet ratified the Constitution, a failure that greatly annoyed the president, who advocated the creation of a strong federal

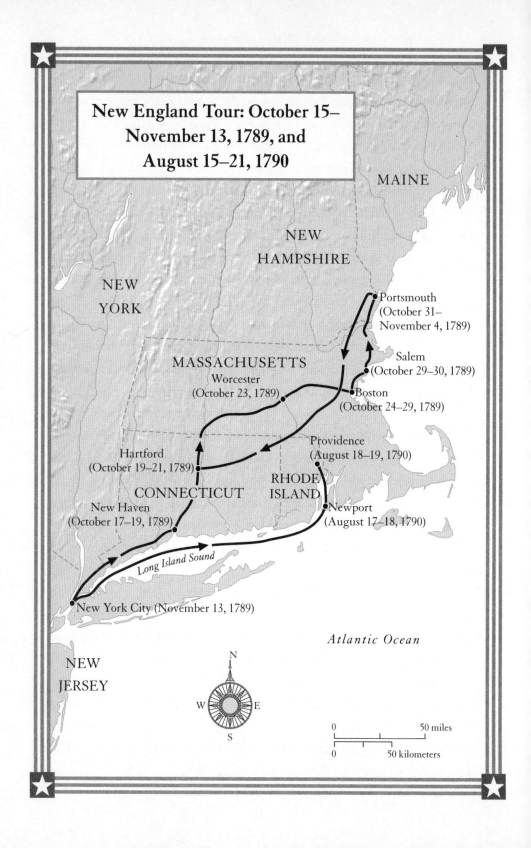

New England Tour: October 15–
November 13, 1789, and
August 15–21, 1790

MAINE

NEW
HAMPSHIRE

NEW
YORK

Portsmouth
(October 31–
November 4, 1789)

Salem
(October 29–30, 1789)

MASSACHUSETTS

Worcester
(October 23, 1789)

Boston
(October 24–29, 1789)

Providence
(August 18–19, 1790)

Hartford
(October 19–21, 1789)

RHODE
ISLAND

CONNECTICUT

New Haven
(October 17–19, 1789)

Newport
(August 17–18, 1790)

Long Island Sound

New York City (November 13, 1789)

Atlantic Ocean

NEW
JERSEY

N

W   E

S

0   50 miles

0   50 kilometers

union. Later, in August 1790, after Rhode Island had finally joined the new government, Washington relented and scheduled a short excursion to Newport and Providence.

As his coach bounced along the rutted roads of New England, he eagerly examined the face of a society that he had not seen since some of the more critical moments of the Revolution. His earlier impressions of the region had not been positive. When Washington accepted command of the Continental Army in 1775 and traveled to Massachusetts to review a force of determined militiamen who had just held their own against the British at Bunker Hill, he found the local soldiers ill trained and too egalitarian for his taste. They did not accept orders; they went home whenever they pleased. In private letters, Washington described the Massachusetts soldiers as "an exceedingly dirty and nasty people." He added that there was "an unaccountable kind of stupidity in the lower class of these people which, believe me, prevails too greatly among the officers."[5]

By 1789 such unflattering memories had faded. Indeed, as anyone who studies Washington closely soon discovers, one of the man's most admirable qualities was his willingness to reassess impressions formed at an earlier time. Unlike many political leaders, he was not afraid to change his mind on the basis of more accurate information. The New Englanders the president encountered on the road now impressed him as hardworking and entrepreneurial. Traveling along the shore of Long Island Sound to New Haven, he recorded in his diary, "We found all the Farmers busily employed in gathering, grinding, and expressing the Juice of their Apples."[6] He watched them driving well-fed cattle to market, harvesting impressive crops, and everywhere showing a commendable diligence that ironically might have come from the very social equality that he had once condemned as bad for military discipline. He took special note of the "great equality in the People of this State [Connecticut]—Few or no opulent Men and no poor."[7]

As these scattered diary entries suggest, Washington brought to the journey a serious and evolving concern for the future of the new republic. At every stop, he performed the expected rituals of political theater—exchanging formal greetings with town leaders and participating in endless toasts—but he also asked questions, listened, watched closely, and filled his diary with trenchant observations about a country trying to make sense of itself after a long period of imperial rule.

—II—

Before reaching Hartford, Washington had begun to consider the state of American manufacturing and was particularly curious about the production of cloth. As he passed through small Connecticut communities along the coast of Long Island Sound, he interrogated likely informants about plans to turn out textiles.[8] What, he asked, were the prospects for the local efforts? Were the people really serious about developing a new industry? In New Haven, Washington inquired about the progress of a "Linnen Manufacture."

Although the response was disappointing, the information does not seem to have discouraged Washington. After all, these small endeavors faced a major challenge in satisfying even minimal consumer demand. In Wallingford, the news was more encouraging. Here, he learned that some enterprising individuals who were trying to produce silk knew enough to plant mulberry trees so that they could feed the worms. Washington concluded that the experiment had the potential to become "beneficial." The entrepreneurs obviously had a long way to go. Fortunately, the results with silk making were better in Mansfield, where "they are further advanced in this business."[9]

Washington's incessant quest for information about manufacturing revealed a central element in his thinking about the nation's future. Although he was a Virginia planter, he had come to realize that the country's prosperity depended on more than the export of crops such as rice and tobacco. By the time he became president, Washington was fully aware that domestic economic development was fundamental to the success of the new government. Like other leaders of more recently liberated colonial societies — Mahatma Gandhi, for example — Washington understood that political independence did not guarantee economic independence. Americans may have freed themselves from British rule in 1783, the year the peace treaty was signed, but they still purchased most of their consumer goods from the former mother country, and these old habits were hard to break. The imported items flooded into the major ports of the United States, draining scarce capital and discouraging efforts to create greater economic self-reliance.[10]

Cloth accounted for the largest household expenditure. The size of this market comes as a surprise to Americans, who imagine that earlier generations were less dependent on the consumer marketplace than we are today. The spinning wheel has become an icon for an imagined self-sufficient world that we have lost. But nostalgia of this sort is unwarranted and reflects profound ignorance about the character of everyday life during the late eighteenth century. When Washington became president, most men and women in this country relied on stores to provide the fabric they needed to dress their families. They demanded credit from merchants and insisted on having access to stylish goods such as colorful cottons and high-end woolens.

Washington was determined to break the cycle of dependence. He knew the solution was not to be found in the encouragement of more spinning and weaving in individual homes because Americans were too busy with other productive activities to waste time making goods that could easily be purchased. Rather, the challenge for the new government was the promotion of large-scale domestic manufacturing. Only in this way could Americans ever hope to escape continued imperial domination. Economic freedom required mills and factories, state-of-the-art technologies, and a reliable labor market. This conviction energized Washington's journey.

As the president also well knew, there was another major obstacle to economic development: Americans lived in a highly speculative environment. Paper transactions, most of them related to land, obsessed wealthy urban financiers as well as ordinary people in search of better lives. Isaac Weld reported that even the richest people in Philadelphia "are not idle or inattentive to the increase of their property, being ever on the watch to profit by the sale of lands, which they have purchased, and to buy more on advantageous terms. It would be a difficult matter to find a man of any property in the country, who is not concerned in the buying or selling of land, which may be considered in America as an article of trade."[11]

Although Washington himself worked hard to sell his own western lands for a good profit, he sensed that none of this frenetic gambling did much to achieve genuine economic independence for the United States. Speculative activities that yielded no tangible product could never provide a proper substitute for manufacturing ventures, which were needed to supply the people with consumer goods competitive in terms of price and quality with European imports. Washington agreed with businessmen such as Peter Colt, a pioneering industrialist from Connecticut, who insisted that as long as American investors diverted capital from useful manufactures to "paper Speculations," American consumers would continue "their disgraceful dependence on Europe . . . [for] ordinary Cloathing."[12]

About such matters Washington lacked the theoretical sophistication of Alexander Hamilton, the country's most brilliant economic thinker, but he fully appreciated that the future prosperity of the United States required a balance between agriculture and manufacturing. Some contemporary Virginians such as Thomas Jefferson disagreed. They worried that the growth of industry in this country could undermine the virtuous independence of yeomen farmers—according to Jefferson, the source of the republic's moral strength—and saddle America with hoards of impoverished laborers. Jefferson recognized the importance of commerce. It was manufacturing that alarmed him.[13] Washington did not share these fears. The country had to feed itself, of course, but it also had to achieve genuine economic freedom. For Americans to buy American goods was a patriotic act. The crucial element in reaching the proper economic balance was labor—or, more precisely, a reallocation of American workers in a way that would not compromise agricultural production.

Only a few months before his first inauguration, Washington outlined his economic program. In an expansive letter to Lafayette, he noted with satisfaction the growth of manufacturing in the United States. Although he did not advocate encouraging this sector at the expense of agriculture, he thought an advance in manufacturing could be achieved if "women, children, & others" left the fields for the factory. He listed a number of promising experimental efforts—in the manufacture of furniture, shoes, glass, and textiles—and in all cases, he insisted that the transformation had led to "no diminution in agriculture." A balance between the two pursuits had been maintained "at a time when greater and more substantial improvements in manufactures were in the making than were ever before known in America." He drew Lafayette's attention to efforts in Connecticut, where impressive projects were in the works to produce "superfine and other broad cloths." As a demonstration of sincerity, Washington observed that he had asked a friend "this day, to procure me homespun broad cloth, of the Hartford fabric, to make a suit of cloaths for myself." And he added, "I hope it will not be a great while, before it will be unfashionable for a gentleman to appear in any other dress. Indeed, we have already been too long subject to British prejudices."[14]

Washington was determined to appear at his inauguration dressed entirely in Hartford cloth. Knowing how much politics depended on performance, he used the occasion to communicate to the public his personal commitment to economic nationalism. The task for finding sufficient yardage fell to his secretary, Tobias Lear. It was a difficult challenge. Lear turned first to Boston. Samuel Breck, who lived there, informed him that "Colonel [Jeremiah] Wadsworth" of Hartford was apparently producing woolen cloth of acceptable quality. Breck also reported that a mill near Boston might meet the president's expectations, but since the factory was just getting started, he could not guarantee a timely delivery. Still, like Colt, Breck associated industrial progress with economic independence. Americans, he predicted, would soon be able to compete with the foreign imports.

Success depended on women. The logic of the argument was compelling. Britain would lose its price advantage as soon as American women joined the labor force. Cold weather would do the trick. Their work, he insisted, "can be had at a less rate than in Europe owing to the length of our winters." The assumption seems to have been that women would help cultivate the fields during the temperate months, and when it got too cold, they would take factory jobs.

The reallocation of labor was the key to progress. Breck noted that during the colonial period, British commercial regulations had promoted female "Idleness." But those days were gone forever. Americans now could promote "manufactures which *their* [British] *Laws* cannot counteract."[15] When Washington met female workers on his tour, he accepted the situation in a remarkably matter-of-fact way. He certainly did not seem shocked that young women would seek employment outside the home. When he visited the Boston Sailcloth Manufactory, he simply noted in his diary that the workers were women and girls. "They are the daughters of decayed families, and the girls are of Character— none other are admitted. . . . This is a work of public utility & private advantage."[16]

Lear needed cloth, however, not a lecture on economic development. Fortunately, he quickly discovered that the Hartford group could in fact supply material suitable for the inauguration. In April 1789, a newspaper reporting on the ceremony in New York City exclaimed, "The cloth is of as fine a fabric and so handsomely finished, that it is universally mistaken for a foreign manufactured superfine cloth." [17] Such fulsome testimonials helped Wadsworth and his partners obtain new orders as well as financial assistance from the State of Connecticut. It awarded the Hartford Woolen Manufactory, originally established in 1788, a tax break and a bounty on all "woolen yarns." Soon the company was advertising a striking range of colors that could be "relied upon," meaning, of course, that the dyes would not run. Agents noted the popularity of "Congress Brown" and "Hartford Grey," but it was soon rumored that Martha Washington had taken a special liking to "London Smoke." Other colors such as "bottle green" were available, but a merchant warned Washington that "the greys & dark browns were too mean and coarse either for you or Mrs. W." [18] Wadsworth apparently had a flair for merchandising. Writing in a newspaper under an assumed name, he proposed, "The gentlemen who are, or shall be, elected to serve in the Senate or House of Representatives of the United States as also the President and Vice President, should all be clothed in complete suits of American manufactured cloth." [19]

The tour of the Hartford mill went well. Washington had developed a warm relationship with Wadsworth during the Revolution, when his organizational skills brought him appointment as the commissary general of the Continental Army. Wadsworth returned to Connecticut after the war, and in 1788 with his partners, Peter Colt and Oliver Wolcott, he opened the first woolen mill in the United States to employ waterpower in processes other than those required to clean the wool. The pioneering project not only used new technology but also managed to persuade shareholders that it could reach hugely ambitious goals for the production of finished cloth.

Washington went from building to building, chatting with the workers and examining the woolens that Wadsworth displayed. The president, who hoped that the Hartford experiment would encourage other Americans to invest in manufacturing, had appropriately good words for what he saw. He declared that the entire enterprise "seems to be going on with Spirit."[20] And to reinforce his words of praise, he ordered a suit for himself and sufficient cloth to make new breeches for his servants.[21] In terms of publicity, the Hartford appearance as well as several other similar events outside Boston were a success. They served to publicize his economic agenda for the nation: strengthen the United States by buying goods made in America. Newspapers in other states picked up the story. The *Daily Advertiser* published in New York City, for example, reported, "The attention which the President of the United States has paid to the several manufacturies in the States through which he has passed, has given a new spur to the manufacturers, as they can be assured both of his encouragement and patronage."[22]

Alas, the buoyant rhetoric did not reflect real conditions on the factory floor. Washington may have publicly put a positive spin on what he saw, but as he confided in his diary, "There [their] Broadcloths are not of the first quality, as yet, but they are good."[23] Like a veteran coach burdened with untested players, the president tried to make the best of the situation. What he discovered, of course, was that Wadsworth and his partners had gotten in over their heads. As one representative for the company later admitted, the original organizers were "totally unacquainted with the various subdivisions of the Labour" and "equally destitute of every kind of Machinery and Labourers for executing such a project."[24]

The company failed to persuade local people to exchange farming for factory work, and in his desperation to recruit an adequate labor force, Wadsworth hired men described as deserters from the British army who claimed expertise in manufacturing that they did not possess. In addition, the company could not obtain a reliable supply of wool, since among other problems, it turned out that sheep did not thrive in Connecticut. Raw materials came from as far away as Spain, and they often proved to be of disappointing quality. Moreover, the dyes ran. Wadsworth lowered prices in order to stimulate sales, but experienced American consumers still purchased British imported cloth. A person knowledgeable in the cloth trade visited the factory in 1794, the year that it went out of business, and concluded, "The fabric was very poor and hard in spinning, and dearer than the British, [which was] loaded with all the expense of freight, insurance, merchant's profits, and nine and a half cents duty." [25]

The Hartford experience might well have discouraged Washington, but that is not what occurred. To be sure, Wadsworth's enterprise had been ill planned and underfunded. But for Washington, it was the challenge rather than the failure that engaged his imagination. In fact, his enthusiasm for manufacturing—his conviction that it could free American consumers from dependence on Great Britain—persuaded him to entertain what for the times was a genuinely radical proposition.

The visit to the Hartford mill was still fresh in Washington's mind when he returned to New York in November 1789 from his tour of the Eastern States. Waiting for the president was an unsolicited letter from a stranger in Wales who advanced an extraordinary plan for American manufacturing and the restructuring of the labor market. The timing was perfect. About the writer, Thomas Howells, not much is known. As a young man he achieved success as a watchmaker, but after living in London for some years, he returned to his native Hay in Wales, where he established several impressive woolen mills, one of which employed nearly eighty workers. Howells seems to have been inspired by what he had heard about the egalitarian character of the United States, and he seriously contemplated moving his entire family to America. [26]

Howells's letter was bold, bordering on the impertinent. The writer, however, was confident that Washington would react positively to the proposal. "I flatter myself," he explained, "[that] you'll readily excuse the Liberty I take in addressing you, when you understand that the following thoughts are the result of a strong attachment to the freedom of America." He quickly got to the point: Howells wanted to transplant to the United States his entire cloth-making business, which he had no doubt "in time will be found of the greatest consequence."

Specifically, he hoped to establish an up-to-date factory in Virginia that would use the latest technology that he had so recently developed in Wales.

Howells anticipated the kind of objections that skeptics might raise. As the Hartford group had discovered, the major problem facing American entrepreneurs was labor supply. People in this country were too scattered. Moreover, they wanted to cultivate their own land, not work in factories for wages. But Howells assured Washington that new inventions in cloth production had reduced the demand for labor. According to the Welshman, "The great improvements which have been made in England in the Woolen and Cotton business by Water-Engines is an amazing saving in labour as much as three fourths through the whole process & in some departments as much as nine tenths."

And then came a truly radical suggestion. What, Howells asked, could the manager of a large textile factory do if he could not find an adequate number of "young white people" to work the machines? How could Virginia in particular solve the problem? The stunning answer was African American slaves. The state had a sizable unfree labor force already in place. Although Howells lived in Wales, he seems to have been aware that after the Revolution, many Virginia planters—including Washington—found it very difficult to market tobacco as they had done during the colonial period for a profit. In an effort to adjust to changing conditions, they turned increasingly to wheat. The results were encouraging; however, as they soon discovered, cereal cultivation did not require the intensive, year-round attention that tobacco demanded. And because large numbers of slaves no longer made as much economic sense as they had in the past, a number of Virginia planters seriously began to entertain the idea of manumitting their bondsmen.

This shift in thinking about labor presented Howells with an opportunity.[27] "I would propose," he continued in his letter to Washington, "that those Gentlemen who are disposed to emancipate their Negroes would appoint some of their younger ones for that business and give them their freedom after a service of seven years as an Apprentice." The plan contained a built-in incentive for hard work: as soon as the blacks had completed their apprenticeships, they would "remain in the business and become useful Members of Society."

Howells assured Washington that he would encourage the industrial training of slaves only if he could not find enough white workers. But both men surely knew that this was not about to happen. The proposition asked Washington to put aside almost two centuries of bondage and racism in the interests of accelerated economic development. A new form of capitalism demanded a new social structure. Howells augmented the deal by offering to move the most advanced machines to Virginia. He was also prepared to transport "a sufficient number of my best Workmen to take under their care those young people who might be willing to be instructed in the several departments of the business." And the only things that the writer asked in return were a short-term subsidy from the state government and a promise of land for the workers he would transfer from Britain. Failure was out of the question. The enterprise promised to "bring the woolen manufactory to a degree of perfection in a much shorter time than could be expected." [28]

One might have predicted that Washington would reject the scheme out of hand. After all, even allegedly enlightened Virginians such as Jefferson were notoriously touchy on the subject of slavery. The slaves at Mount Vernon numbered in the hundreds, but the president showed no inclination to ignore Howells. After witnessing the recent progress in textile manufacturing in New England, he jumped at the possibility of establishing mills in Virginia. He immediately wrote to Beverley Randolph, then the governor of Virginia, endorsing Howells's plan. The Hartford experience had opened Washington's eyes; he had seen the future. Textile mills had the capacity to transform the face of Virginia society. "If a greater quantity of Wool could be produced," he informed Randolph, "and if hands (which are often in a manner idle) could be employed in the manufacturing of it, a spirit of industry might be promoted, a great diminution might be made in the annual expenses of individual families, and the Public would eventually be exceedingly benefitted." [29]

Washington did not specifically mention employing African Americans in the enterprise—much less letting them work in the factory to gain freedom—but that aspect of Howells's proposal could not have remained a secret. After all, the president enclosed a full copy of Howells's letter with his own endorsement to Randolph. The governor well understood the implications of the plan. Washington urged Randolph to pursue the enterprise with the members of the Virginia legislature, observing only, "I do not pretend to determine how far that Plan may be practicable & advisable; or, in case it should be deemed so, whether any or what public encouragement ought to be given to facilitate its execution." [30]

Whatever Randolph's personal opinion may have been, he could hardly have ignored Washington's immense prestige. Howells's plan—described as a "Letter from the President of the United States, on the subject of a certain proposal made by a foreigner, for the establishment of a woolen manufactory within the State"—reached the Virginia House of Delegates early in December 1789. The legislators recommended a subsidy for Howells. The business about slaves working in factories for freedom did not raise an alarm, at least not in public. Randolph agreed that current agricultural practices were often inefficient, and he thought that "the Ability of the young and old who are disqualified for the severe Toils of the Field [might] . . . be useful in manufactures." [31]

Within a few days of receiving the governor's letter, Washington suddenly backed away. He remained enthusiastic about industrial development in the United States, but to his profound embarrassment, he had learned that his dealings with Howells raised the possibility that the president might be engaged in a conspiracy to break international law. "I am told," Washington informed Randolph, "that it is a felony to export the Machines, which it is probable the Artist [Howells] contemplates to bring with him." The discussion had to stop immediately. "It certainly would not carry an aspect very favorable to the dignity of the United States," he concluded, "for the President, in a clandestine manner, to entice the subjects of another Nation to violate its laws."[32]

Of course, when Washington departed from Hartford, his mind focused on how to jump-start the development of manufacturing in the United States, he did not have any ideas about the risk of breaking the law. We can certainly commend his integrity, for as our own history suggests, a lesser leader might have compromised honesty in the name of national prosperity. But that was not an option Washington could seriously entertain. More to the point, we encounter in Hartford a man open to new, even radical ideas about the country's future. The first leg of his journey to the Eastern States had encouraged him, as well as those people who read in the newspapers of his visit to the Wadsworth mill, to imagine a new, much more complex America.

— III —

Washington's traveling party left Hartford early on the morning of October 21. The president took the road north to Springfield and then, as he passed through the small village of Brookfield, Massachusetts, he received "an Express" from the governor of the state, John Hancock, "giving notice of the measures he was about to pursue for my reception on the Road, and in Boston."[33] This innocuous note, which could have been interpreted as nothing more than an indication of Hancock's desire to welcome the president of the United States to Massachusetts, triggered a controversy that might strike modern Americans as petty, even risible. But for the two antagonists, the contest was quite serious. During the first year of Washington's presidency, it raised fundamental questions about federal authority and state sovereignty that to this day generate bitter disagreement.

Washington had known the governor for a long time. Before signing the Declaration of Independence—affixing a signature much larger than that of any of his colleagues at the Second Continental Congress—Hancock had won widespread respect throughout New England as an uncompromising advocate of colonial rights. Lord North branded him and Samuel Adams as the two most dangerous rebels in America, a decision that served to inflate Hancock's reputation as a true patriot. But for all his efforts to organize resistance in Boston, he never quite made it into the first rank of American leaders. The huge signature suggests the source of the problem. Hancock's sense of entitlement amazed—sometimes embarrassed—his colleagues.

Hancock's vanity seemed to know no bounds. Contemporaries quickly learned that a little flattery could usually persuade him to support policies that promised to advance his career. People such as John Adams knew how to play on Hancock's egotism. When the American Congress moved in 1775 to appoint a commander of the Continental Army, Hancock assumed that he would receive the appointment. Fully aware of Hancock's hopes, Adams hinted that he could help make it happen. It made no matter that Hancock had no military experience. As he waited for his appointment, Adams threw his support to Washington, and the nakedly ambitious Hancock never forgave him for nominating the much more qualified Washington for the post.

Like Patrick Henry, Hancock returned to his home state, seemingly content for most of the Revolution to be a major fish in a smaller pond. Drawing on his own funds, he built up what would be regarded today as a political machine, and his ability repeatedly to win elections in Massachusetts depended in no little part on the timely distribution of favors. One historian describes Hancock's political style as "paternalistic public theater." He does not appear to have had a clear ideological agenda. His vanity required the loyalty of the crowd; to achieve this, he purchased for the town expensive bells and fire engines and financed out of his own pocket projects that brought employment to men who had no work.[34]

Despite his continuing popularity in Boston, Hancock's desire for national fame remained a driving force long after the end of the Revolution, and even though he had waited to the very last moment before declaring in public where he stood on the ratification of the Constitution, he convinced himself that he still had a chance to become the first vice president of the United States. His maneuvering served largely to annoy Adams. Nothing came of the intrigue except perhaps a further lowering of his reputation outside of Massachusetts, where his populist policies kept the local voters in line. He ran sixth in the polls for vice president and received not a single vote in Massachusetts. James Madison informed Thomas Jefferson at the time of the first national elections, "Hancock is a weak, ambitious courtier of popularity, given to low intrigue."[35] This assessment may be too harsh, but there is no question that Washington knew in advance that Hancock might present a problem. As one man who attended the Massachusetts Ratifying Convention observed, Hancock's character was "not entirely free from a portion of caprice."[36]

Although Hancock eventually voted for the Constitution—the result of complex backroom deals—he remained suspicious of the federal government. Its power threatened his own political base, and during the debates over ratification, Hancock strongly defended a doctrine of state sovereignty. Exactly where he drew the line between the federal government and state authority remained fuzzy, but he seems to have persuaded himself that Washington had arrived in Massachusetts as a sort of foreign ambassador and as such, the president was obliged to treat the governor as the dominant political figure in his own state. Washington, of course, regarded such views as fatuous nonsense, the kind of thinking he associated with local demagogues. The whole point of the Constitution in his opinion had been the establishment of a strong union.[37]

The governor lost no time in an attempt to gain the upper hand. While Washington was still on the road, Hancock raised several extremely sensitive issues touching on preeminence. First, he urged Washington to stay with him during the entire Boston visit. For someone who did not understand the jockeying for dominance, the gesture might have been seen as an act of generosity. This was the kind of hospitality one would expect him to offer a traveler on a long and difficult trip—except, of course, the president had made it abundantly clear from the moment he took office that he would not stay in private homes. In his response to the governor, Washington explained politely that he had already engaged a house in the city. "From a wish to avoid giving trouble to private families," the president wrote, "I determined, on leaving New York, to decline the honor of any invitation to quarters which I might receive on my journey." [38] The political game of chess played on a board of etiquette was just getting under way.

Hancock then insisted that Washington attend a welcoming dinner at the governor's house as soon as the president reached Boston. In other words, he assumed that within the Commonwealth of Massachusetts, it was proper for a president to pay his respects to the governor. Washington, of course, thought this plan insulted the dignity of the presidency. He reasoned that if he accepted Hancock's invitation, he would establish a precedent that would haunt future presidents of the United States. By having the first meal in a state capital with the governor, Washington would signal that governors somehow outranked presidents, an intolerable conclusion that more recent governors have had to relearn.

Samuel Breck, a young man who watched the drama unfold, later observed in his diary: "Great importance was attached by Governor Hancock to the importance of *state* sovereignty, and he carried his notions of *state* independence so far as to expect that Washington, Chief Magistrate of the Union, should pay him the first visit." [39] The President did express his willingness to have "an informal dinner" with Hancock, but he deliberately left the question of timing open.[40] As Washington visited Worcester and Cambridge, the touchy issue of the first meal was left hanging.

The governor also informed Washington that he had planned an elaborate military review to honor the president. Hancock knew this was a key point of contention. Without any discussion, he seized control of the presentation of the army—at the very least, a provocative symbolic move. In a note, he advised Washington that he, Hancock, on his own authority, had ordered "proper escorts to attend you." And as an expression of the people's love for their president, the governor explained that "a military parade has been determined on, & a body of about 800 men, will be under arms at Cambridge on the day of your entering Boston." How could Washington object? Hancock had thought of every detail, even historical context. "The troops," he wrote, "will occupy the ground on which the continental army was formed for your reception in the year 1775."[41] As one newspaper that supported the governor announced, "His Excellency the Governor, on the first information of the intention of The President, issued his orders for paying every military honor to the illustrious visitant."[42]

Washington did object. Although the American people celebrated his accomplishments as head of the Continental Army, he did not feel entirely comfortable greeting the local troops, who after all, were not under his command. He informed General John Brooks, a Revolutionary veteran who now served as an officer in the Middlesex Militia, of his misgivings. He had the greatest respect for Brooks's military record, and perhaps because of their long relationship, Washington did not want to embarrass the veteran officer. Still, as he told Brooks, since "I conceived there was an impropriety in my *reviewing* the Militia, or seeing them perform Manoeuvres otherwise than as a private Man, I could do no more than pass along the line." It was not clear whether Washington thought that the review raised serious constitutional issues about presidential authority or he was just annoyed that Hancock had turned the visit into a kind of circus. The president clearly would have preferred a simpler welcome, but as he confessed in his diary, "Finding this ceremony was not to be avoided, though I made every effort to do it, I named the hour of ten to pass the Militia."[43] The occasion turned out to be far grander than Washington had anticipated. A leading national newspaper exclaimed that at General Brooks's request, the president would "review three brigades of the MIDDLESEX Militia . . . [and] It is said, that this review will exhibit upwards of 1000 men in COMPLETE UNIFORM."[44]

As Washington and Hancock were taking a measure of each other, a third group suddenly entered the controversy. Representatives of the Boston Town Committee dispatched agents to meet the president on the road near Worcester, and these men announced that whatever the governor had planned, they envisioned a quite different agenda. They informed Washington that they had organized a grand parade in which thousands of ordinary people would participate, and although they did not solicit his ideas on how the event would unfold, they told Washington in general terms the character of the celebration that they had arranged.

The spokesmen for the town seemed most concerned about assuring Washington that he would be completely safe in Boston. Perhaps their visitor feared that adoring crowds might get out of control. As the Boston Town Committee explained in its note to the president on October 21, "The Town of Boston desirous of Expressing in a Public manner their Joy at being honored by your presence, and of preventing disorders which might otherwise arise from the eagerness of the Citizens to behold so Illustrious a Character, have Found it necessary to arrange the Citizens in their several Professions for your reception."[45]

The whole discussion about possible disorder seems a little odd. In fact, Washington may not have understood what the spokesmen were getting at. Not until he actually reached Boston did it become fully apparent just what it meant to organize all the citizens of the city by profession. The Boston Town Committee may have had another issue in mind. As they well knew, critics of republican government—in Great Britain as well as America—insisted that it always promoted popular unrest, even anarchy. In 1787 a member of the British House of Commons insisted, for example, that it was unsafe to live in the United States. "At present," he announced, "it was so difficult to decide whether the United States of America were under one government, whether they consisted of many discordant governments, or whether they were under no government at all." At about the same time Britain's counsel in New York wrote home with the alarming news that "mobs, tumults and bodies of men in arms are on tip toe in various parts of the country."[46] By promising an orderly affair, the committee indicated an awareness of its responsibility to demonstrate that Americans could be trusted. Washington certainly did so. The committee was relieved to learn that although "the President was desirous to come into the town in a private manner—yet to gratify the inhabitants, he cheerfully altered his arrangements so as to coincide with those of the town."[47]

However accommodating the president, the turf battle between the Boston Town Committee and the governor continued, and it almost ruined the entire visit. On Saturday, October 24, Washington arrived in Cambridge, where he reviewed a large number of local militiamen. Following the presentation of the troops, Washington expected to travel a short distance to Boston, and according to the president's diary, just before reaching his destination, members of an "Executive Council"—Hancock's representatives—met him. Samuel Adams, who was then the lieutenant governor and Hancock's political ally, led the way into the city, an official act that Washington called "in every degree flattering & honorable."[48]

The diary masks what actually occurred. To make his way to the center of Boston, Washington had to cross a narrow causeway known as the Neck, a feature of the local landscape long since removed by urban development. At the entry to the Neck, vehicles containing members of the Boston Town Committee blocked the way, and the group declared that it had no intention of clearing the road until the town's representatives had assurance that they—and not the Governor's Council—would control the festivities scheduled to begin shortly. The rivals argued. A delay of a few minutes turned into an hour on this cold and wet day. Soon Washington lost patience, and turning to his traveling secretary, William Jackson, he demanded to know whether there was an alternative route into Boston. None could be found. Just at the moment when the entire visit threatened to collapse, the two sides reached an understanding that seems to have ceded full management of the parade to the town.[49] Washington crossed the Neck as if nothing had gone wrong. As we shall see, the massive celebration that the town had organized was a stunning success, but before reconstructing the grand parade, we first need to discover how Hancock and Washington finally settled their differences over state sovereignty.

At the conclusion of his first long day in Boston, during which he had reviewed many thousands of ordinary Americans who marched in a parade, an exhausted Washington went to the house he had rented on the corner of Tremont and Court streets, and there he waited for the governor to appear. The president assumed that Hancock would share a meal, a relaxed but highly symbolic reunion. That did not happen. Not only did the governor not show up, he had the audacity to send word that he would appreciate it if Washington would come to dinner at his house. Hancock had apparently organized a large party to which he had invited "the principal citizens of Boston . . . [and] the officers of the French squadron then in port."[50] Washington would have none of it. He finally had supper with the lieutenant governor, Samuel Adams. It does not take much imagination to comprehend how awkward the occasion was for both men.

The next day, Hancock and his political allies realized that they had made a huge mistake. The president was not about to compromise. Men representing the governor rushed to Washington's lodgings, desperately trying to explain why Hancock had not appeared for the expected dinner. The problem, they insisted, was Hancock's health. He had suffered a sudden attack of gout. In Boston, the governor's gout was something of a joke, since these attacks seemed always to occur when Hancock was trying to manipulate political rivals. No doubt, he did suffer from this problem, but Washington was not moved by the plaintive claims that Hancock "had not been in a condition to call upon me as soon as I came to town."[51] After all, if the governor had really experienced such discomfort, then how could he have possibly organized such a grand dinner party at his own home? If Hancock was well enough to receive so many guests, Washington reasoned, he could surely have taken a little time to visit the president. The moment for polite exchange had passed. An angry Washington informed the governor's representatives "in explicit terms that I should not see the Governor unless it was at my own lodgings."[52]

Hancock had to act quickly to save face. Still insisting that the gout had almost immobilized him, he announced to Washington that he was now prepared to "hazard everything" for "the desirable purpose" of welcoming the president to the Commonwealth of Massachusetts. To this declaration, Washington responded with the cool formality that the confrontation demanded: "The President of the United States presents his best respects to the Governor, and has the honor to inform him that he shall be at home till 2 o'clock. The President of the United States need not express the pleasure it will give him to see the Governor; but, at the same time, he most earnestly begs the Governor will not hazard his health on the occasion."[53]

The heavy-handed repetition of Washington's full title in a short note—President of the United States—revealed that the communication concerned rival interpretations of political power rather than a matter of dinner etiquette. Hancock got the point. But to the last, he played the part of a martyr. He arrived at Washington's house carried on the shoulders of two large servants, his legs completely wrapped in red flannel. Later, Hancock's wife insisted that Washington broke down in tears when he realized how much pain the governor endured by going out on a cold October day. No corroborating evidence survives to suggest that Washington felt any emotion other than the satisfaction of having bested his theatrical rival.[54] A Boston newspaper that supported Hancock tried valiantly to deflect public attention away from the governor's blundering assertion of state sovereignty. A so-called correspondent explained that "there has been no circumstance in the life of our worthy Governor, which could have tried his feelings so much as his bodily indisposition at this happy moment: When the citizens of the State, with one voice, are paying their respects and applauses to the man, who has led in the defense of the rights of America, and of the human race."[55] As is so often the case in such controversies, then and now, the governor's friends insisted that the whole business about competing dinners "was a mere falsehood invented to injure him."[56]

Partisan appeals could not disguise the fact that Washington had won the battle over the first dinner. He exposed the governor's claims as little more than a case of inflated ego. The people of Boston ignored the farce, however. Their attention focused entirely on the president. As one witness to the controversy observed, "The Popularity of the President seemed to bear everything down, like a torrent."[57] Other governors quickly appreciated the fundamental issue at stake: governors, even in their own states, did not outrank the president of the United States. Samuel Breck, a boy at the time, recounted a story about John Langdon "who, at the time Washington was travelling in 1788 [1789], was chief magistrate of the state of New Hampshire. This gentleman, hearing of the etiquette that Hancock wished to establish, chose to show his disapprobation of it by meeting Washington with a large escort of cavalry on the very frontier of his state, and accompanying the President to Portsmouth and showing him personally every attention."[58] Langdon had learned how to greet a president of the United States.

—**IV**—

However significant Washington's duel with Hancock was in establishing the preeminence of the president throughout America, the people of Boston had other things on their minds during his visit. They staged an amazing parade in Washington's honor, the likes of which had never before been witnessed in this country. Ordinary men and women had a very good time, of course, but even as we reconstruct this celebration, we should appreciate the broader political importance of their impassioned welcome. Their enthusiasm helped neutralize Hancock's schemes, since if the people had in fact taken his part in the controversy with Washington, they would have called into question the popular foundation for the new federal government. They most definitely did not do so. They communicated loudly to Washington that they were willing to give a strong union a chance to succeed.

That the fullest descriptions of a Washington parade come from Boston is no surprise. Massachusetts had long been an impressively literate society—adult male literacy rates topped 90 percent at this time—and by the 1790s, the state supported a large number of newspapers. For us, that was a very good thing, since many people who took part in the grand celebration failed to provide as much detail about the visit as did the major journals. Participants regularly informed distant friends that if they wanted to know more about Washington's stay in Boston, they should find a newspaper account. In a letter, for example, John Adams explained to Abigail, who was then in New York and eager for intelligence from Massachusetts, that "I write no Particulars, because the News papers will give you the details." This unsatisfactory statement is doubly frustrating because Adams ended his note without fully explaining what he meant when he insisted that Washington's "Journey will do much public good."[59]

For almost everyone who participated in the event, Washington held a special place of honor. They credited him with saving Boston from destruction at the beginning of the Revolution. As commanding general of the Continental Army in 1776, he had applied military pressure on the British force occupying the city in such a way that it became impossible for the occupation soldiers to defend it. The British negotiated a peaceful departure, sailed away to Nova Scotia, and left Boston relatively undamaged. Since many Americans had predicted that the enemy might burn the city to the ground, the happy result was declared a great accomplishment, and so when Washington returned many years later, the people of Boston were determined to thank him for preserving the city as well as for accepting the presidency.

On Saturday, October 24, representatives of the Boston Town Committee took charge of the president's visit, literally pushing the governor's agents aside. This was an important victory for the people of Boston. A group of local dignitaries led Washington's little caravan across the Neck into the city proper. The president was mounted on a magnificent charger. The weather did not cooperate. One man described the day of Washington's arrival as "unusually cold and murky." But no one complained. Patient spectators were quite sure that they were witnessing a special historical moment.

It would have been a pity to allow inclement weather or an annoying squabble with the governor to compromise the celebration. The people of Boston had put a lot of work into the arrangements. One man reported, "For the last 10 days we have done nothing but prepare for, and enjoy the Visit of the best of Men."[60] Advertisements in the newspapers urged members of various societies of workingmen—more like guilds than modern unions—to make appropriate plans well in advance of the president's visit. For example, one announcement called on "All Masters of Vessels within the Town of Boston . . . to meet at the Bunch of Grapes, on the morning of the arrival of the PRESIDENT, there to form, and fall into the Procession, immediately after the Marine Society." Common seamen received similar instructions from the officers of the Marine Society.[61] The people of Boston seemed determined to present themselves to the president as a community of hardworking artisans and laborers—this was their message, their side of the conversation with the president. They were free citizens, not slaves. And throughout the day, they repeatedly signaled that it was they who were responsible for the city's commercial achievement. Indeed, their interest in the nation's future economic development—in shipbuilding and the Atlantic trade—complemented Washington's conviction that a strong union would promote greater prosperity for all Americans.

Local organizers scheduled the Boston procession to begin promptly at noon. As might be expected, the participants had to appear at designated assembly points well in advance of the official start. By ten in the morning, many people invited to take part in the parade were in place. It is impressive that so many participants—a huge percentage of the city's population—had sorted themselves out in so short a time. In any case, delays were inevitable. Like Washington, the townsmen who planned to march endured a long wait in the cold.

Finally, at about one o'clock in the afternoon, with cannon booming and church bells ringing, the president commenced his ride into the city center. A group of soldiers identified as "the Independent Company of Light Infantry" preceded him, as did a small marching band that the officers of the visiting French warships had contributed to the event. The musicians represented "His Most Christian Majesty," Louis XVI, King of France, who would soon fall victim to a revolution in part sparked by the American example. Once the troops had reached the end of the parade route, they opened ranks and faced inward, "which being done, an avenue was formed, which reached from the Neck to the State House, for The President, &c. to pass through." In addition to the soldiers, "school boys," monitored by their teachers, took up positions along the street, forming a kind of youthful honor guard. It was only when everyone was in place that "his Highness, on horseback, dressed in his military uniform" entered the heart of Boston. Following the president—presumably also riding on horseback—were his secretaries Jackson and Lear, whom the newspapers described as members of Washington's "suite."[62]

It struck some observers as noteworthy that at this grand moment, one of the state's most successful political figures, John Adams, was nowhere to be seen. A person identified as a correspondent to the *Herald of Freedom*, a local newspaper, wanted to know "the reason why, when all this parade is making to receive the FABIUS [Washington] of the age . . . the great, the wise and patriotic ADAMS should be wholly neglected." The writer seemed to be suggesting that Washington might somehow be responsible, a charge that had no merit. But seeking to explain why the vice president was missing, the commentator concluded, "The same honors which wait on a WASHINGTON would be well bestowed on the VICE-PRESIDENT, and the GOOD MAN, who now employs our whole attention would be doubly satisfied, by seeing his compatriot and friend bedecked with some of the laurels which are heaped on his own head."[63] There is no evidence that Washington was aware of the problem. After all, he had offered Adams a seat in his carriage when the president's party left New York. The offender was probably Governor Hancock, a longtime political rival of Adams, but the oversight proved just a passing issue. Later in the festivities Adams would receive the public recognition he so eagerly desired.

By the time Washington rode into Boston, a very large crowd had assembled. It is impossible to judge precisely the number or character of the men and women who lined the street. Without question, a very large percentage of the city's population—then around eighteen thousand—either participated in the parade or watched those who marched. What we do know is that contemporaries praised the social diversity of the people who endured the cold. This was America as it should be seen: different sorts of men and women and all well behaved. "We are happy to announce," declared the *Massachusetts Spy*, "that all classes of citizens have been assiduous to show every respect to the man, whom they consider, under Providence, as the defender of their rights."[64] Another Boston paper added, "The Joy of all ranks of people is extreme, upon the prospect of our beloved President's arrival."[65] Women apparently had the best view of Washington. Perhaps they wanted to avoid the inevitable pushing and shoving on the street. In any case, witnesses reported that "the windows of the houses from the entrance of Boston, at the Neck to the State House, and down Cornhill and State Street, were filled with ladies."

Not surprisingly, such an event offered an unexpected though welcome opportunity to make money. Entrepreneurs eager to rent viewing space had constructed special galleries in front of some buildings on the parade route. These temporary structures, thrown up in only a day or two, were beautifully carpeted and decorated with appropriate plant material. Women took seats on these structures and on the tops of houses. They waved wildly as the president passed. Many wore special ornaments for the occasion. How they communicated the rules of fashion so swiftly is not known—done, of course, without the benefit of electronic networking—but on the day of the celebration, it was reported that the women honored Washington by wearing special sashes depicting American eagles and laurel leaves.

A few privileged spectators watched Washington from windows located in buildings opposite the Massachusetts State House, where the president was expected to review the entire parade. These were the best seats available. Convenience, of course, came at a cost. Just as with modern forms of entertainment, the most desirable locations "were let for a very good price."[66] But even for people willing to spend money on the celebration, it was a long day. Many had taken up viewing positions early in the morning, and despite the inhospitable weather, they remained in viewing positions until at least four in the afternoon, when it was getting dark.

Even for hearty Bostonians, sitting through the entire procession of workers and dignitaries was an ordeal. The damp and the chill took a toll. Within a few days, large numbers of people came down with colds, which they termed, in honor of the moment, "the Washington cold."

One woman who had been present for the entire afternoon told Abigail Adams, "Everybody who was at the parade the Day the president entered Boston took a cold. People stood at the windows, some of them Six hours, waiting for his arrival—Having got a good situation, they were afraid to leave it lest they should not be able to recover it again; The Day was dreadful raw & uncomfortable."[67] The experience probably did Washington, still recovering from a dangerous illness, no good. Two days later, on October 26, he scribbled in his diary: "The day being Rainy & Stormy—myself much disordered by a Cold and inflammation of the left eye, I was prevented from visiting Lexington (where the first blood in the dispute with G. Britain was drawn)."[68]

As during his earlier visit to Gray's Ferry Bridge, Washington endured in Boston a carefully staged event, which the people of the city probably regarded as the high point of the day. Various local figures had decided long before the president arrived that it was not enough for Washington simply to ride through the center of the town. The occasion required a grand and highly symbolic moment that powerfully expressed how the community felt about the new government and its leader. This was a poignant setting in which one encounters the popular political imagination of post-Revolutionary America taking shape and finding new ways to give voice to abstract ideas about the meaning of republicanism. Without the slightest hint of irony, one commentator observed, "When an occasion presents itself, in which the people of the United States can testify to distinguished merit, their respect and esteem—they have never known to let it pass unimproved." The writer then asked, what "was to be expected from them when an opportunity offered of personally paying their tribute to a Man, in whose character, whatever is Great and Good—whatever dignifies and adorns human nature, are so happily united?"[69]

While Washington was still traveling, various suggestions about how best to honor the "Great and Good" circulated in Boston. Fortunately for him, the more ambitious ones do not seem to have generated much public enthusiasm. A proposal for a huge monument came from

Judge James Sullivan, a highly respected judge and future governor of Massachusetts. At a town meeting, he urged the citizens of Boston to construct "a permanent Triumphal Arch as the entrance of the Town, to remain a lasting memorial of this pleasing event."[70] Sullivan recommended that the arch carry the words "His Most Patriotic Majesty," a curiously inappropriate declaration for an elected official.

But Sullivan had a grander ideological agenda. He noted that Washington probably did not have long to live, or as he stated bluntly, "it is our misfortune to be assured that he will, in a few years, resign himself to the universal conqueror, and join the congregation of the dead." The challenge, therefore, was not simply commemorating Washington's undeniable greatness, but, rather, preparing the republic for a time when it had no leaders of Washington's caliber. "Who will succeed him," explained the judge, "we cannot tell." And so, the true purpose of the great arch—despite the bizarre inscription "His Most Patriotic Majesty"—was to remind people not to give their presidents any power that they were not willing to grant "to even the worst of men." The point seems to have been that while the people could "trust" Washington "with unlimited power," they could not expect to do so ever again since Washington was a unique figure in political history.[71]

No doubt, the judge meant well. Given the constraints of time and money, however, the permanent installation he had in mind was not feasible. In a letter published in Boston's *Independent Chronicle*, one of Sullivan's supporters argued that a civic committee should be formed "for making arrangements to promote a subscription for this purpose." The case for the great arch appeared self-evident: "If built of stone, it would add not only a lasting monument of respect, but [also] a durable ornament to the town." The writer assured readers that funds for the project would be forthcoming. Indeed, the money "might be raised in a few hours, as without doubt every wealthy citizen would willingly subscribe for completing so glorious a purpose."[72] Nothing came of the plan, at least not in 1789.

Nor did anyone seriously push for another, even more striking possibility. Lucy Cranch wrote to her aunt, Abigail Adams, that one group in Boston had put forward a prospectus calling for the erection of "a Colossal statue which would represent General Washington—and all the people were to walk under it."[73] Perhaps the inspiration for this construction was the Colossus of Rhodes, one of the seven wonders of the ancient world. Chroniclers described that victory monument, long since destroyed, as the tallest statue ever built. Since we do not have a blueprint for the Boston colossus, we cannot know how high the Washington statue would have been. What is certain is that the president would have been extremely embarrassed if he had had to witness the city's entire population marching in solemn procession between his legs.

Although the members of the Boston planning committee seem to have been wedded to the notion that Washington's visit was a kind of modern-day Roman Triumph in which the revered leader would pass through a great arch, they discarded ideas for a colossus or a permanent stone monument. But even though they scaled back on size and expense, they were determined to present the president with an impressive symbolic display. At the time, no one characterized the final elaborate results as strangely out of place for a New England city. The committee authorized construction of what was called "The Triumphal Arch," a creation much grander than the one that Washington encountered earlier that year in Trenton.

Charles Bulfinch, who went on to become one of the most celebrated architects in the United States and is associated with many striking neoclassical buildings in Boston and Washington, D.C., was responsible for the design of the arch. He was eager to make his mark. Indeed, the arch was Bulfinch's first public commission, and he seems to have allowed his imagination extraordinary freedom. He mixed classical themes with patriotic ornamentation that called attention to the creation of a new republican government.[74] The edifice spanned an entire street from side to side. According to a contemporary report, a central triumphal arch, which served to focus the viewer's attention, was eighteen feet tall and fourteen feet wide. On each side of this impressive opening, Bulfinch placed a smaller arch, each seven feet wide. Local carpenters probably framed out this temporary structure in wood. Today nothing survives. Other than newspaper accounts, the only depiction that we have of the arch is a small print that appeared in a monthly magazine. The sketch is surprisingly lifeless. Two people are present to give the picture perspective, but the print fails to communicate the excitement of the crowd as Washington, dressed in full military uniform, passed through the arch on his great white charger.

The complex symbolic message that the structure communicated—not only to Washington but also to the people of Boston—struggled uneasily with Bulfinch's basic classical design. He honored the federal union by mounting thirteen stars on the frieze, which had been painted blue. Above that, he constructed what was described as "a handsome white dentule cornice." Perhaps at the urging of the Boston Town Committee, Bulfinch included several inscriptions that seemed appropriate for the day: "To the Man who unites all hearts" and "To Columbia's favourite Son." Then, as we can see from the print, he added on the right side of the street where the construction was tied to the State House "a Trophy, composed of the arms of the United States, of the Commonwealth of Massachusetts, and our French Allies, crowned with a laurel wreath." Over these decorative elements, Bulfinch inserted the words "Boston relieved March 17, 1776." One wonders why a local newspaper had to explain that the date was a "proof of a grateful remembrance of the services to this town by the illustrious President in his military character." Perhaps historical memory was already slipping in the new republic.

Topping the entire creation was a huge canopy rising another twenty feet above the arches on which Bulfinch placed an American eagle. One account insisted that the whole patriotic spectacle "captivated the eye of the beholder, [and] added much to the testimonials of the respect of the day." What is not revealed in the print is a special gallery, placed below the canopy, designed for "a select choir of singers of both sexes." According to the plan, after Washington passed under the main arch and had taken his place on a reviewing stand located in front of the State House, the hidden choir would burst into song: "Great Washington, the Hero's Come."[75]

All went well. In his diary, Washington noted in detail the dimensions of the triumphal arch. But riding through the Bulfinch structure was only the start of a very long day. After dismounting, he entered the State House, where the Massachusetts legislature met, and from the Senate chamber, he walked out onto a raised gallery—really a temporary reviewing stand—that overlooked the crowd assembled around the great arch. This stand is clearly visible on the right side of the print. "Seven large Pillars," an echo of the Roman theme, supported a gallery projecting out from the second floor of the State House. The event's planners called this observation deck "The Colonnade"; the president referred to it as a "Balcony." Here, in the open air, Washington sat in a chair that allowed him to see and be seen by the people.

What might have struck the president as peculiar were the decorations carefully arranged around him. As one witness recorded, "At the back of this gallery, which was covered with rich carpeting, stood erected on a pedestal a handsome figure, emblematical of the season, of the Goddess of Harvest, holding the Cornucopia, or horn of plenty." The newspapers mentioned "other emblems," but no one bothered to describe their character. On the outside of the Colonnade, where the spectators could see it, hung a banner proclaiming, "The Man of the People."[76]

The notion that Washington, a wealthy Virginia planter, should be welcomed in Boston as a "Man of the People" probably owed a lot to Thomas Dawes, a popular political figure who claimed in city affairs to speak for the local artisans and laborers. It is not surprising, therefore, that the Boston Town Committee commissioned Dawes to oversee the design of the reviewing stand as well as the Goddess of Harvest. He was an extremely interesting, though somewhat mysterious, individual.

During the years leading up to the Revolution, Dawes had helped to organize semisecret resistance efforts. After the United States achieved independence, he continued to serve as a kind of backroom politician, making deals and influencing appointments. But he was also a talented architect. In fact, Dawes taught Bulfinch, his gifted student, the basic elements of building and design.[77] The claim that Washington was a man of the people should be interpreted as an ideological appeal. In all the swirling rhetoric about "His Majesty," the banner reminded the president that he represented the American people—not a privileged segment of the population but all citizens of the republic; at least, that was Dawes's hope.

Then, what for the president was a pleasurable ordeal, the grand procession, began. Several days before Washington had arrived, broadsheets had been distributed throughout Boston spelling out the exact order of the different groups that would pass the reviewing stand. Although it is hard to estimate the number of participants in the parade, the figure must have been in the thousands. First came various elected officials. Members of the learned professions followed: clergymen, physicians, and lawyers.

But it was the tradesmen, manufacturers, and artisans of Boston who dominated the spectacle. Large groups of workers representing the major trades passed by the president's gallery; they carried hand-painted flags identifying their crafts. Some presented colorful banners with "mottoes"—a kind of advertising—while others exhibited coats of arms. The marchers appeared in alphabetical order, so that the bakers and blacksmiths welcomed the president before the wharfingers and wheelwrights did. They certainly impressed Washington. He noted in his diary that the choir's performance was "followed by the different Professions, and Mechanics . . . with their Colours [who marched] through a lane of the People which had thronged about the Arch under which they passed."[78]

The entire procession echoed early modern European events in which the guilds celebrated in public their own proud histories. But whatever the parallels to an older social hierarchy may have been, the people who marched in Boston did not possess royal charters giving them special privileges or social status. These tradesmen, manufacturers, and artisans were free workers, and in a modernizing economy, they informed the president that the nation's future depended on commerce.

For hours during this cold and dreary day, they continued to march through the Bulfinch arch and then, when they reached the Colonnade, cheered the president. The card makers displayed a motto, "United to extend the Manufactures of our country." The carvers declared, "The Arts flourish under Liberty." The coppersmiths simply celebrated "Union." The lemon dealers encouraged "Success through Trade." Some tradesmen tried to advance their own businesses. The paper stainers, for example, announced, "May the fair daughters of Columbia deck themselves and their walls with their own manufactures." And the hairdressers, waving a flag on which they had painted "a wig, razor and comb," reminded the president of an undoubted truth: "By Fashions we live." The crowd remained on the street until the last group of workers marched by carrying "the Columbian flag." Everyone seemed pleased with how Boston presented itself to the president. As night was falling, "The multitude . . . dispersed, highly satisfied with the occasion of their assembling, and fully participating in the joy of the day."[79]

Participants and spectators had witnessed an extraordinary celebration of republican equality. The artisans and mechanics testified that in this post-Revolutionary society that disdained aristocracy—the claim that because of bloodlines some men are better than others—free workers could in fact compete to achieve a better life. The simplicity of their appearance made the point; they arranged themselves only by the letters of the alphabet. As one commentator observed, "The more free the constitution of any country, the less we see . . . of the inferiority of various classes of men in the presence of their superiors in rank."[80]

At the end of the day, a military escort accompanied Washington to the house where, much to the governor's annoyance, the president had elected to stay. Revelers were still out in the streets. Fireworks lit up the night skies, and candles illuminated many windows. The president was tired. He had come to Boston to proclaim the union. The people had responded not only to a Revolutionary leader, but also to the invitation to support the new constitutional government. No doubt he slept well. He could not have known at that moment, of course, that two young couples had just decided to name their newborn sons "GEORGE WASHINGTON." The boys were christened during his visit.[81] The journey to discover America was off to a promising start.

One marvelous recollection captured the spirit of the moment. During the 1820s, Samuel Breck, who had been a young man at the time of Washington's visit to Boston, remembered taking a leisurely walk in the evening after the grand parade. His companion happened to be Henri Jean Baptiste, vicomte de Pontèves-Giens, commander of a squadron of French naval vessels. The two men passed the house where Washington resided. Breck noted, "All was quiet around it. No guards, no noise, no parade of visitors whatever." How could one explain such calm after a day of extraordinary celebration? "'Ah,' said the good Pontèves, 'this is the residence of the chief magistrate of your nation, reposing with confidence in the midst of his fellow citizens, and protected by their love, a defense infinitely better than bayonets. In my country,' he added, 'the smallest general would have had the house surrounded by sentinels.'"[82]

—V—

Washington returned to New York City from his whirlwind tour of the Eastern States convinced that the nation was making very good progress. What he had seen in Massachusetts, Connecticut, and New Hampshire provided persuasive evidence—at least, to him—that the country was rapidly repairing the physical damage suffered during the Revolution. Commerce was rebounding; manufacturing showed promise. In early January 1790, he summarized his thoughts about the state of the nation. In a wide-ranging and unusually reflective letter to Catharine Macaulay Graham, a highly respected British historian, he reported that he had "found the Country, in a great degree, recovered from the ravages of War—the Towns flourishing—& the People delighted with a government instituted by themselves & for their own good."

The fragmentation of civil society, which he had feared so deeply during the 1780s, had not occurred. In fact, in moving prose rare in Washington's correspondence, the president argued that the new government had preserved the original goals of the Revolution. He recognized, of course, that although the system established by the Constitution was not "absolutely perfect," it was still "one of the best in the World." For Washington, the reasons for success were obvious: the people enjoyed "free & equal Representation." Moreover, "an efficient & responsible Executive" had guided them through a difficult transition.

The claim about executive competence may sound self-serving, but Washington was not bragging about his own contribution to securing the union. Without the support of the people, his own efforts would have achieved nothing. They had in fact responded to the challenge. It was "next to a Miracle," he thought, that so many citizens, scattered over such a large territory and "so different in their habits," had expressed such impressive "unanimity and good will." At this moment, he could honestly say that if he had in fact somehow contributed to "the felicity of my Country," then he was satisfied that his public career had done some good. As he explained to Graham, the strength of the union "will be the only real compensation I can receive in the closing Scenes of life." [83]

We have no reason to question Washington's sincerity at this moment. He may, of course, have wanted to provide a British commentator with positive news about the United States. There was no doubt, however, that the journey to the Eastern States had raised his spirits. Alas, his sanguine mood did not last long. During early 1790, a number of contentious issues that had not disturbed the relative tranquility of the first year of his presidency came to a head, and the unity that Washington cherished began to give way to public disagreement, incipient faction, and threats to the stability of the union.

In mid-January, Hamilton released his *Report on Public Credit*. In this brilliantly innovative document, Washington's secretary of the treasury argued that if the United States hoped to gain the trust of the nations with which it traded, it would have to establish a solid credit rating. But since the country remained saddled with a huge public debt incurred during the Revolutionary War, the prospects for economic progress seemed doubtful. To address the problem, Hamilton proposed that the federal government fund at full face value all the promissory notes issued to the soldiers during the war and that it assume the war debt for which the various states were liable. The plan at once strengthened the union and secured the nation's credit.

Almost immediately, James Madison and other leading Virginians cried foul. They pointed out that many impoverished soldiers had sold their promissory notes at a fraction of face value. The discounted notes were now in the hands of speculators who stood to make a lot of money if Hamilton's scheme became law. The debate in Congress over the fairness of the plan turned old friends into political enemies. What saved the day was a compromise negotiated by Hamilton and Jefferson. According to this agreement, Hamilton could have his way with funding the war debt if he and his allies accepted a southern location for the permanent capital of the United States, something the Virginians wanted very badly. While these divisive issues played out, a group of Quakers submitted a petition to Congress calling for the abolition of the slave trade. The proposition thoroughly frightened southern representatives, who, as they would do repeatedly, threatened to leave the union if the federal government dared to interfere with human bondage. Congress tabled the petition, but the bitterness and mistrust remained. And to add to the political volatility was the question of what Americans should make of the French Revolution, which seemed to be generating alarming new levels of violence.[84]

While Congress debated these vexing issues, Washington again fell ill. Much like the experience of the previous year, his illness was so serious that close colleagues in New York feared that he would be dead before the summer. After a bad spell in mid-April, the president appeared to rally, so much so that he began exercising. But then the dangerous symptoms returned, and by the end of May, people anticipated that he would not recover. As in 1789, they were wrong. Part of the appeal of a short journey to Rhode Island was the prospect that a voyage on the Long Island Sound might restore his health.[85]

It was ironic that in the midst of these personal and political trials, Washington decided to visit Rhode Island. He directed some of the least flattering remarks in his correspondence to that state. It not only had adopted during the 1780s fiscal policies that struck Washington as grossly irresponsible, but had also shown annoying reluctance to ratify the Constitution. Repeated efforts to persuade the legislature to join the union had failed, and it was not until late May 1790 that the small farmers of Rhode Island, who feared the new government would burden them with heavy taxes, allowed their representatives to accept the Constitution.

William Loughton Smith, a South Carolina congressman who accompanied Washington on the Rhode Island tour in August 1790, could not believe the political culture that greeted him. He reported that the people he encountered "are generally anti-Federal, and ignorant, and dislike any government which calls on them for taxes; in fact, they seem to care very little for what government prevails or whether there is any at all, and would prefer that which required the least taxes."[86] Washington had no patience for such narrow parochialism. In a letter written in January 1790, he railed against the state of affairs in Rhode Island. Only "the little State of Rhode Island" still remained outside the union. "How long she will be able to stand in that forlorn condition," he observed, "must depend upon the duration of that infatuation and evil policy of which she appears to have been guided." [87]

Washington invited a small group of political figures to travel with him. The composition of the party suggested that he was trying to persuade influential people to work together in the future. Although the divisions would in fact prove too deep to repair, Washington thought that a relaxing journey that took the rivals away from the hothouse environment of the capital might help to reduce the mistrust that had yielded legislative paralysis. One newspaper expressed hope that he was correct. The *Massachusetts Spy* noted, "Although the very difficult affairs of this session [of Congress], the most important in the civil history of the Union have not been transacted in the time, nor in the manner many earnestly desired, it is to be hoped that the public apprehension and jealousies will subside, and that all good men will cultivate that national spirit which diffused such a luster over the first session." [88] The junket included Thomas Jefferson, who was deeply skeptical of Hamilton's economic program. Joining him were Congressman Smith; George Clinton, the governor of New York; John Blair, a member of the Virginia Supreme Court; and several presidential secretaries. They sailed up the Long Island Sound on Captain Brown's *Hancock*. If the name of the ship stirred memories of an earlier standoff over state sovereignty, no one recorded it. The plan called for a short stay in Newport, followed by a stop in Providence.

For our purposes, Newport is the main focus of our attention. When the *Hancock* reached Rhode Island, an artillery company discharged thirteen cannon. The number, of course, expressed a new political reality, not a hope, as it was in 1789. When the president and his party landed, an impressive group of local dignitaries greeted them. "A large and respectable committee from the town, and Reverend Clergy, received the President on the wharf," reported the city's newspaper, "and with the citizens, in procession, escorted him to his lodging." The hosts were eager to show Washington that the people of the state could be gracious and cooperative. They organized a feast, which sparked a long, obligatory round of toasts.[89]

For all the enthusiasm for his visit, the president must have realized immediately that Newport had suffered more during the war than had almost any other American city. Long occupied by British forces, it had seen its once-flourishing Atlantic trade destroyed. Many people left Newport during the Revolution, and those who stayed had to endure daily insult as well as property destruction. One might have thought the arrival of a French army in 1780 would have altered the situation for the better. The French were certainly easier to live with than the British troops had been, but at the end of the day, large numbers of soldiers who had to be lodged and fed drained the community's dwindling resources. Independence brought an end to the suffering, but as anyone could see, Newport would never again become the prosperous commercial center it had been before the conflict with Great Britain.

Washington walked the streets of Newport, admiring the many architectural treasures that it has to offer. One building in particular caught his attention, an impressive structure known as the Touro Synagogue. He probably knew very little about the history of Newport's Jewish community. Late in the seventeenth century, a number of Sephardim—Jews of Iberian background—moved from Barbados to Rhode Island. From the first, authorities in colonial Rhode Island expressed a willingness to tolerate the newcomers. In 1684 the legislature informed the Jews that "they may Expect as good Protection here, as any Strainger being not of Our Nation residing amongst us in this his Majesties Collony Ought to have, being Obedient to his Majesties laws." Although the Jews had no trouble fulfilling this expectation, they had a hard time establishing themselves in the community. It was not until the middle of the eighteenth century that their population reached about two hundred. Some 10 percent of Newport's merchants were Jews.[90]

During the mid-1750s, the group felt confident enough to organize a synagogue. They appointed Isaac Touro as "hazan," or reader, and plans were announced for the construction of a new place of worship. The members of the congregation envisioned an impressive building. The problem they faced was that there was no architect in the colony who knew how to design a synagogue. Fortunately, the synagogue's supporters turned to Peter Harrison, a gifted artist who happened to be Episcopalian. He is remembered today for, among other things, his magnificent Brick Market Building and Redwood Library, both still standing in Newport. He threw himself into the Touro commission. Trained in England in the neo-Palladian tradition that was then very popular throughout the Atlantic world, Harrison closely studied how Jewish rituals defined space within the synagogue. He had models from Europe to guide him, but mostly, he proved a good listener.

The work went slowly, largely because funds for the building were hard to raise. The synagogue was finally dedicated on December 5, 1763. People of other faiths participated in the ceremony, and they praised Harrison's magnificent accomplishment. The editor of the *Newport Mercury* reported that he could hardly contain his enthusiasm. "The Order and Decorum, the Harmony and Solemnity of the Musick, together with the Handsome Assembly of People, in an Edifice the most perfect of the Temple Kind perhaps in America, and splendidly illuminated, could not but raise in the Mind a faint Idea of the Majesty and Grandeur of the Ancient Jewish Worship mentioned in Scripture."[91]

The moment of majesty and grandeur did not last long. The War for Independence took a terrible toll on the Jews of Newport. Occupation disrupted normal business patterns, and some Jewish merchants left the city in search of more promising commercial opportunities. A few Jews sided with the British. The Touro congregation never recovered from the American Revolution; by 1782 there were only six Jewish families left in Newport.[92] But somehow, through it all, the temple survived. A visitor who toured Newport just a year before Washington arrived was shocked by the state of the city. "The whole appearance of the place is shattered and out of repair," the anonymous traveler observed. And yet, the synagogue stood out among the ruins. "The Jews synagogue is the most ornamented of them all [churches in the town], and the best building of the kind which I have seen. The portico is supported by pillars of the Ionic order. The inside is rich and elegant." He praised the large brass chandelier that hung over the reading desk. Equally impressive were the "highly ornamented brass candlesticks." He noted that the gallery for women was splendidly "enclosed with a carved network, supported by pillars, and over the gallery another range of pillars support the roof."[93] Harrison had included twelve columns of classical design, which he had learned represented the twelve tribes of Israel.

In contrast to the beautifully crafted interior, the outside of the building seemed remarkably plain. That was no accident.[94] The members of the congregation did not want to draw attention to the magnificence inside. Harrison had done very well. Sadly, his life soon came undone. On the eve of the Revolution he moved to New Haven, Connecticut, where he became a vocal supporter of the British Empire. Local patriots decided to silence Harrison. Soon after a mob ruined his house, he died. Harrison, who deserves recognition as one of America's foremost architects, was buried in an unmarked grave.

During his tour, the surviving members of the Touro congregation greeted Washington at the synagogue. The spokesman, Moses Seixas, read a formal statement of welcome. His words are worth quoting fully since they not only addressed the challenge of religious toleration in the new nation, but also inspired Washington to respond in what was surely one of his more thoughtful and elegant declarations. Seixas opened by incorporating the president's Revolutionary leadership of the American people into Jewish history. "With pleasure we reflect on those days — those difficult days of difficulty, & danger when the God of Israel, who delivered David from the peril of the sword, shielded your head in the day of battle." The winning of independence boded well for the Newport Jews:

> Deprived as we heretofore have been of the invaluable rights of free Citizens, we now (with a deep sense of gratitude to the Almighty disposer of all events) behold a Government, erected by the Majesty of the People—a Government, which to bigotry gives no sanction, to persecution no assistance—but generously affording to All liberty of conscience, and immunities of Citizenship: deeming everyone, of whatever Nation, tongue, or language, equal parts of the great governmental Machine.

Seixas specifically thanked the new administration for "all the Blessings of civil and religious liberty." And he closed by asking "the Angel who conducted our forefathers through the wilderness into the promised land" to guide Washington at the moment of death—like Joshua— "into the Heavenly Paradise to partake of the water of life, and the tree of immortality." [95]

These were moving words quite different in character from the formulaic exchanges that Washington endured when he entered cities such as Boston or Richmond. He might have responded politely without putting too much thought into the exercise, but he did not do so. In fact, drawing on the writings of John Locke, the president put forward in splendid clarity what he regarded as the philosophic foundation for religious toleration in the new republic. His declaration has enduring value. Washington believed that the United States had achieved something unique in the world of nations. The American people provided "mankind examples of an enlarged and liberal policy: a policy worthy of imitation." And the key element in this new social order was rights—the rights that every man or woman enjoys simply by virtue of having been born. These rights are not a gift from a government to the people. Even if the entire constitutional system collapsed, they would still possess basic rights. "It is now no more that toleration is spoken of, as if it was by the indulgence of one class of people, that another enjoyed the exercise of their inherent natural rights." Seixas and the Jews of Newport need not worry, "for happily the Government of the United States, which gives to bigotry no sanction, to persecution no assistance, requires only that they who live under its protection should demean themselves as good citizens, in giving it on all occasions their effectual support." He wished "the Children of the Stock of Abraham" the best for the future, and although the little congregation did not in fact prosper—most of the Jews left Rhode Island for New York—Washington's message stands to this day as a condemnation of those who think that social class defines fundamental human rights and that governments have the authority to decide which faiths it will tolerate.[96]

—VI—

Washington rushed back to New York. He had to move his entire family to Philadelphia, the new temporary capital of the United States. He had completed the tour of the Eastern States, and although Rhode Island tried his patience, he concluded that the great majority of the American people supported the creation of a stronger union. The trip had not healed the growing ideological mistrust that separated John Adams from Thomas Jefferson, Alexander Hamilton from James Madison. Washington hated the sniping among friends. None of this, however, caused him to doubt that the American people provided humanity with powerful examples of the benefits to be derived from living under a strong republican government.

CHAPTER VI

Signs of Trouble:
The Road South

In the wake of his successful New England tour, George Washington had high expectations for his journey through the southern states. After all, he was a Virginian, and there is no question that he felt more comfortable in the South than he had in the North. But while he continued to champion his vision for a strong union—one that he insisted must include the new settlements west of the Appalachians—Washington encountered challenges on the road, some quite unexpected, which with hindsight, we can see as harbingers of political and social forces that in time would compromise national solidarity.

The journey started well enough. In Richmond, Washington encouraged construction of a canal that promised to link the new western settlements to established ports in the East, a commercial connection that he argued would further strengthen the union. But as he traveled south toward Charleston, the unexpected news that a Pennsylvania law might free the slaves that the president had brought to Philadelphia from Mount Vernon distracted his attention and raised hard questions about the role that slavery would play in the nation's future. And although the people in the communities along the road organized splendid welcoming ceremonies—as impressive as anything he had witnessed in the North—a major argument between John Adams and Thomas Jefferson over the implications of the French Revolution for

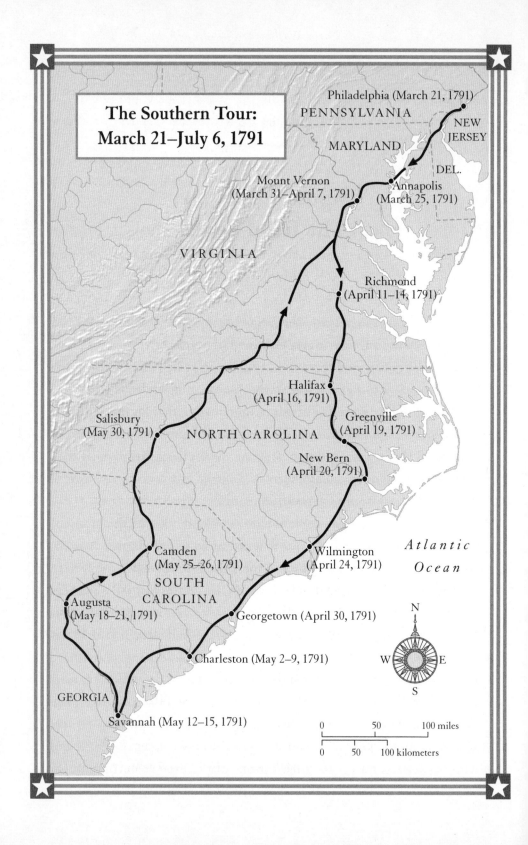

The Southern Tour:
March 21–July 6, 1791

Philadelphia (March 21, 1791)

PENNSYLVANIA

NEW JERSEY

MARYLAND

DEL.

Mount Vernon
(March 31–April 7, 1791)

Annapolis
(March 25, 1791)

VIRGINIA

Richmond
(April 11–14, 1791)

Halifax
(April 16, 1791)

Salisbury
(May 30, 1791)

NORTH CAROLINA

Greenville
(April 19, 1791)

New Bern
(April 20, 1791)

Camden
(May 25–26, 1791)

Wilmington
(April 24, 1791)

Atlantic
Ocean

SOUTH
CAROLINA

Augusta
(May 18–21, 1791)

Georgetown (April 30, 1791)

Charleston (May 2–9, 1791)

N

W   E

S

GEORGIA

Savannah (May 12–15, 1791)

0   50   100 miles

0   50   100 kilometers

the United States publicly revealed that however much Washington had discouraged political infighting of this sort, he could not in fact control ideological differences that promoted the very fragmentation that he most feared.

—I—

The Southern Tour, carried out during spring 1791, occurred within a dramatically different political framework than had the New England trip. During the first year of Washington's presidency, the American people seemed unsure how the new Constitution would affect their lives. In an effort to give the republican experiment a chance to succeed, they tried to moderate serious differences. But by 1791, the political climate had shifted. Fundamental disagreements about the proper direction of the country divided former friends and agitated the public. It was in this unsettled atmosphere that George Washington once again set out to discover what the American people were thinking about the federal government that they had so recently ratified.

The journey began with surprisingly little ceremony. Newspapers reported only that late on the morning of March 21, 1791, the president's small caravan had departed Philadelphia for the southern states. The tour, by far his most ambitious undertaking, took Washington to Charleston and Savannah, to places he had never visited during the Revolution, and then, turning north from Georgia, he stopped at various backcountry communities such as Augusta and Camden, Charlotte and Salem—small settlements without long histories.

The only thing that Major Jackson and the others traveling with Washington knew for certain was that the trip would be extraordinarily difficult. Few people before this time had attempted such a demanding undertaking, and those who survived the ordeal complained bitterly about aggressive mosquitoes, frightening reptiles, and primitive lodging.

Although it might have been easier for the president to sail directly to South Carolina, travel by boat was never a serious option. Washington's goal remained, as it had been during his earlier excursions, to perform the presidency for Americans scattered over thousands of miles and thereby to affirm the benefits the people would derive from a strong federal union.

The staging of the presentation was much more elaborate than it had been during the first trip to Boston. The entourage was larger, the props more elaborate. Washington sat in a new coach driven by John Fagan, who was described as "tall and burly in person." Like many other teamsters who had long experience with poor roads and stubborn animals, Fagan was also irascible. He had come to the United States as a Hessian soldier, but this military background did not bother Washington, who after all was most interested in employing someone who knew how to negotiate rough roads. Fagan did a fine job controlling the high-spirited four-horse team. Major Jackson, Washington's secretary, was present throughout the journey. James Hurley served as postilion, the person who rode next to the lead horses pulling the coach.

Washington also brought two slaves, Giles and Paris, who had served him at Mount Vernon and during his recent trip to New England. The president expected Giles to act as the postilion, but as soon became clear, an injury kept Giles from performing in this capacity. Paris, much younger, seems to have ridden a horse behind the baggage cart, which among other objects contained Washington's Continental uniform, which he donned just before entering a town. Paris was responsible for the welfare of a favorite white charger, as well as for a number of other horses that accompanied the president over almost two thousand miles of treacherous roads.[1] Amazingly, all eleven animals survived the arduous journey without mishap.

Although some southern political figures expressed surprise on hearing the news that Washington would in fact visit the region, his intentions were never really in doubt. Early in his first term as president, he vowed to travel to all thirteen original states. The only question was scheduling. The journey had to take place when Congress was not in session. Still, when Major Jackson informed William Blount, a respected leader from North Carolina, that the president intended to tour the South during spring 1791, Blount trumpeted the information as if no one had expected it. The timing was propitious. Washington sensed the need to address growing regional differences.

Ever since Washington had toured New England, southerners grumbled that he had not given enough attention to their states. Early in 1790, one correspondent from Virginia reminded the president, "Your friends to the Southward fondly hope [to have], the pleasure of a Visit—I do not know that we shall not otherwise become a little jealous." [2] Blount certainly saw the trip in terms of regional competition. He warned his associates to convince "the Overseers of Roads and Ferry-Keepers to *mend their ways* and repair, or rebuild boats. If the greatest attention is not paid him [Washington], he will be greatly disappointed and mortified for to the North, the contention has been who should pay him the most [respect]." [3]

Although Washington did not seem concerned about which region of the country greeted him most effusively, he realized that the character of the southern trip was significantly different from the one that had taken him to Boston and Newport. It was not that ordinary Americans in the South greeted him less enthusiastically. In Charleston and Savannah, Georgetown and Richmond, events honoring the president were as elaborate as any he had encountered in New England. Throughout the South, the people organized grand parades and impressive receptions.

Still, there was no denying that the context of the journey had changed. Political consensus that had marked the first months in office proved fleeting. Hard issues about the location of the capital, the funding of the national debt, and the collection of taxes strained old friendships and inflamed regional jealousies. Despite his frequent censure of faction, Washington found himself slowly drawn into contentious debates that turned cabinet members against one another and sparked angry exchanges in Congress.

Washington's planning for the final journey reflected this increasingly fractious political climate. To be sure, he still recorded in his diary impressions of local commerce, river navigation, and soil quality, but he also collected intelligence about the public's reaction to specific federal legislation. The Excise Bill Congress passed early in 1791 was especially worrisome. The act was part of Alexander Hamilton's ambitious economic reforms. It authorized raising the money desperately needed to pay down the national debt, and although the legislation enjoyed James Madison's support, it irritated a great number of Americans who lived in the southern backcountry and thought they had a God-given right to distill whiskey without having to pay the new excise tax.

For Washington, these contentious issues seemed to threaten the union. If large numbers of Americans refused to obey federal law, the nation could well return to the chaotic situation that it had experienced before the ratification of the Constitution. Tobias Lear, Washington's personal secretary, understood the political situation. He believed that the Southern Tour could remedy the growing discord. Lear expected that the journey would "have the same happy effect" on the union as had the New England trip. Like Washington, Lear knew that "something of a soothing nature is much wanted in the Southern States." The members of Congress representing the region had complained not only about "an additional duty on distilled Spirits," but also about Hamilton's plans to establish the Bank of the United States. They claimed that the federal government had assumed too much power. It was Washington's burden to persuade these critics that they had nothing to fear. "It is to be hoped," Lear explained, "that the presence of our chief Magistrate will, like the vivifying influence of a vernal sun, dispel the gloom of discontent and give a new spring to that spirit which can alone conduct us to tranquility and greatness."[4]

—II—

Soon after Washington completed his tour of Rhode Island, he and his family moved to Philadelphia, the temporary capital of the United States. The location of the permanent home of the federal government had been an extremely divisive issue. Not surprisingly, different groups in Congress advanced the interests of their own states, and it was not until July 1790 that Alexander Hamilton and Thomas Jefferson were finally able to hammer out an agreement that placed the capital along the Potomac River. The decision involved a complex compromise on funding the national debt, so at the end of the day, Jefferson assured his allies that the capital would be on the Virginia border while Hamilton advanced his ambitious economic plans.[5] The final resolution pleased Washington, of course, since the Federal City, as it was then called, would be near Mount Vernon. Even better, the legislation known as the Residence Bill authorized him to select the precise site for the capital. While commissioners worked out the details of the survey and purchase of the land, the president and Congress conducted their business in Philadelphia, a wealthy, cosmopolitan city that Washington thoroughly enjoyed.

These developments in no way hindered the president's determination to complete a tour of the South, an enterprise that the general called his "line of march." Old friends from the time of the Revolutionary War invited him to stay with them, but he firmly reminded them of his intention never to accept lodging in a private home. As he told Colonel William Washington, a cousin and distinguished veteran, the president would adopt the same rule in the southern states as he had in New England, "which was not to incommode any private family by taking up my quarters with them during my journey—I am persuaded you will readily see the necessity of this resolution, both as it respects myself and others—It leaves me unembarrassed by engagements, and by a uniform adherence to it, I shall avoid giving umbrage to any by declining all such invitations of residence." Both William Washington and

Edward Rutledge warned the president that his plan was impractical, since the region had in fact few "Public Houses" worth his attention.[6]

On this matter, the president did not give way. The friends did have a point, however, one that underscores the personal sacrifices Washington made on his tour. In his diary, a congressman from South Carolina recorded the indignities he faced in taverns on the road from Philadelphia to Charleston. Every night ferocious "bugs" attacked him, and in one primitive establishment, he wrote, "I was kept awake a great part of the night by bugs and fleas, and the united groaning and grunting of the hogs under the window."[7]

Washington scheduled his departure from Philadelphia in anticipation of a congressional recess. He could not be away from the capital while the legislature was still in session. But another factor figured centrally in his plans. He knew that the summer heat and humidity of the Deep South would make travel insufferable. As he informed William Washington, he wanted at all costs to avoid "the warm and sickly months."[8] That decision, however, raised other problems. If he left the capital in late March and reached Charleston and Savannah in mid-May, he would be forced at the start to travel particularly unpleasant muddy roads in Maryland and Virginia. He explained to his friend David Humphreys on March 16, "I am about to set out tomorrow or next day on a tour through the southern States. I am under the necessity of commencing my journey with very bad roads in order that I may take such advantage of the season as to be leaving the southern extremity before travelling shall be rendered disagreeable and perhaps dangerous by the heat."[9] He devoted extraordinary attention to the details of travel. Before he left Philadelphia, Washington told colleagues where he would be on any particular day. His projections depended in large part, of course, on good luck. A serious accident or major storm could ruin the best-laid plans.[10]

Unlike the tour of the Eastern States, where the distances between cities were not great, the Southern Tour presented almost insurmountable difficulties with communication. For several months, the president would be several hundred miles away from the nation's capital, and in the event of an emergency—an attack on an American naval vessel by Great Britain, for example—it would be imperative to contact Washington. He fully appreciated the problem. In a letter addressed to three cabinet members—Alexander Hamilton, Thomas Jefferson, and Henry Knox—he reiterated his precise schedule. He intended to be in Richmond on April 11, New Bern on April 20, Charleston on May 2, and so on. Washington admitted that the "route of my return is at present uncertain," but he did not believe that the possibility of being extremely hard to reach in the event of a crisis should be a major obstacle to the continuance of government.

The three cabinet members in Philadelphia had the responsibility to decide just how serious the threat to the United States might be. "I have to express my wish," the president wrote, "if any serious and important cases should arise during my absence, (of which the probability is but too strong) that the Secretaries for the Departments of State, Treasury, and War may hold consultations thereon, to determine whether they are of such a nature as to require my personal attendance at the seat of government." If they concluded that they really needed the president, he promised to "return immediately from any place at which the information may reach me." Washington must have known that this advice was grossly inadequate. If a crisis had occurred while he was in Augusta or Camden, for example, he would not have been able to reach the nation's capital for a very long time.

There was another possibility: the cabinet members might conclude that they could deal with an emergency without consulting the president. This was dangerous constitutional ground. Still, Washington trusted his colleagues, and he advised them that if they should "determine that measures, relative to the case, may be legally and properly pursued without the immediate agency of the President, I will approve and ratify the measures." Even considering that the business of government during a congressional recess was not too demanding, Washington's plan put a lot of pressure on his advisers. What if they made a mistake? Or advanced a policy affecting foreign relations that later embarrassed the president? He had given the trio carte blanche to make administrative decisions without consultation with the executive officer elected by the people. Almost as an afterthought, Washington remembered John Adams, the vice president. "Presuming that the Vice-President will have left the seat of government for Boston," Washington noted, "I have not requested his opinion to be taken on the supposed emergency."[11] Of course, if Adams happened to remain in Philadelphia—an unlikely event—Washington advised the three cabinet appointees to include the vice president in the discussions. There was no sense in these instructions that Adams outranked the others in the constitutional structure.

Both Jefferson and Lear hoped that the mail would keep the president adequately informed of what was happening in Philadelphia. The system worked reasonably well during the early stages of Washington's journey. As we shall see, he received some distressing news from the capital while he was in Richmond. But as he journeyed deeper into the Carolinas, communication became increasingly tenuous. Jefferson sent a number of important letters to Washington, but because of a last-minute change in travel plans, the correspondence never reached him.[12] The president did not realize the extent of the problem until he returned, and found waiting for him in Fredericksburg a bundle of official mail. More to the point, mail addressed to the president—possibly containing confidential political intelligence—could not be secured from inquisitive eyes. As Washington observed, "The letters, which will have to pass through *many* hands, may find *some* who are not deficient in curiosity."[13]

Washington's striking new coach also distinguished this trip from the earlier journey to New England. When he traveled to Boston, he employed a vehicle that he had used for a number of years. It had provided good service, but the president now wanted a more stylish coach. This is not surprising. Although he was a modest person, he loved fine objects, many of them imported from Great Britain and sold at prices that only the wealthiest planters could afford. He filled Mount Vernon with finely crafted items that he had seen described in the kind of upscale magazines that engrossed the members of the gentry. Before the Revolution, when an English merchant foolishly tried to unload goods on Washington that were not of the best quality or reflective of current cosmopolitan fashion, the future president complained, "You may believe me when I tell you that instead of getting things good and fashionable in their several kinds, we often have Articles sent Us that could only have been used by our Forefathers in the days of yore." [14] When he learned that the leading coach maker in Philadelphia had just imported two vehicles of the latest style, Washington could hardly contain his excitement. He immediately purchased one. The other coach came into the possession of Samuel Powel, then mayor of Philadelphia. [15]

Washington instructed the Clark brothers, the nation's leading coach makers, to refurbish the imported coach thoroughly. As with so many other aspects in his life, the president oversaw every detail. The vehicle, sometimes described in contemporary documents as a "chariot" or "a new lightweight traveling coach," served as a key prop in the new political theater. However much Americans of the period yammered about republican simplicity, opulent displays of wealth impressed ordinary people and ambitious local leaders. [16] In such matters, little has changed over the last two and a half centuries. Certainly Washington understood that his special coach would help focus popular attention on him and, more important, on his appeal for a strong federal government. The vehicle was large. Pulled by four special reddish-brown horses with black manes and driven by a coachman sitting high above the road in a box, it projected for a southern audience power and taste. Washington had it equipped with venetian blinds and black leather curtains. He also demanded that the Clarks paint it a cream color, and most unexpectedly, the president ordered the craftsmen to reproduce on four external panels Giovanni Battista Cipriani's *Four Seasons*.

Washington's artistic demands strike a discordant note for two reasons. First, Cipriani, an Italian painter who spent most of his professional career working in London, filled his canvases with amorous cupids and nymphs, soft, almost sensuous scenes that seem hugely out of character for Washington. Perhaps the president wanted Americans to appreciate how much he knew about celebrated European artists. But there was a second problem with his choice. Cipriani had already provided elaborate ornamentation for one of the most famous coaches in the eighteenth-century world, the so-called golden state coach, which transported the royal family on important occasions. No one in Philadelphia made the connection between Washington's coach and George III's—at least, not in the newspapers—but although Americans had a weakness for extravagance, the decorations on the coach seemed oddly aristocratic. The final element in the preparation was the display of the Washington family crest, another reminder of wealth and status. Washington outfitted the slaves in "bright livery of red and white."[17]

Contemporaries praised the new coach without reservation. One newspaper described it as "a superior specimen of mechanical perfection." And Lear insisted that it was "a most beautiful & elegant Chariot, said to be the handsomest altogether that had been made in this Country."[18] The one dissenter was Thomas Jefferson. Although he voiced no complaint about the provocative Cipriani panels, he felt compelled to warn Washington that the new coach was not properly designed to traverse the rough roads of the southern states. The problem was height. Jefferson predicted that the vehicle would tip over as soon as it encountered a large rock. Whether Washington put much stock in Jefferson's opinions on such practical matters is not known, but the caution played on his mind. Soon after he left Philadelphia, Washington informed Jefferson, "I am much indebted to your kind concern for my safety in traveling—no accident has yet happened either from the high hanging carriage, or the mode of driving." [19] After all, during the first leg of the trip, the Great White Coach had successfully navigated "roads exceedingly deep, heavy & cut in places by the Carriages which used them." [20]

Washington may have underestimated the dangers of travel through the South. The first of two near-fatal accidents had nothing to do with the design of the Great White Coach. Rather, the cause was gross incompetence, a factor that more careful planning might have avoided. Washington decided to cross the Chesapeake Bay on March 24 so that he could attend a large reception in his honor at Annapolis. The traveling party engaged several vessels to transport the coach and baggage wagon. He ordered his slave Paris to wait with several horses for a later crossing, and at three o'clock in the afternoon, Washington boarded the larger of two "Ferry Boats."

The president sensed almost immediately that the crew did not know what it was doing. As night fell, a great storm swept over the bay. Before it subsided, the two boats, which had made slow progress, became becalmed, neither able to return to Rock Hall nor reach the safety of Annapolis. About eight o'clock the wind suddenly picked up. Washington called it a "gale." By this time, the boats were at the mouth of the Severn River, a short distance from their destination. Because of "the ignorance of the People on board, with respect to the navigation" of the Severn, the president's vessel ran aground near Queensbury Point. With great effort, the crew managed to free the ferry. Disaster still loomed. As Washington explained in his diary, the sailors "having no knowledge of the Channel and the night being immensely dark with heavy and variable squalls of wind—constant lightening & tremendous thunder—we soon grounded again on what is called Horne's Point [Horn Point] where, finding all efforts in vain, and not knowing where we were we remained, not knowing what might happen, 'till morning." [21]

Washington did not report whether he felt himself to be in mortal danger. The threat of death never perturbed him. However, spending the night on a boat in uncomfortable quarters bothered him greatly. The next morning he complained about "having lain all night in my Great Coat & Boots in a birth [berth] not long enough for me by the head, & much cramped." Daylight found the boat, which was still unable to free itself, about a mile from Annapolis. Spectators appreciated the potential tragedy that was unfolding, but there was nothing they could do. Finally, "a sailing boat" came to the rescue, and the president landed in Annapolis with his baggage in remarkably good condition. He ordered another boat to return to Horn Point "to take off two of my Horses & Chariot, which I had left aboard." However, since Fagan did not know of Washington's plan, he tried to transfer the Great Coach onto a much smaller "Sailing Boat." During the off-loading, the boat capsized, nearly drowning Washington's traveling party. It was not until midday that the president learned that the coach and "all my other horses" were safe. The governor of Maryland had apparently tried to reach the president during the storm but was forced to turn back "when it grew dark and squally." [22]

No one made much of a fuss over the situation, which, of course, would have changed American history. A newspaper provided a brief account of the near disaster on the Severn River. In the inflated rhetoric of the time, it assured readers, "The guardian angel of America was still watchful; and we are happy in assuring our countrymen that the health of their dearest friend has not been at all affected by an accident far more distressing to those who were apprized, or rather apprehensive, of his situation, than to himself." [23] The Annapolis reception went ahead as planned. Although the guests who came to honor the president may have wondered why the most important person in the United States had nearly died the day before on a boat manned by an inexperienced crew, they seem to have acted as if nothing out of the ordinary had happened.

On March 27, Washington sent Martha a fuller, more personal account of his long night on the bay, and when Lear expressed curiosity about the event, the president refused to repeat what he had already told his wife. "For the history of our travels & adventures *so far*," he instructed, "I refer you to a letter I wrote to Mrs. Washington from Annapolis yesterday." [24] That letter has not survived, probably because Martha destroyed all of her personal correspondence with her husband after he died.

Washington then hurried off to the proposed site of the new Federal City. The negotiations with local landholders were both tedious and acrimonious, and it required the president's full diplomatic skills to advance the project. The talks concluded well, and on the evening of March 30, Washington arrived at Mount Vernon, where he rested for a week before setting off for the Carolinas and Georgia. On April 7 he announced in his diary, "Recommenced my journey with Horses apparently well refreshed and in good spirits." [25] He was eager to renew the journey.

— III —

Had Washington been superstitious, he might have canceled the trip soon after leaving Mount Vernon. To reach Richmond, his first major stop, he had to cross the Occoquan River at Colchester. Before the Occoquan silted up sometime during the middle of the eighteenth century, Colchester had been a modestly prosperous tobacco port, but over the years, the business activity moved to Alexandria. A ferry still operated, however, and on the morning of April 12, Fagan drove the Great Coach onto the boat.

Perhaps because the trip across the river was short, no one bothered to unhitch the four horses, a serious mistake. Moreover, the person charged with calming the horses did not do his job. The unnamed bungler may have diverted his attention to the president or to the many spectators watching from small boats. In any case, the lead horse bolted when the ferry was fifty yards from the farther shore. Washington called it "swimming water," meaning that the water was not too deep.

General consternation erupted. As one would expect, Washington never lost his composure, but it was a close thing. He noted in the diary that the lead horse "with much difficulty . . . escaped drowning before he could be disengaged." One after another, the other three horses followed the "struggling" animal into the water. Before anyone could react, "they all got over board harnessed & fastened as they were and with the utmost difficulty they were saved." The president declared it a miracle that "the Carriage escaped been [being] dragged after them." He praised the many spectators who rushed to help.[26] Although Washington may not have been in danger of drowning, he knew that a major accident would have ended the southern journey. As had been the case after the perilous crossing of the Chesapeake Bay, no one speculated about the implications for the entire nation had Washington ended his days in the Occoquan River.

The president set out the next morning at 6:00 a.m. The road took him through Fredericksburg, where he spent time visiting his sister Elizabeth. He was still traveling in familiar territory. Old friends poured into the streets to welcome the local planter who had become a national celebrity. Fredericksburg's mayor wished Washington well on his trip. He chose his words wisely, assuring the president, "The long and fatiguing journey you have undertaken will further manifest your unremitted attachment to that country, whose obligations to you can be better felt than described, and we trust will not only influence the present generation to admire public and private virtues, from your example, but teach your successors how to watch over the welfare of this extensive union."[27]

The mayor was shrewd to draw attention to the prospect of an extensive union. The challenge of incorporating the huge territory beyond the Appalachian Mountains into the United States weighed heavily on Washington's mind. When he reached Richmond, he enjoyed the cannon salute and the massive illumination of the city, but his thoughts were on a canal then under construction.

For more than two decades Washington had viewed water transportation between the original states and the western territory as vital to the nation's future. He put forward a sophisticated argument: if rivers such as the James and the Potomac could be opened to commerce from the Ohio Valley—in effect, turning rivers into canals—they would link frontier farmers with eastern merchants and a huge Atlantic marketplace. The unobstructed flow of goods would work to increase everyone's prosperity. Washington himself stood to gain. He owned thousands of acres beyond the mountains, and reliable canals promised to increase the value of his land. Moreover, if the James or the Potomac became the major conduits for domestic trade, Virginia would flourish, always a pleasing prospect for Washington.

Washington's logic contained another key step: he believed that political identity depended in large part on the federal government's ability to advance the economic interests of its citizens. If the settlers who were then rushing to Kentucky and Ohio concluded that they could do better by trading their produce with the Spanish in New Orleans, they would probably do so. It made no matter that the Spanish were Catholic or that an absolute monarch ruled the empire. Emotional and family ties to the original thirteen states could not in themselves guarantee allegiance.

Political loyalty always came down to economic interests. The expansive vision of union that Washington championed depended ultimately on developing the bonds of commerce. He stated the argument forcefully in a 1785 letter addressed to James Warren, a prominent political figure in Massachusetts. The goal of the correspondence was to persuade Warren of the need for a strong central government. Washington stressed the role that canals would play in this transformation. "The great Works of improving and extending the inland navigations of the two large Rivers, Potomack & James, which interlock with the Western Waters, are already begun, and I have little doubt of their success," he stated with a sense of confidence that was surely premature. "The consequences to the Union, in my judgment, are immense," Washington continued, "& more so in a political, than in a Commercial point; for unless we can connect the New States, which are rising to our view in the Regions back of us, with those on the Atlantic by interest," the nation will fragment into separate competitive regions. Indeed, unless the United States could find a means to "make it easier & cheaper" for the western farmers "to bring the product of their labour to our Markets," they would turn to the Spanish, or even the British in Canada. If they did this, "they will be quite a distinct People, and ultimately may be very troublesome neighbours to us."[28] Warren, who had supported the American cause during the Revolution, must have seen the implicit connection between Great Britain before the war and the United States under the Confederation. Parliament had restricted colonial trade, only to discover that its American policy sparked thoughts of independence. Washington was suggesting that if the new government treated the western settlements like colonies, they too might break away.

It was from this perspective that Washington studied the rivers of Virginia and Maryland. He struggled to locate their headwaters and speculated about what it would take to connect them to the Ohio Valley. And he gave close attention to the fall line on the Potomac and the James—the point in a river's course where harder upland formations meet softer sedimentary rocks, creating a rapid or a fall. At such points, the rushing current and the exposed boulders create an impassable barrier for boats carrying trade goods. On the James, the fall line occurs near Richmond. The future of the union, Washington insisted, depended on finding a way to tame the rocks.

During the 1780s, Washington focused most of his attention on the Potomac River. His interest in the project had originated at a time before the Revolution when as a young man, he had explored the lands to the west of the mountains. It came as no surprise that as soon as he accepted the presidency, he put forward ambitious plans for water transportation. In a burst of enthusiasm, he communicated to Jefferson in 1789 his "ideas of the practicability, importance, & extent of that navigation."

The intensity of Washington's commitment may have surprised Jefferson, who also shared the president's expansive vision of western settlement. According to Washington, even at this late date, it was hard to find reliable surveys "of the Country between the sources of the Potowmac and the navigable waters, that fall into the Ohio." Still, although he had received reports of "the many falls, rapid water and rugged banks," he remained confident that the project was feasible. Since "there is an abundance of water," he wrote, "I should conceive that with the aid of Canals & Locks, it might be accomplished."

Like many other overly eager entrepreneurs, Washington filtered the intelligence he obtained through the lens of inflated hopes. He confided to Jefferson that his preliminary research demonstrated persuasively that "the distance between the Eastern & Western Waters is shorter, and that the means of communication are easier, than I had hitherto represented or imagined."[29] The skeptics—and there were many—simply did not know what they were talking about when they pointed out how far the headwaters of the Potomac and James were from the Ohio River. Success seemed to be only a matter of will.

Washington knew that there were three specific problems to surmount before the canals could become operational: the projects required a huge infusion of capital, cooperation between the states that claimed the rivers, and access to the latest technology required for the construction of locks. Washington threw himself into the challenge. He lobbied vigorously to persuade the legislatures of Maryland and Virginia to support the Potomac plan. The results of these efforts were mixed. Taxpayers in neither state wanted to pour massive funds into the canal. Their grumbling demonstrated to Washington once again the need for a strong central government that could assume the lead in such ventures.

To raise capital, Washington helped organize the Potomac Company and later the James River Company for which he served as president between 1785 and 1795. In his capacity as businessman, he sold shares to friends and neighbors. For many of them, his passionate sales pitch must have been nearly irresistible. Despite his efforts, however, the companies were always underfunded.[30] Even more intractable was the issue of technology. British engineers understood the complex construction of locks, but few showed interest in moving to the United States and working for companies that could barely meet a payroll. Various Americans accepted positions as engineers. They generally could claim no experience in canal building, and fewer still possessed the managerial talents required to keep large numbers of unskilled workers on the job.[31]

Despite Washington's optimistic reports to potential shareholders, the progress on the Potomac was disappointing. Tons of dynamite hardly made much difference in opening the river to commerce. And then, quite unexpectedly, Washington stumbled on what he believed was the answer to all the problems. He learned of a brilliant, somewhat cranky inventor living in what is now West Virginia who had designed a boat that propelled itself forward without the aid of a motor. James Rumsey—the kind of appealing figure we have encountered repeatedly during Washington's journeys—recognized that a vessel that could sail upstream around the falls on special sluiceways would remove the need for expensive and complex locks.

Washington was so excited by the news that in 1784 he traveled many miles from Mount Vernon to Bath, Virginia, just to meet Rumsey, the man who he hoped possessed the technology to secure the union. Although locals apparently called the inventor "Crazy Rumsey," he and Washington had a productive conversation. "Remained at Bath all day," Washington noted in his diary, and viewed "the Model of a Boat constructed by the ingenious Mr. Rumsey, for ascending rapid currents by mechanism. . . . The Model, and its operation upon the water . . . not only convinced me of what I before thought next to, if not quite impracticable, but that it might be the greatest possible utility in inland Navigation." What made the invention all the more attractive was its simplicity. Washington concluded that any "common boat builder or carpenter" could easily keep the vessel in good working order. It required no more expertise than did a "plow, or any common implement of husbandry on a farm."[32]

Washington was so sure that he had solved the challenge of the rapids and the rocks that he provided Rumsey with a glowing testimonial. Rumsey could not have been more pleased. Although he was extremely clever, he fretted that other wealthier and better-connected inventors would receive credit for his own ideas. In his introduction to his *Short Treatise on the Application of Steam* (1788), Rumsey complained, "A candid public will then consider my situation, thrown by hard fate beyond the mountains, and deprived of every advantage which that grand mover, money, produces."[33] Washington's generous words should have put Rumsey's mind at ease. He announced in a certificate released to the public: "I have seen the model of Mr. Rumsey's Boat constructed to work against a stream; have examined the power upon which it acts; have been an eye witness to an actual experiment in running water of some rapidity; & do give it as my opinion (altho' I had little faith before) that he has discovered the art of propelling Boats, by mechanism & small manual assistance, against rapid currents."[34]

Washington's effusive support for Rumsey reminds us how open he was to new ideas, especially if they served to strengthen the union. He immediately saw the connection between Rumsey's boat and the political future of the settlements beyond the mountains. But his eagerness to find solutions to the problem of river navigation eroded his critical faculties. Rumsey's so-called walking boat was in fact a kind of Rube Goldberg contraption that worked more or less well under perfect conditions. It looked like a huge water spider. A paddlewheel activated a group of long poles that in relatively shallow water gripped the river bottom and literally walked the boat forward. Later tests revealed that Rumsey's boat could not navigate the strong Potomac current, and Rumsey, who was frustrated by having to oversee the day-to-day management of the company, gave up entirely on the pole boat.[35]

Even without Rumsey, Washington pushed ahead. Although he

always thought the Potomac River would provide the best water route to the West, he encouraged efforts to develop commercial transportation on the James River. As with the Potomac, the problem was how to conquer the falls, a formidable obstruction located near Richmond. In 1785 a group of prominent Virginians formed the James River Company, but they made little progress in solving the engineering issues associated with building locks. In 1789 the enterprise was reorganized as the James River and Kanawha Canal Company. Washington served as president, a largely honorary position. The directors included prominent figures such as John Marshall and Edmund Randolph. The prospect of a good financial return may have blinded them to the immensity of the task.

The Kanawha River was in fact a tributary of the Ohio River, several hundred miles from Richmond. Establishing a commercially viable link between it and the James presented a huge challenge. During the early stages of construction, the directors concentrated their resources on Richmond. They relied on slave labor. The company investors owned some of these workers, but many others were rented from local planters eager to find some way other than growing tobacco to use their bondsmen. For the African Americans, it was probably a very bad deal. Breaking rock was dangerous as well as onerous.[36] And it is not surprising that after two years, the canal—which paralleled the James River—had only reached the little community of Westham, a distance of about seven miles.

Several accounts of the canal as it appeared in 1791 have survived. Congressman William Loughton Smith, returning from the nation's capital to his home in South Carolina, viewed the construction site only a short time before Washington arrived. He noted that the James River at Richmond was "full of rocks and shoals." To avoid these obstructions, the workers concentrated on "cutting a canal along the river." The company had assembled a large labor force. Smith reported seeing "ninety Negroes . . . constantly employed, with four overseers and a head manager." He had never encountered a scene as dramatic as this.

"I rode as far as the spot to which the canal ends," he noted in his diary. The description of the sight was almost Dante-esque, a vision of massive human activity punctuated by dynamite explosions. "The roaring of the water over the rocks and the noise of the workmen working below," Smith observed, "with the explosions made in blowing the rocks up, render the scene curious and pleasing." He predicted that Richmond would become a flourishing commercial center "when the navigation with the country is entirely open." He estimated the completion only a year or two away.[37] The company missed the goal by more than half a century.

For Washington the Richmond visit allowed him a chance not only to inspect the canal's progress, but also to remind the nation of the importance of inland transportation for the union. Dr. James Currie, who lived in Virginia, provided an account of the president's Richmond tour for his friend Thomas Jefferson. The company directors engaged a boat for the occasion, he explained, and from the river, Washington was able to inspect the new locks. The organizers, who clearly understood how to stage an event, dressed the men who rowed the president up the James in impressive "red Coaties." Special speed trials were arranged. Currie assured Jefferson that the time the boats "took in passing the 2 locks was 7 minutes and 4 seconds by a stop watch."[38] Although in his diary entry for April 12, Washington ignored the colorful costumes, he did carefully tabulate the depth of the water and the width of the locks, and while the quality of the work seemed satisfactory, he wondered why the locks were so expensive. "They cost, according to the Manager's . . . account about £3000, but I could see nothing in them to require such a sum to erect them."[39]

We have no way to know whether Washington really thought the canal would be completed in only three more years. He probably sensed that the task would take much more time and a lot more money, which in fact it did. But the point of the Richmond visit was not to inventory difficulties and excuses. His public and widely reported appearance on the river was much like his earlier tours of the textile mills in New England: he used these theatrical moments to communicate his vision for the country. He encouraged Americans to think expansively. The country's unity depended on a harmony of economic interests.

— IV —

While well advanced on his tour of the South, Washington encountered another problem quite unexpectedly, which in the fullness of time would destroy the union he cherished. The issue was slavery. The president was so much a part of a culture that accepted unfree labor that he did not comprehend the immensity of the danger. But the warning signs were there. After all, his own slaves suddenly became an embarrassing problem for Washington while he was on the road from Richmond to Wilmington, North Carolina. The alarm bells first sounded when Paris challenged the authority of a white man.

During the entire journey—to New England as well as the South— Washington's slaves had remained virtually invisible, appearing only as coachmen wearing the colorful livery of the president. On this occasion, however, a young slave emerged from the background with a genuine personality. Perhaps because Paris was not feeling well—a doctor's bill documents the special care he received from a physician in Wilmington— he began quarreling with John Fagan, the irritable driver who was not about to take backtalk from a slave.[40]

Although Washington may or may not have been an understanding master by the standards of the period, he certainly refused to side with a slave who defied a white man's authority. No sooner had the president completed the Southern Tour than he informed Lear, "Paris has become so lazy, self willed & impudent, that John [Fagan] (the Coachman) had no sort of government of him; on the contrary, John says, it was a maxim with Paris to do nothing he was ordered, and every thing he was forbid."[41] Because Paris did not know his place, Washington demoted him from his position as a coachman, and when the traveling party returned to the capital, Paris remained at Mount Vernon. The president ordered another slave to "take the Waggon box in place of Paris."[42]

Washington's impatience with Paris may have owed something to Hercules, a slave who had stayed in Philadelphia cooking for the president's family during Washington's long absence in the South. No one accused Hercules of sloth or at that time of disrespect. Because of events not of his own making, however, the talented slave forced Washington to confront a subject he would rather have avoided. However he may have regarded his own slaves, he did not want slavery—as an institution that supported much of the new nation's economy—to become a topic for national debate. It was an explosive issue.

However much the nation's political leaders wished the problem would just go away, Americans discovered that slavery could not easily be ignored. It touched their lives almost every day and was woven into the fabric of the society. One could proclaim that the Revolution had defended the rights and liberty of all men, but the truth of the matter was that people such as Paris and Hercules did not enjoy the freedom celebrated by the patriotic white citizens of the republic.[43] Some scholars have argued that we should not judge eighteenth-century slaveholders such as Washington and Jefferson from the perspective of a modern culture that champions civil rights. We are told that we live in a different world, that we have different standards.

Such assertions are misleading. The slaveholders of the early republic knew that slavery was wrong, but they lacked the moral courage to reform a labor system that profited a small group in society at the expense of so many black workers who fully understood the benefits of freedom. As long as the country's leaders conspired to ignore slavery, they could pretend that it did not threaten the union. But it did. On the road to Wilmington, Washington confronted the fundamental tensions between race and freedom. Indeed, Hercules forced the president, who regarded securing the federal union as his highest goal, to compromise his own integrity to preserve slavery.

The crisis began when a letter from Lear reached Washington while he was still in Richmond. (This was one time when the mail system actually worked. The president may have later wished that it had not functioned so well.) Lear informed the president that the attorney general of the United States, Edmund Randolph, had just had a conversation with Martha. He informed her that three of his own slaves—Randolph too came from Virginia—had raised an extremely troublesome issue. They brought to his attention a Pennsylvania law allowing slaves transported into the state to sue for their freedom after only six months' residence. If a slave left Pennsylvania for whatever reason during this period, the clock restarted. Randolph warned that the slaves who had come up to Philadelphia from Mount Vernon "might follow the example." The news deeply disturbed Martha, who had not the slightest interest in freeing her slaves.[44]

While Washington was inspecting the locks on the James River, his trusted secretary, Tobias Lear, was busy in the nation's capital gathering additional information about the implications of the Pennsylvania law. Like any other personal assistant to the president, Lear was eager to head off trouble before it became a public issue. He went directly to the attorney general. Together they reviewed the precise wording of the statute. Randolph concluded that the intentions of the state legislature were distressingly clear, at least for the slaveholders who had come to Philadelphia to do the nation's business. The lawmakers declared, "If a Slave is brought into the State and continues therein for the space of six months, he may claim his freedom, let the cause of his being brought [to Pennsylvania] be what it may." There was no wiggle room, even for members of Congress.

When Lear reported his conversation to the president, somewhere in North Carolina when he received the letter, the secretary assured

Washington that the local abolitionist society supported by the Quakers had announced that it would not attempt to inform slaves "which belong to the Officers of the General Government or members of Congress" about the liberating potential of the Pennsylvania legislation. Lear did not put too much stock in that pledge. After all, there were many other people in Philadelphia who hated slavery. These agitators, Lear explained, were eager to counsel slaves about obtaining freedom. They were a real danger, since they were prepared to "use all means to entice them [the slaves] from their masters."

After a thorough review of the situation, the attorney general concluded that he could do nothing to protect the nine slaves that Washington had brought to the capital from Mount Vernon. But he also noted that the situation might not be as dire as it had initially seemed. Washington might get around the law by taking his slaves out of Pennsylvania before the end of six months. According to the person charged with enforcing the nation's laws, if "before the expiration of six months, they [the slaves] could, *upon any pretense whatever*, be carried or sent out of the State, but for a single day, a new era would commence on their return, from whence the six months must be dated for it requires an *entire* six months for them to claim that right."

After having consulted Martha, Lear set in motion an elaborate plan of deception. He immediately returned one unnamed slave to Mount Vernon. Martha clearly supported the idea of removing other slaves from Philadelphia, if only for a single day, and she agreed to transport two of them to New Jersey, a few miles away from Washington's home in the capital. For Hercules, however, the challenge was more complex. Lear decided to put forward a cover story to persuade this extremely valuable slave—he was the chief cook for the president's household— that his services were now required at Mount Vernon.

According to the plan, Lear would tell Hercules that since Washington would soon return from his Southern Tour, it would be desirable for him to be in Virginia to receive his master. And the secretary added to sweeten the fictive message that when Hercules was back at Mount Vernon, "he will have it in his power to see his friends." Behind the nefarious scheme lay a mean-spirited test: if Hercules balked—if he insisted that he preferred serving the Washington family in Philadelphia—"it will be a pretty strong proof of his intention to take advantage of the law at the expiration of six months." [45]

Lear need not have worried about disappointing Washington. After all, he acted on direct orders from the president. We may wish that Washington had not personally authorized the plan to fool the slaves. Disingenuousness seems out of character, but we must remember that he was a product of a culture that either applauded such behavior or turned its back on the people who were defined as property. In any event, Lear followed the recommendations for a scheme of deception put forward in Washington's April 12 letter. It makes for painful reading. The letter rehashed all the ambiguities inherent in a system that relied on slave labor. On the one hand, Washington thought that his own slaves were basically loyal, a common conceit among masters. On the other hand, the slaves could not be completely trusted. The best of them were always susceptible to provocateurs who failed to understand that attacks on slavery threatened the stability of the entire union.

Almost every passage of the letter betrayed Washington's deep sense of fear and insecurity. First, he recognized that even if the Pennsylvania law had exempted his slaves from the six-month rule, it made no difference. The city contained too many troublemakers who would try their best to persuade the slaves that they were entitled to freedom. He doubted that his slaves would listen to such arguments, but just in case he had misjudged their commitment to him and his wife, he urged Martha to send all but the most essential workers back to Mount Vernon as soon as possible. All the talk of freedom threatened his entire estate. Martha owned most of the Washington slaves—they were called dower slaves—and if any of these men or women ran off, the president would be held personally responsible for the monetary loss. He had to consider the financial risk. Would people born into bondage—whose children had little hope of freedom—find liberation desirable? Had he not treated them well? Offered them food and clothes? One could never be sure. "The idea of freedom," he observed, "might be too great a temptation for them to resist. At any rate it might, if they conceived they had a right to it, make them insolent in a State of Slavery." These gnawing uncertainties justified deception. Back to Virginia they would go.

Even with the plan in place, Washington remained uneasy. He did not want the public, even his colleagues in the government, to know that he had authorized a design based on untruth and manipulation. "I wish to have it accomplished," he told Lear, "under the pretext that may deceive both them and the Public." He knew he could count on his wife. The three of them would conspire to thwart the conspirators. Secrecy was essential. The whole issue had to be removed from the stage of public opinion. "I request that these Sentiments and this advice may be known to none but *yourself & Mrs. Washington.*"[46] One might inquire at this point why Washington was so sensitive about public opinion. Did he want to preserve a reputation for truthfulness so carefully crafted over a lifetime? Or did he feel that gulling slaves out of their freedom might not sit well with many ordinary Americans, the kinds of people who turned out on the streets to welcome him and march in celebratory parades?

The trio of conspirators quickly discovered that their plan had no chance. Hercules exposed the plot. What little we know about him suggests that he was a person of immense charm. He was also a distinguished chef, able at a moment's notice to prepare an impressive meal for Washington's guests. Martha's grandchild, who as a boy called Hercules "Uncle Harkness," described the "celebrated *artiste*" of the kitchen as "a dark-brown man, little, if any, above the usual size, yet possessed of such great muscular power as to entitle him to be compared with his namesake of fabulous history." No one dared cross Hercules when he was working in the kitchen. Like his master, he was a stickler for detail. He planned every aspect of the huge presidential dinners in advance. George Washington Parke Custis, Hercules's young admirer, claimed that the slave's "underlings flew in all directions to execute his orders, while he, the great master-spirit, seemed to possess the power of ubiquity, and to be everywhere at the same time." Perhaps because he was so valuable, the president allowed Hercules special privileges that may have softened the fact that the man remained a slave. For example, he received about two hundred dollars a year from selling "the slops [waste food] of the kitchen."

Custis observed that while Hercules was "homely in person," he liked to outfit himself in the very latest fashions. Indeed, by the standards of the time, Hercules was something of a fop. In other words, as the popular song went, he was a person who stuck a feather in his hat and called himself macaroni—a person of cosmopolitan tastes. About his consumer desires, a wonderful record survives. Apparently, Hercules liked linen of "exceptional whiteness and quality, then black silk shirts, ditto waistcoat, ditto stockings, shoes highly polished, with large buckles covering a considerable part of the foot, blue coat with velvet collar, and bright metal buttons, a long watch-chain dangling from his fob, a cocked-hat, and gold-headed cane." These items, much the same things Washington himself would have desired, "completed the grand costume." During his off hours, Hercules loved to strut about on the streets of Philadelphia. Strangers whom he encountered did not know what to make of a black man decked out like a member of the city's elite. Again, as Custis remembered from a distance of sixty years, "Many were not a little surprised on beholding so extraordinary a personage, while others who knew him would make a formal and respectful bow, that they might receive in return the salute of one of the most polished gentlemen and veriest dandy" of the town.[47]

In fact, Hercules enjoyed such a good life in Philadelphia that it was easy for many white people to forget that he was a slave. Washington's plan to avoid the law, however, brought home the chef's dependence on a master. On May 22, Lear informed the president that he had had a conversation with Hercules. The secretary followed the planned script. "Hercules has been told," Lear explained, "that it is necessary for him to be at Mount Vernon on your return there, as his presence at that time will be indispensable there & he can be very well spared here." He therefore ordered Hercules to be in Virginia as soon as possible. The conspirators would have preferred to send him by ship, but no vessels were then leaving Philadelphia for the Potomac River. The slave would have to take a stagecoach.

Everything was going according to plan. Except that Hercules would have none of it. A person who had built up such a large network of friends—whites and blacks—was bound to get wind of the conspiracy. Lear was naive to think otherwise. Perhaps other household slaves overheard discussions of the Pennsylvania statute and considered among themselves how best to react. In any case, just before he was scheduled to leave Philadelphia, Hercules confronted Lear. As the secretary reported to Washington on June 5—the returning president had just crossed the boundary between North Carolina and Virginia— "somebody, I presume, insinuated to him [Hercules] that the motive for sending him home so long before you was expected there, was to prevent his taking advantage of a six months residence in this place." Why, the slave asked, would anyone doubt his integrity? Did the president think that slaves had no sense of honor? Hercules protested that it would never have occurred to him to take advantage of the possibility of gaining his freedom.

The slave's performance was so moving that Lear concluded that there was "no doubt of his sincerity." Even Martha begged forgiveness from Hercules, offering to let him remain in Philadelphia "till the expiration of six months and then go home." After Hercules calmed down, Martha and Lear reaffirmed their willingness to let him stay, and then, after Washington had completed the Southern Tour, they persuaded him to go back to Mount Vernon once again to cook for his master.[48] As the drama unfolded, the president, who at his own inauguration insisted, "no man should ever charge me *justly* with deception," discovered what could happen to the best-laid plans.[49]

Through the whole negotiation, Lear had played his part, but the situation in which Washington had placed him was a source of great embarrassment. Lear came from New Hampshire, a state that generally found slavery repellent.[50] While the president was still on the road, championing a strong federal union, Lear wrote a letter that attempted unsuccessfully to bridge the gap between conscience and duty. Like many subordinates over the centuries, he allowed his personal relationship with Washington to triumph over principle. The attempted manipulation of Hercules disgusted him. "You will permit me now, Sir, (and I am sure you will pardon me for doing it) to declare," he wrote, "that no consideration should induce me to take these steps to prolong the slavery of a human being had I not the fullest confidence that they will at some future period be liberated, and the strongest conviction that their situation with you is far preferable to what they would probably obtain in a state of freedom."[51] If Lear really thought that slavery under Washington was better than freedom in Philadelphia, he did not understand the world of Hercules and Paris.

Hercules may have had a plan of his own. At the end of Washington's presidency in 1796, Hercules refused to return to Mount Vernon. He disappeared into the back streets of Philadelphia. His master showed no sympathy. Blaming the unfaithful slave for running away—for claiming freedom—the president announced, "The running off of my cook has been a most inconvenient thing to this family, and what renders it more disagreeable, is, that I had resolved never to become the master of another slave by *purchase*, but this resolution I fear I must break."[52] Neither Martha nor George forgave Hercules. Long after Washington had retired, he still tried to lure his ungrateful slave back into service. Nothing worked. The years passed. In 1798, Washington asked an agent (a kind of private detective) to discover where "Hercules our Cook" might be hiding. If possible, the master of Mount Vernon hoped that Hercules might be captured and sent back to Mount Vernon. He warned his contact to remember, however, "if Hercules was to get the least hint of the design, he would elude all your vigilance."[53] Not until 1801, several years after Washington's death, did Martha finally give up hope of again seeing her favorite chef.[54]

When Hercules disappeared, several of his own family members remained in bondage at Mount Vernon. During the period of Washington's retirement, a group of French noblemen visited the plantation, and there they encountered a young girl who happened to be Hercules's daughter. A servant accompanying the French aristocrats—his name was Beaudoin—interviewed the child. A fragment of that exchange appeared in a diary kept by one of the other guests. "The general's [Washington's] cook ran away, being now in Philadelphia, and left a little daughter of six at Mount Vernon. Beaudoin ventured the opinion that the little girl must be deeply upset that she would never see her father again; she answered, *Oh! Sir, I am very glad, because he is free now.*"[55]

—V—

While Washington traveled farther south during the spring of 1791, enjoying the hospitality of people throughout the Carolinas and Georgia, a drama that would change the character of American politics was unfolding in Philadelphia. The curious confrontation in the capital raised the question of how political dissent fit into a republican government. Should one see political figures who challenged the president's policies as enemies—as threats to the union—or were they simply what the British called members of the loyal opposition?

What triggered the crisis was a celebrated confrontation between two European writers, Edmund Burke and Thomas Paine, over the meaning of the French Revolution. Their highly public debate unexpectedly inflamed political differences in the United States, setting old Revolutionaries at odds and encouraging the kind of partisan bickering that Washington believed could undermine the nation's unity. He had good reason to fear that powerful European states were looking to take advantage of the military weakness of the new republic. But whatever his concerns, the issues that divided Europe made their way to the United States. They spilled over into domestic debates, amplifying discord and creating deep, even conspiratorial suspicions about the intentions of men who had once worked together to secure the Revolution.

On July 14, 1789, a mob stormed the Bastille, the hated symbol of autocratic and corrupt rule. At first, commentators throughout the Atlantic community welcomed the event, and many predicted that the bold resistance of the French people would bring about significant reforms. Almost no one foresaw the massive violence known as the Terror. With the publication of *Reflections on the Revolution in France* on November 1, 1790, Burke sounded an alarm. In a long, passionately argued essay, he warned English readers not only of the possible excesses of the French Revolution, but also of the danger that ideas put forward to justify the assault on an aristocratic regime would spread to Great Britain. That it was Burke who launched such a strident critique surprised many admirers who associated him with his earlier defense of American rights. In passionate speeches before Parliament delivered before the Revolution, he had argued that if British rulers did not negotiate in good faith with the colonists, they would demand independence—which is, of course, exactly what they did. He later excoriated the corruption of British administrators in India. And so, it came as a shock to many Americans that Burke would furiously execrate the French people who were contending for their constitutional rights.[56]

Reflections is a discursive piece. It lacked the stylistic polish associated with Burke's earlier productions. Moreover, the author did not always get his facts correct, and critics suggested that he had allowed emotion to distort the analysis. Whatever personal animus energized his writing, the final product did in fact provide a coherent defense of monarchical society in France. Even before Robespierre turned the demand for ideological purity into an excuse for mass executions, Burke asserted that the revolutionary dream of reinventing the entire political system would come to no good. He argued that the French should look to England for inspiration. The celebrated British constitution, he insisted, reflected a valuable heritage that linked the living generation to the wisdom of those who had come before. Government was a compact between the living and the dead. The aristocracy and an established church were not institutions to be taken lightly. Burke insisted, "We look up with awe to kings; with affection to parliaments; with duty to magistrates; with reverence to priests; and with respect to nobility."[57] The French were foolishly trying to escape their own history. As Burke explained, "People will not look forward to posterity, who never look backward to their ancestors."[58]

Paine challenged Burke on almost every point. The man who had written *Common Sense* had left the United States in 1787, and as the self-proclaimed Revolutionary voice of the age, he took up residence in Paris, where he announced that he had encountered the same liberating spirit that had originally sparked the American Revolution.[59] His response to Burke—*The Rights of Man* (Part 1)—revisited many of these ideas. The book defended the French attempt to overthrow the ancien regime and corrected some of Burke's factual errors. But it did much more: Paine denied the legitimacy of monarchy and the aristocratic privileges that it fostered. In prose that ordinary readers could readily understand, he observed, "If I ask a man in America, if he wants a King? He retorts, and asks me if I take him for an idiot?"[60]

The notion that some men inherit the right to rule others made no sense to Paine. As he stated, "Men are born and always continue free, and equal in respect of their rights. Civil distinctions, therefore, can be founded only in public utility."[61] The French had a splendid opportunity. They could correct the errors of the past, rid themselves of oppressors who claimed superior status on the basis of birth, and return sovereignty where it properly belonged—to the people. Paine even questioned the maldistribution of wealth in society. The rich had no business crushing the poor. As he argued, "Government does not consist in contrast between prisons and palaces, between poverty and pomp, it is not instituted to rob the needy of his mite, and increase the wretchedness of the wretched."[62] Perhaps it is no wonder that Paine is still regarded in some circles in the United States as a threat to a comfortable social order.

Without seeking Washington's permission, Paine dedicated *The Rights of Man* to the president. Each copy—and the book sold very well—opened with the words: "I present you a small Treatise in defense of those Principles of Freedom which your exemplary Virtue hath so eminently contributed to establish." Although the act appeared presumptuous, it did not immediately create an embarrassment for the administration. After all, Paine stressed a direct connection between the American and French Revolutions. In Paris, he had experienced the intoxicating "ardour of Seventy six [1776]" once again. But Paine also had his eye on the marketplace. The book represented a welcome source of income, and Washington's name was guaranteed to help sales. In fact, when Paine finally got around to telling Washington that he had taken "the liberty of addressing my late work" to him, he provided Washington with the latest sales figures. "I have printed sixteen thousand copies," he reported. "When the whole are gone, of which there remain between three and four thousand, I shall then make a cheap edition, just sufficient to bring in the price of printing and papers, as I did by Common Sense." As a special present, Paine sent Washington "fifty Copies as a token of remembrance of yourself and my Friends."[63]

Paine need not have bothered. More than a month earlier, copies of *The Rights of Man* had reached Philadelphia. Everyone discussed the controversial title. On May 8, Lear wrote to Washington, recounting a heated conversation he had just had with Colonel George Beckwith during one of Martha Washington's weekly receptions. Lear thought the whole exchange amusing, and his report was certainly intended to entertain the president, who was then staying in Charleston. Beckwith—Lear called him Beckworth—had been a secret British agent during the American Revolution, and in the years following the peace, he carried out delicate assignments in North America for the British government. Since he and his superiors viewed Paine not only as a dangerous troublemaker but also as a direct threat to British security, he wondered whether the dedication to Washington carried a deeper meaning. Beckwith wanted assurance that "*everything* in that Book did not meet the President's approbation."

Lear feigned ignorance. What possibly could Beckwith mean? The agent observed the obvious: "Because there are many things in it which reflect highly on the British Government & administration, and as it is dedicated to the President, it may lead to a conclusion that he approves of those things." Lear parried, noting that since Washington had not yet read Paine's work, it would be "absurd to suppose, *merely from the circumstance of its being dedicated to him*, that he approves of every sentiment contained in it." The secretary concluded the conversation by urging Beckwith to take his concerns directly to Paine, who was then living in France.[64]

It was Thomas Jefferson who turned a minor diplomatic squabble into a domestic political crisis. On the same day that Lear recounted in detail his conversation with Beckwith, Jefferson sent a letter to the traveling president. Like a schoolchild who knows that he or she has done something bad and now wants to minimize the damage, the Secretary of State opened with the comforting observation that over the previous week, he had witnessed not "one single public event worthy of communicating to you." But on second thought, there perhaps was a minor thing worth reporting: everyone in Philadelphia was talking about Paine. The newspapers were taking sides, some pro-Paine, some pro-Burke, and in the excitement of discussion, Jefferson confessed that he had managed—according to him quite unintentionally—to alienate Vice President John Adams.

From Jefferson's perspective his "indiscretion" seemed of no great importance. As he recounted for Washington the complex story, John Beckley, who lived in Philadelphia, had arranged with Jonathan Bayard Smith for the first publication of *The Rights of Man* in the United States. Before sending it off to the press, Beckley gave a copy to James Madison, who in turn shared it with Jefferson. He returned the manuscript to Smith with a short covering letter. In this note, Jefferson explained that he was "extremely pleased to find it [Paine's book] will be reprinted here [in the United States], and that something is at length to be publicly said against the political heresies which had sprung up among us. He has no doubt our citizens will rally a second time round the standard of Common Sense." It was the reference to political heresies that caused the trouble. Were there really people in the Washington administration who did not support the republican values that Paine defended so passionately?

Much to Jefferson's surprise, his endorsement was included in the book when it was issued several days later. What he regarded as an unfortunate mistake—the release of a private note to the public—immediately transformed the publication into a highly partisan affair, which turned personal differences over the future of republicanism in this country into an excuse for faction. Whether Jefferson's actions were calculated to promote his political agenda or simply an unfortunate accident cannot be discerned.

There was no question, however, that Jefferson and Madison had grown tired of Adams's pronouncements, which seemed to favor a highly structured social order that many Americans associated with monarchy. Adams protested that he wanted nothing to do with kings and aristocrats, but Jefferson did not believe him. In his account of the affair, Jefferson noted diplomatically that he had always regarded Adams "as one of the most honest & disinterested men alive." And he still held to that opinion even after Adams's "apostasy to hereditary monarchy & nobility."

According to Jefferson, Adams had brought the censure on himself by publishing several long essays in praise of British institutions. As was often the case with Jefferson, he tried to take the high moral ground, suggesting that others had caused the problem. After all, as Jefferson reminded Washington, it was he, not Adams, who was the true republican. "I certainly never made a secret of my being anti-monarchical, and anti-aristocratical: but I am sincerely mortified to be thus brought forward on the public stage, where to remain, to advance or to retire, will be equally against my love of silence & quiet, & my abhorrence of dispute."[65]

Adams, of course, was surprised to learn of Jefferson's abhorrence of dispute. When his rival finally sent a note of apology, the vice president noted that Paine's work, which Adams really did find obnoxious, had been republished in all the newspapers. It seemed almost as if someone was using *The Rights of Man* to advance a personal political agenda. And since the work carried Jefferson's endorsement, Adams could not help but regard the whole episode as "a direct and open personal attack upon me, by countenancing the false interpretation of my Writings as favoring the Introduction of hereditary Monarchy and Aristocracy into this Country."

The entire exchange was hurtful. Why, Adams wondered, had Jefferson not spoken to him personally—as a colleague—about their differences? "You and I have never had a Serious conversation together that I can recollect concerning the nature of Government. The very transient hints that have ever passed between Us, have been jocular and Superficial, without ever coming to any explanation."[66] To further inflame matters, Adams's son John Quincy wrote a series of essays under the pen name Publicola, defending his father's views. The tone was aggressively adversarial. Noting Jefferson's admiration of Paine, John Quincy declared, "If . . . Mr. PAYNE is to be adopted as the holy father of our political faith, and this pamphlet is to be considered as his Papal bull of infallible virtue, let us examine what it contains." [67] Jefferson and Adams, two men who had so long defended the principles of the American Revolution, had no political discussions for a very long time after this crisis.

—VI—

How, we might ask, at the conclusion of Washington's extensive tour through the South, can we place the totality of his achievement in a larger political and personal context? What does the journey reveal about the man and American society at a critical moment that we did not already know? What in fact does it tell us about the origins of our own political culture? What exactly is his message for us?

For the president in 1791, the answer was obvious. He was greatly relieved just to have made it back to Mount Vernon without another major mishap. Like a general returning from an arduous campaign, he seemed genuinely pleased that he had taken the new federal government to the American people. He had in fact gathered information about the reception of the new government, and what he learned during the endless receptions was universally positive. We might wonder occasionally whether the people he encountered told him the truth. Perhaps many of them exaggerated the level of popular support for the federal government. But discounting that, Washington was not discouraged by anything he had seen or heard.

As soon as he returned home, the president dispatched letters to his closest colleagues reviewing his recent experience in the South. He awarded himself high marks for advance planning. He took particular pride in having maintained a precise schedule, day after day over sandy and dusty roads, which tested the endurance of men and horses. [68] The Great White Coach showed remarkably few signs of wear and tear. Not once did he mention to friends the unpleasant events—the accidents on the Chesapeake Bay or Occoquan River or the distasteful negotiations with Paris and Hercules, for example. Alexander Hamilton received the fullest account of the southern trip. The president insisted that the success of the entire venture resulted from a mixture of luck and skill. As he explained to Hamilton, "The improbability of performing a tour of 1700 miles (—I have rode more), with the same set of horses without encountering any accident . . . appeared so great that I allowed eight days for casualties."[69] In this recounting, no such casualties had occurred.

A few weeks later, Washington again celebrated his good fortune. He informed David Humphreys that he had "performed a journey of 1887 miles without meeting any interruption by sickness, bad weather, or an untoward accident." How the president calculated the total mileage is not known, but he had added 187 miles to the grand total. One can forgive Washington's hyperbole. It was in fact amazing that he and the horses "kept up their full spirits to the last day."[70]

As Washington well knew, the story of his journeys to the new nation was not simply a tale of personal survival. From a political perspective, the enterprise had paid valuable dividends. Along the roads of America, he had repeatedly asked the people he encountered how they felt about the new federal government. Did they support a strong system that made demands on them in the form of taxes? Did they share his optimism about the future prosperity and strength of the union? Did they see the dangers of fragmentation? The results, of course, were highly impressionistic. But whatever the sources of insight, the president was able in 1791 to conclude to his own satisfaction that the United States was in good shape—certainly in better shape than it had been under the Confederation during the 1780s. "I am much pleased," he concluded, "that I have taken this journey as it has enabled me to see with my own eyes the situation of the country thro' which we traveled, and to learn more accurately the disposition of the people than I could have by any [other source of] information."[71]

Throughout his journey, to both the North and South, Washington witnessed largely contented Americans, busy making a living and confident about the prospects of bettering their lot in the new republic. At the end of his journey of discovery, he could look back on the scores of conversations he had had from New Hampshire to Georgia—with workers in the woolen mills of New England, many of them women, members of the town committees sitting on the reviewing stands of Boston and Portsmouth, Jewish leaders in Newport anxious about religious toleration, entrepreneurs in Richmond supervising slaves building a canal that might one day connect the settlements beyond the mountains to the Atlantic ports, and hundreds of women who honored him at receptions where they made it clear that they too were part of the larger political culture. He had carried a vision for a strong central government to the people, and they had responded enthusiastically.

Washington summarized his general impressions for Humphreys, the Revolutionary veteran with whom he had begun the journey from Mount Vernon to New York several years earlier. "The country appears to be in a very improving state," the president reported, "and industry and frugality are becoming much more fashionable than they have hitherto been." Republican government was good for the American people. Whatever others may have told him about growing discontent, he found the situation to be quite different. "Tranquility reigns among the people," he told Humphreys. They expressed the hope that the "general government" would flourish. However fearful of anarchy the Americans may have been in the past, they now "begin to feel the good effects of equal laws and equal protection."[72]

Washington understood, of course, that the nation still faced serious problems. He recognized that securing the Revolution was an ongoing process. The union could never be taken for granted. Always threatening were the grumblers who could not imagine a broader political horizon than their own states. As we have seen, the president labeled these parochial figures "demagogues." It was they, and not the American people, who posed the greatest peril for the nation. As Washington explained in his diary, "The manners of the people, as far as my observations, and means of information extended, were orderly and Civil." On those rare occasions when they complained, "it was not difficult to trace the cause to some demagogue, or speculating character."[73] Washington had no expectations that ambitious troublemakers who played on the emotions and prejudices of ordinary men and women would disappear. The demagogues would continue to claim that their self-serving rhetoric spoke to the common good. Washington was fully aware of the histrionic character of these appeals, as were many Americans who had participated in his journey of discovery.

We need not accept Washington's largely optimistic appraisal. After all, we know what he could not possibly have known. Soon after his return from the southern states, the regional divisions that he so feared became more manifest. Instead of pursuing national solidarity, the members of his own cabinet turned on each other, and like members of a dysfunctional revolutionary family, they encouraged faction, often by airing personal political differences in newspapers that aggressively took sides on the major issues of the day: the implications for the United States of the French Revolution, the efforts of the federal government to encourage domestic manufacturing, the expansion of slavery to the new western states, and the demand of the states for greater sovereignty.[74] Such developments disappointed, even angered Washington during the last years of his life. The controversy over the spread of slavery later tore at the fabric of the nation. Abraham Lincoln faced the very kinds of problems about which Washington had warned. He too defended union above all else.

Despite these developments, we should not lose sight of Washington's remarkable inventiveness. His bold journey—his insistence on reaching out to the American people—established a precedent that presidents who have followed him cannot easily ignore. At a critical moment in our country's history when fragmentation was a genuine threat, he devised an innovative means to communicate a vision for the future of the United States that resonated persuasively among ordinary men and women from New Hampshire to Georgia. His great insight was seeing the need to perform his office on a new national stage. That is his legacy. We can conclude that about one thing John Adams was absolutely correct: Washington was indeed a great "actor of the presidency." His message has enduring significance for all Americans. A great nation like the United States must always remain more than the sum of its parts. A strong union is our shared Revolutionary heritage.

Hiding in Plain Sight

George Washington's return to Philadelphia in 1791 was not the end of the story—at least not the story of the Great Coach in which he took such pride. Like the relics of a medieval saint, the vehicle continued to speak to the American people about a moment at the start of the nation's long history when unity seemed to have trumped division. During the nineteenth century, sectionalism came close to destroying the country for which Washington had sacrificed so much. In this context the coach provoked the popular imagination. It became a symbol of an earlier, more unified America, and its preservation took on greater significance as the federal government came under attack from many quarters.

We know that the coach made it through the long southern trip in surprisingly good condition. When Washington finally arrived back in the nation's capital, David Clark greeted him. Clark was eager to know how the vehicle on which he had spent so many hours working had stood up to the terrible southern roads. He got under the coach, examining the suspension and wheels. John Fagan, the irritable driver, leaning down from the box, shouted, "All right, Mr. Clark; all right, sir; not a bolt or screw started in a long journey and over the devil's own roads." Washington participated in the round of congratulations. He shook Clark's hand, assuring the master craftsman that his coach had been thoroughly tested on "a great variety of very bad roads."[1] For the remaining years of Washington's presidency, the coach appeared at important state occasions. But however much pleasure it brought to Washington, it did not serve any obvious function after he finally retired to Mount Vernon in 1796. Someone drove it back to Virginia, where it was stored. Birds and moisture took a greater toll on the coach than had so many miles on the road to Georgia. And then it disappeared.

As early as 1802, people began to ask what had happened to the Great Coach. It seemed wise to begin the search at Mount Vernon. After Washington died in 1799, his wife, Martha, tried to maintain the huge estate, but without his firm hand, the operation quickly deteriorated. At her death, the executors of the estate put the coach up for auction. The legal records at the time described it as an "elegant chariot."[2] After the sale, the trail became very hard to follow. Rumors circulated about the coach's location and condition, but no one knew for certain where it had gone.

One writer announced that he had it on good authority that the Great Coach had somehow been transported to New Orleans. There, through an amazing piece of bad luck, it found itself positioned between British soldiers attempting to take the city during the War of 1812 and American defenders. Bullet holes testified to the ferocity of the battle. In his *Annals of Philadelphia and Pennsylvania in the Olden Time* (1842), John F. Watson recounted the sad fate of the vehicle. "It became in time a kind of outhouse," Watson explained, "in which fowls roosted; and in the great battle of New Orleans, it stood between the combatants, and was greatly shot-ridden."[3] Alas, no one could verify the account, and searchers understandably turned their attentions to more plausible explanations.

After years of frustration, the quest took an unexpected turn. Elizabeth Steel, an illiterate woman who had worked for several years as a servant in the family of Colonel John Hare Powel, claimed that she knew exactly where to find Washington's coach. She asserted that while in the employ of the Powels, she had actually seen the vehicle. Some people immediately expressed skepticism. Steel's affidavit referred to a period between 1842 and 1850, and although it was possible that she provided an accurate account, it was noted, "her memory was *very* defective." The Powels did not support her testimony. In fact, they described her as simply a "talkative old person." To those who reflected on the matter, it seemed that Steel had confused the missing Washington coach with one in the possession of the Powel family at the time that the president purchased his vehicle. But as had occurred repeatedly during the Middle Ages, the desire to locate an authentic relic overruled common sense, and people who should have known better declared that they had at last located the real object.

Armed with Steel's testimony, the coach's current owner, Benjamin Richardson, began displaying it at various festivities as the genuine Washington Coach. Richardson was a peculiar man. He originally purchased the coach to enhance his extensive collection of "curios and relics," but perhaps sensing that the new acquisition might generate income, he threw himself into historical reenactment. Dressed in a Continental Army uniform, he would ride in parades in the Washington Coach. Even friends described Richardson as "eccentric, and illy balanced mentally." He certainly seemed to enjoy playing the part of Washington.

Whatever his state of mind may have been, Richardson was cunning enough to bring the coach to the Centennial Exhibition held in Philadelphia in 1876. The organizers of this grand event, one of the most important in American history, celebrated not only the accomplishments of the Revolutionary generation, but also the impressive industrial progress the United States had made following the Civil War. And so they placed the coach in one of the main exhibition halls. It provided a splendid link between the nation's noble past and its prosperous, presumably united future. After the Civil War, it spoke once again for the Union. For only twenty-five cents, members of the public could sit in the coach. An African American interpreter, no doubt unaware of his role as Paris, stood ready to answer questions. It was reported that the

Prince of Wales, who was then visiting the United States, declined an invitation to take a ride in the coach. Perhaps the prince had second thoughts about the propriety of being seen in a vehicle once owned by a colonial liberator.

During the last several decades of the nineteenth century, the coach appeared in parades. The doubts about its authenticity remained, however. It was sold and resold. Finally, it came into the possession of Augustus Frey, described as a "dealer in real estate, insurance, stocks, bonds, and commercial paper." He offered to sell the coach to the Mount Vernon Association for the handsome sum of $10,000. After reviewing the evidence, that group turned down the offer, observing at the time, "They believed it was the property of a neighbor of General Washington, a Colonel Powel." Rejection did not discourage Frey. In 1901 he persuaded the Michigan chapter of the Mount Vernon Association to pay $350 for the coach. After it underwent minor repairs in New Jersey, the coach was carried to Mount Vernon, where a large sign informed visitors that it was the "Carriage Exhibited at the Centennial Exposition, Philadelphia 1876, as 'WASHINGTON'S WHITE CHARIOT.'"[4]

Finally, the parties contesting the coach's authenticity turned to one of the leading historians of the day, J. Franklin Jameson. As one of his admirers declared, Jameson "has done more than any living man to promote sound historical research in America."[5] That assessment seems a little over the top. There was no question, however, that he enjoyed broad professional respect and welcomed the chance to pick up extra money as a consultant. In a letter written in 1908, he noted that "a nice old lady"—presumably Mary Stevens Beall—had recently approached him and asked him to settle definitively the dispute over Washington's coach. The research turned out to be undemanding, something that a good graduate student could have done in a day or two. But in the swirl of claims and counterclaims, Jameson offered undoubted expertise.

After examining the records, including those related to New Orleans and the illiterate servant, Jameson came to the conclusion that

Washington had never owned the coach on display at Mount Vernon. He dismissed every piece of evidence offered in support of its authenticity. He could find only a copper medallion "formerly affixed to one of the doors of his coaches." It was a section of the original painting of the *Four Seasons*, which Washington had treasured in 1791. Jameson thought the artwork an embarrassment. It "bears a group of cupids said to be by Cipriani, but anyhow, very ugly and apparently of the African race. Thus, as you will see, the cause of history in the United States is progressing with great éclat."[6] The coach displayed at Mount Vernon was in fact the Powel coach, not Washington's.

Jameson's findings begged the question of what had actually happened to the president's coach. The answer was hiding in plain sight. After analyzing printed sources that were readily available to anyone willing to examine them, Jameson focused attention on the auction held soon after Martha's death. He found that George Washington Parke Custis, the president's step-grandson, had purchased the item, which even then was in terrible shape. Custis had little more than a sentimental attachment to the coach, and as it continued to deteriorate, he decided to sell it to William Meade, then bishop of the Protestant Episcopal Church in Virginia. Meade wrote a book entitled *Old Churches, Ministers, and Families in Virginia*, and it was that publication that finally settled the mystery. The bishop explained that he had come into possession of the coach about fifteen years after Washington died. "In the course of time," Meade recounted, "from disuse, it being too heavy for these latter days, it began to decay and give way."

People in the area had apparently known all along of the coach's existence. They came to the bishop requesting mementoes—in other words, tangible, personal connections linking them to the hero of the Revolution. Under these circumstances, Meade decided to have the coach "taken to pieces and distributed among admiring friends of Washington who visited my house, and also among a number of female associations for benevolent and religious objects, which associations, at their fairs and on other occasions, made a large profit by converting the fragments into walking sticks, picture frames, and snuff boxes."

In no way did Meade's actions embarrass him. After all, he had turned a wreck into a gold mine. A spoke from one of the wheels alone brought in $140. The bishop retained one object. "Besides other mementoes of it," Meade reported, "I have in my study, in the form of a sofa, the hind seat, on which the General and his lady were wont to sit on."[7] Lost in Meade's narrative were Major Jackson, Tobias Lear, Paris, Giles, John Fagan, and all the others we have met who once accompanied Washington on his journey to America.

Notes

—PROLOGUE—

1. J. P. Brissot de Warville, *New Travels in the United States* (London, 1792), ix.
2. *Diaries of George Washington*, ed. Donald Jackson and Dorothy Twohig (Charlottesville, VA, 1979), vol. 5, 452–53. Also see Papers of George Washington, Presidential Series, vol. 3, to Edward Rutledge, January 16, 1791, 236.
3. See Richard J. Ellis, *Presidential Travel: The Journey from George Washington to George W. Bush* (Lawrence, KS, 2008); Sandra Moats, *Celebrating the Republic: Presidential Ceremony and Popular Sovereignty, from Washington to Monroe* (DeKalb, IL, 2010).
4. GW Papers, vol. 4 (January 9, 1790), 552, emphasis added.
5. Marcus Cunliffe, *George Washington* (Boston, 1958). The best character studies are Edmund S. Morgan, *The Genius of George Washington* (New York, 1982), Robert Middlekauff, *Washington's Revolution: The Making of America's First Leader* (New York, 2015), and Paul K. Longmore, *The Invention of George Washington* (Charlottesville, VA, 1999). The most detailed account of Washington's life remains Douglas Southall Freeman, *George Washington:*

A Biography, 7 vols. (New York, 1948–1957). More recent biographies include Ron Chernow, *Washington: A Life* (New York, 2010), and Joseph J. Ellis, *His Excellency: George Washington* (New York, 2005). More narrowly focused studies are Harlow G. Unger, *"Mr. President": George Washington and the Making of the Nation's Highest Office* (Boston, 2013), and Edward Larson, *The Return of George Washington: George Washington's Ascent to the Presidency: 1783–1789* (New York, 2014).

6. GW Papers, vol. 5, 50 (January 24, 1790).

7. Cited in Leonard D. White, *The Federalists: A Study in Administrative History* (New York, 1961), 100.

8. GW Papers, vol. 3, 49 (May 10, 1789). On the centrality of the concept of "union" in American political thought at this time, see Douglas Bradburn, *The Citizenship Revolution: Politics and the Creation of the American Union, 1774–1804* (Charlottesville, VA, 2009). Also see Don Higginbotham, *George Washington: Uniting a Nation* (Lanham, MD, 2002).

9. A list of some surviving places that Washington visited on his tours can be found in William G. Clotworthy, *In the Footsteps of George Washington: A Guide to Sites Commemorating Our First President* (Blacksburg, VA, 2002), 322–72.

10. *Diaries of GW*, vol. 6, May 2, 1791, 127.

11. Max S. Edelson, *Plantation Enterprise in Colonial South Carolina* (Cambridge, MA, 2011).

12. Archibald Henderson, *Washington's Southern Tour, 1791* (Boston, 1923), 139.

— CHAPTER I: THE POWER OF PUBLIC OPINION —

1. *Diaries of George Washington*, eds. Donald Jackson and Dorothy Twohig (Charlottesville, VA, 1979), 5, 460–61.

2. George Washington Parke Custis, *Recollections and Private Memoirs of Washington* (Bridgewater, VA, 1859), 397.

3. *Diaries of GW*, vol. 5, 456.

4. Ibid., 453–54.

5. Ibid., 452–53.

6. *Writings of James Madison*, ed. Gaillard Hunt (New York, 1904), 270.

7. *Adams Family Correspondence*, ed. Margaret A. Hogan, et al. (Cambridge, MA, 2008), vol. 8, 412.

8. Ibid., 421.

9. Ibid., 426.

10. Stephen Decatur Jr., *Private Affairs of George Washington: From the Records and Accounts of Tobias Lear, Esquire, His Secretary* (Boston, 1933), 56.

11. Ray Brighton, *The Checkered Career of Tobias Lear* (Portsmouth, NH, 1985).

12. *An Oration, to Commemorate the Independence of the United States of North-America* (Philadelphia, 1786), 28.

13. GW Papers, vol. 2, 74–75.

14. *Writings of GW*, ed. John C. Fitzpatrick (Washington, DC, 1931–44), vol. 31, 449–450. Also see Robert C. Alberts, *The Golden Voyage: The Life and Times of William Bingham 1752–1804* (New York, 1969).

15. *Diaries of GW*, vol. 5, 460–61.

16. Garry Wills, *Cincinnatus: George Washington and the Enlightenment: Images of Power in Early America* (New York, 1984).

17. *Writings of GW*, vol. 30, 23–24.

18. *Diaries of GW*, vol. 5, 445.

19. Ibid., 446–47.

20. On the weakness of the Confederation, see Jack N. Rakove, *The Beginnings of National Politics: An Interpretive History of the Continental Congress* (New York, 1988).

21. Rosemarie Zagarri, ed., *David Humphreys' "Life of General Washington"* (Athens, GA, 1991), xix.

22. Ibid., 49, 50.

23. Cited in Douglas Southall Freeman, *George Washington: A Biography* (New York, 1954), vol. 6: *Patriot and President*, 169.

24. *Pennsylvania Packet* (Philadelphia), April 24, 1789.

25. *Independent Gazetteer* (Philadelphia), April 21, 1789.

26. *Pennsylvania Packet*, April 24; *Independent Gazetteer*, April 21; *Freeman's Journal* (Philadelphia), April 29. Also see Freeman, *George Washington*, vol. 6, 170–73; James Thomas Flexner, *George Washington and the New Nation* (Boston, 1969), 175–76.

27. *Pennsylvania Packet*, April 24, 1789.

28. Ibid., May 1, 1789; Freeman, *George Washington*, vol. 6, 174–76.

29. *Pennsylvania Packet*, May 1, 1789; Custis, *Recollections*, 393–94.

30. Boudinot to his wife, April 24, 1789, Boudinot Family Collection, online, courtesy of the Princeton University Library.

31. Quoted in Freeman, *George Washington*, vol. 6, 183.

—CHAPTER II: INVENTING A NEW THEATER OF POLITICS—

1. George Washington Parke Custis, *Recollections and Private Memoirs of Washington* (Bridgewater, VA, 1859), 366–68. I thank Mary Thompson, research historian at Mount Vernon, for her generous assistance in reconstructing Washington's love of the theater.

2. *Diaries of George Washington*, ed. Donald Jackson and Dorothy Twohig (Charlottesville, VA, 1979), vol. 5, 500–502.

3. The complete list can be found in Washington's *Rules of Civility*, which have appeared in many modern editions.

4. See Edmund S. Morgan, *The Meaning of Independence: John Adams, George Washington, and Thomas Jefferson* (New York, 1976), 29–58; Paul K. Longmore, *Invention of George Washington* (Charlottesville,

VA, 1999); Edward G. Lengel, *Inventing George Washington: America's Founder in Myth and Memory* (New York, 2011); and Robert F. Dalzell Jr. and Lee Baldwin Dalzell, *George Washington's Mount Vernon: At Home in Revolutionary America* (New York, 2000).

5. *Writings of George Washington*, ed. John C. Fitzpatrick (Washington, DC, 1931–1944), vol. 33, 73.

6. Ibid., vol. 30, 168–69.

7. Papers of George Washington, Presidential Series, vol. 2, 62.

8. David Waldstreicher provides valuable insights into this problem in "Federalism, the Styles of Politics, and the Politics of Style," in Doran Ben-Atar and Barbara B. Oberg, eds., *Federalists Reconsidered* (Charlottesville, VA, 1999), 99–117.

9. GW Papers, vol. 2, 246–47.

10. Ron Chernow, *Washington: A Life* (New York, 2010), cited 566.

11. Adams to Rush, June 21, 1811, in John A. Schutz and Douglass Adair, eds., *The Spur of Fame: Dialogues of John Adams and Benjamin Rush, 1805–1813* (Indianapolis, 1966), 196–97.

12. Ibid., 106–107.

13. Cited in Page Smith, *John Adams* (New York, 1962), vol. 2, 754.

14. Cited in Stanley Elkins and Eric McKitrick, *Age of Federalism: The Early American Republic, 1788–1800* (New York, 1993), 536.

15. Cited in Chernow, *Washington*, 575.

16. Linda Grant DePauw, ed., *Documentary History of the First Federal Congress of the United States of America* (Baltimore, 1972), vol. 1, 28–29.

17. James H. Hutson, "John Adams' Title Campaign," *New England Quarterly* 41 (1968): 34; and Kathleen Bartoloni-Tuazon, *For Fear of an Elective King: George Washington and the Presidential Controversy of 1789* (Ithaca, NY, 2014).

18. Cited in Kenneth R. Bowling and Helen E. Veit, eds., *The Diary of William Maclay and Other Notes on Senate Debates* (Baltimore, 1988), xiii.

19. DePauw, ed., *Documentary History*, 1, 27–28.

20. Cited in Elkins and McKitrick, *Federalism*, 47.

21. GW Papers, vol. 2, 249.

22. Ibid., 250.

23. Ibid.

24. Cited in Hutson, "Title Campaign," 33.

25. Cited in Chernow, *Washington*, 576.

26. GW Papers, vol. 3, 199. For a detailed account of the battle over the ratification of the Constitution in Virginia, see Pauline Maier, *Ratification: The People Debate the Constitution, 1788–1789* (New York, 2011), 255–319.

27. GW Papers, vol. 3, 199.

28. Joanne B. Freeman, *Affairs of Honor: National Politics in the New Republic* (New Haven, CT, 2001), 45–47.

29. GW Papers, vol. 3.

30. Ibid., 323.

31. Ibid., 322–23.

32. Ibid., 321–22. Freeman provides a good account of how very ambitious men tried to sort themselves out according to honor and character in *Affairs of Honor*, 1–61.

33. GW Papers, vol. 2, 247.

34. Ibid., 247–49.

35. Cited in Elkins and McKitrick, *Federalism*, 49–50.

36. GW Papers, vol. 5, 463.

37. Ibid., 354–56.

38. Ibid., vol. 3, 322.

39. Ibid., vol. 5, 526–27.

40. Ibid., vol. 2, 246.

41. Ibid., 313–14.

42. Ibid., vol. 3, 323.

43. Ibid., 76–77.

44. Stephen Decatur Jr., *Private Affairs of George Washington: From*

the Records and Accounts of Tobias Lear, Esquire, His Secretary (Boston, 1933), 27.

45. Rosemarie Zagarri, ed., *David Humphreys' "Life of General Washington"* (Athens, GA, 1991), 57.

46. GW Papers, vol. 4, 1.

47. Ibid., 162.

48. *Boston Gazette and Country Journal*, October 19, 26, 1789.

49. GW Papers, vol. 4, 214.

50. *Daily Advertiser* (New York City), November 14, 1789.

51. *Herald of Freedom*, October 23, 1789.

52. *Boston Gazette*, October 19, 1789.

53. GW Papers, vol. 7, 212–13.

54. Ibid., vol. 2, 114.

55. *Gazette of the United States*, June 4, 1791.

56. *Daily Advertiser*, November 14, 1789; *Connecticut Courant*, November 2, 1789.

57. *Connecticut Courant*, November 2, 1789.

58. GW Papers, vol. 7, 236–37.

59. *Writings of GW*, vol. 30, 251.

60. Washington Papers, Library of Congress, October 24, 1789.

61. *Diaries of GW*, vol. 6, 21–22.

62. Ibid., 134.

63. Ibid., vol. 5, 494.

64. *Gazette of the United States*, November 12, 1787.

65. *Herald of Freedom*, November 17, 1789.

66. *Independent Chronicle* (Boston), November 27, 1789.

67. *Diaries of GW*, vol. 5, 472, 493, 495, 497.

68. Ibid., vol. 6, 113, 115, 158.

69. J. P. Brissot de Warville, *New Travels in the United States of America, 1788*, ed. Durand Echeverria (Cambridge, MA, 1964), 153.

70. *Diaries of GW*, vol. 6, 112.

71. Louis B. Wright and Marion Tinling, eds., *Quebec to Carolina in 1785–1786* (San Marino, CA, 1943), 256.

72. Ibid., 277.

73. Isaac Weld Jr., *Travels through the States of North America* (London, 1799).

74. Marquis de Chastellux, *Travels in North America in the Years 1780, 1781, and 1782*, trans. Howard C. Rice (Chapel Hill, NC, 1961), vol. 2, 573.

75. Barnet Schecter, *George Washington's America: A Biography through His Maps* (New York, 2010); Kariann Akemi Yokota, *Unbecoming British: How Revolutionary America Became a Postcolonial Nation* (New York, 2011).

76. Christopher Colles, *A Survey*, ed. Walter A. Ristow (Cambridge, MA, 1961), 45, 76.

77. *Diaries of GW*, vol. 5, 461.

78. Archibald Henderson, *Washington's Southern Tour*, 1791 (Boston, 1923), 295–96; Jethro Rumple, *A History of Rowan County, North Carolina* (Westminster, MD, 2009, originally 1916), 178.

— CHAPTER III: THE SCRIPT —

1. Barnet Schecter, *George Washington's America: A Biography through His Maps* (New York, 2010).

2. Patrick Griffin explores Revolutionary state building in his provocative *America's Revolution* (New York, 2012). Also see Howard G. Brown, *Ending the French Revolution: Violence, Justice, and Repression from the Terror to Napoleon* (Charlottesville, VA, 2007), and Tim Harris, *Restoration: Charles II and His Kingdoms, 1660–1685* (New York, 2006).

3. These topics have generated a rich historical literature. Among the most helpful works for me are Max M. Edling, *A Revolution in*

Favor of Government: Origins of the U.S. Constitution and the Making of the American State (New York, 2008); Woody Holton, *Unruly Americans and the Origins of the Constitution* (New York, 2008); and Jack N. Rakove, *Original Meanings: Politics and Ideas in the Making of the Constitution* (New York, 1997).

4. Don Higginbotham, *George Washington: Uniting a Nation* (Lanham, MD, 2002), 35–39.

5. Papers of George Washington, Presidential Series, vol. 1, 6.

6. J. P. Brissot de Warville, *New Travels in the United States of America, 1788*, ed. Durand Echeverria (Cambridge, MA, 1964), 344. See Jack N. Rakove, *The Beginnings of National Politics: An Interpretive History of the Continental Congress* (New York, 1979).

7. *Writings of George Washington*, ed. John C. Fitzpatrick (Washington, DC, 1931–1944), vol. 30, 95–96.

8. Ibid., GW to James McHenry, July 31, 1788, 30.

9. GW Papers, Confederation Series, vol. 5, 80. See Eric Nelson, *The Royalist Revolution: Monarchy and the American Founding* (Cambridge, MA, 2014), chap. 5.

10. GW Papers, Presidential Series, vol. 8, 359, GW to David Humphreys, July 20, 1791.

11. Ibid., Confederation Series, vol. 4, 212 (August 15, 1786).

12. *Massachusetts Magazine*, vol. 3, June 1791, 359–61.

13. GW Papers, Confederation Series, vol. 4, 131–32.

14. Ibid., vol. 5, 63.

15. See Holton, *Unruly Americans*.

16. GW Papers, Confederation Series, vol. 4, 4.

17. Ibid., 299.

18. *Writings of GW*, vol. 30, 21.

19. GW Papers, Confederation Series, vol. 4, 295.

20. Ibid., vol. 4, 300. A valuable account of Washington's worries about the state of the nation before the meeting of the Constitutional Convention can be found in Douglas Southall Freeman,

George Washington: A Biography (New York, 1954), vol. 6, chaps. 2 and 3.

21. T.H. Breen, *American Insurgents, American Patriots: The Revolution of the People* (New York, 2010).

22. GW Papers, Confederation Series, vol. 4, 41, GW to Marquis de Lafayette, April 15, 1786.

23. Drew R. McCoy, *The Elusive Republic: Political Economy in Jeffersonian America* (Chapel Hill, NC, 1980).

24. P. J. Marshall, *The Making and Unmaking of Empires: Britain, India, and America c. 1750–1783* (New York, 2007).

25. GW Papers, Confederation Series, vol. 4, 212. On strong state liberalism, see Stephen Holmes, *Passions and Constraints: On the Theory of Liberal Democracy* (Chicago, 1997), and "Can Weak-State Liberalism Survive?" in Dan Avnon and Avner de-Shalit, eds., *Liberalism and Its Practice* (London, 1999), 31–49. Also see John A. Hall, *The Importance of Being Civil: The Struggle for Political Decency* (Princeton, NJ, 2013). Hall explains, "Sheer intellectual provincialism makes many forget that settled existence depends on the rule of law being guaranteed by effective state power" (20).

26. *Diaries of George Washington*, ed. Donal Jackson and Dorothy Twohig (Charlottesville, VA, 1979), vol. 6, 155, 158.

27. GW Papers, Confederation Series, vol. 5, 115.

28. Ibid., 79–80.

29. Ibid., 145 (emphasis added). Max M. Edling provides a forceful and original analysis of the framers' goals at Philadelphia in *A Revolution in Favor of Government*.

30. GW Papers, Confederation Series, vol. 5, 146.

31. Ibid., see letter to Charles Carter, December 1787, 492.

32. GW Papers, Presidential Series, vol. 1, 262.

33. See Herbert J. Storing and Murray Dry, eds., *The Anti-Federalists: Writings by the Opponents of the Constitution* (Chicago, 1985).

34. Gaillard Hunt, ed., *Writings of James Madison* (New York, 1904),

vol. 5, 267. For a detailed account of ratification in the various states, see Pauline Maier, *Ratification: The People Debate the Constitution, 1787–1788* (New York, 2010).

35. *Writings of GW*, vol. 30, 23.

36. *The Federalist: The Famous Papers on the Principles of American Government* Benjamin F. Wright, ed., (Cambridge, MA, 1961), 106.

37. Hunt, *Writings of Madison*, 244.

38. Ibid., 256–57.

39. Ibid., 267.

40. I am drawing here on the insights of Jack N. Rakove, who more than any other scholar of the Constitution has appreciated how public opinion transformed political culture during the period of ratification. He argues persuasively: "Conceived though the Constitution may have been to check popular excesses, its ratification came to depend on a form of popular politics that marked almost a quantum leap beyond what had proved practical theretofore. The year and a half that separated the adjournment of the Federal Constitution from the assembling of the First Congress had provided a remarkable education in the possibility of conducting politics on a scale that would have seemed inconceivable as late as 1786." See his "The Structure of Politics at the Accession of George Washington," in Richard Beeman and Edward C. Carter II, eds., *Beyond Confederation: Origins of the Constitution and American National Identity* (Chapel Hill, NC, 1987), 261–94, quotation 293.

41. *Independent Chronicle* (Boston), December 9, 1790; GW Papers, Presidential Series, vol. 3, 321; *Writings of GW*, vol. 30, 73.

42. Forrest McDonald, *The Presidency of George Washington* (Lawrence, KS, 1974), 6.

43. *Gazette of the United States*, September 26, 1789.

44. Breen, *American Insurgents*.

45. The most insightful study of nationalism in the United States after the Revolution is John M. Murrin, "A Roof without Walls: The Dilemma

of American National Identity," in Beeman and Carter, eds., *Beyond Confederation*, 333–48. As Murrin explains, "American national identity was . . . an unexpected, impromptu, artificial, and therefore extremely fragile creation of the Revolution" (344). Also see T.H. Breen, "Interpreting New World Nationalism," in Don H. Doyle and Marco Antonio Pamplona, eds., *Nationalism in the New World* (Athens, GA, 2006), 41–60, and Peter Onuf, *Jefferson's Empire: The Language of American Nationhood* (Charlottesville, VA, 2000).

46. *Gazette of the United States*, September 26, 1789.

47. GW Papers, Presidential Series, vol. 5, 287, 524.

48. Ibid., Confederation Series, vol. 4, 131.

49. *Diaries of GW*, vol. 6, 155.

50. For a good account of the aggressive new journalism of this period, see Jeffrey L. Pasley, *"The Tyranny of Printers": Newspaper Politics in the Early American Republic* (Charlottesville, VA, 2002).

51. GW Papers, Presidential Series, vol. 8, 350 (emphasis added).

52. Ibid., Presidential Series, vol. 4, 24.

53. *Diaries of GW*, Vol. 6, 138.

54. *Gazette of the United States*, June 4, 1791.

55. Rufus W. Griswold, William G. Simms, and Edward D. Ingraham, *Washington and the Generals of the American Revolution* (New York, 1856), 271.

56. The original story appeared in the *Columbian Herald*. No copies of that publication have survived. The Maryland piece was dated June 17, 1791.

57. *Diaries of GW*, vol. 5, 492.

— CHAPTER IV: VOICES OF THE PEOPLE —

1. See Simon P. Newman, *Parades and the Politics of the Street: Festive Culture in the Early American Republic* (Philadelphia, 1997).

Newman correctly observes that although we know a lot about the nation's leaders during this period, we "have all but ignored those who were ruled, apparently regarding these Americans as essentially powerless spectators who were outside of and thus in some sense apart from the political process" (xi).

2. *Maryland Journal*, May 31, 1791.

3. Ibid.

4. Theodore Sizer, ed., *Autobiography of Colonel Trumbull* (New Haven, 1953), 170.

5. Ibid., 170–71.

6. Ibid., 171.

7. Ibid.

8. Papers of George Washington, Presidential Series, vol. 10, May 5, 1792.

9. *Connecticut Courant*, November 2, 1789.

10. Daniel S. Lamson, *History of the Town of Weston, Massachusetts* (Boston, 1913), 113.

11. Charles H. Bell, *History of the Town of Exeter, New Hampshire* (Exeter, 1888), 100.

12. *Gazette of the United States*, November 18, 1789.

13. Cited in Archibald Henderson, *Washington's Southern Tour, 1791* (Boston, 1923), 103.

14. *Middlesex Gazette* (Middletown, Connecticut), November 14, 1789.

15. *Maryland Journal*, November 10, 1789.

16. Ibid., April 19, 1791.

17. See Joseph J. Ellis, *His Excellency: George Washington* (New York, 2005), 195–97.

18. Lucy Cranch to Abigail Adams, October 23, 1789, in Margaret A. Hogan, et al., eds., *Adams Family Correspondence* (Boston, 2007), vol. 8, 428.

19. *Dunlap's American Daily Advertiser* (Philadelphia), May 31, 1791.

20. *General Advertiser*, June 7, 1791.

21. "Letter Describing Washington's Visit to Salem in 1789" (from N. Fisher, a woman writer to her brother), *Historical Collections of the Essex Institute*, vol. 67 (1931), 299–300.

22. *Massachusetts Spy*, November 5, 1789, April 21, 1791; *Connecticut Courant*, November 2, 1789; Samuel Blachley Webb, *Correspondence and Journals of Samuel Blachley Webb*, ed. Worthington Chauncey Ford (New York, 1894), III, 142; *Massachusetts Centinel*, cited in Marvin Sadik, *Christian Gullager: Portrait Painter to Federal America* (Washington, DC, 1976), 35; *Boston Gazette*, October 19, 26, 1789; *Gazette of the United States*, October 24, 1789; *Columbian Centinel*, October 27, 1789; *Middlesex Gazette*, November 14, 1789; *Herald of Freedom*, October 23, 1789; *Connecticut Courant*, October 26, 1789; *Freeman's Journal*, July 13, 1791; *New-York Packet*, November 7, 1789; GW Papers, Presidential Series, vol. 4, 282.

23. *Independent Chronicle*, October 22, 1789.

24. *Massachusetts Magazine* 2, (January 1790): 94.

25. *Gazette of the United States*, November 14, 1789.

26. *Autobiography of Charles Caldwell* (Philadelphia, 1855), 89–97.

27. Sarah Knott, *Sensibility and the American Revolution* (Chapel Hill, NC, 2008).

28. *Middlesex Gazette*, November 14, 1789.

29. *Maryland Journal*, April 19, 1791.

30. *Herald of Freedom*, November 10, 1789.

31. Ibid., October 27, 1789.

32. *Dunlap's American Daily Advertiser*, May 31, 1791.

33. "Letter Describing Washington's Visit," 299.

34. *Dunlap's American Daily Advertiser*, May 31, 1791.

35. Mona Ozouf, *Festivals and the French Revolution* (Cambridge, MA, 1988), 9. Also see David Waldstreicher, *In the Midst of Perpetual Fetes: The Making of American Nationalism, 1776–1820*

(Chapel Hill, NC, 1996); Sean Wilentz, ed., *Rites of Power: Symbolism, Ritual, and Politics since the Middle Ages* (Philadelphia, 1985); and Simon P. Newman, *Parades and the Politics of the Street: Festive Culture in the Early American Republic* (Philadelphia, 1997).

36. *Boston Gazette*, October 26, 1789.

37. *Gazette of the United States*, November 21, 1789.

38. *Essex Journal* and *New Hampshire Packet*, October 21, 1789.

39. The fullest analysis of these parades can be found in Jurgen Heideking, *The Constitution before the Judgment Seat: The Prehistory and Ratification of the American Constitution, 1787–1791* (Charlottesville, VA, 2012), 340–78.

40. *Boston Gazette* and *Country Journal*, February 11, 1788.

41. *New Hampshire Gazette*, June 26, 1788.

42. *Columbia Herald*, May 29, 1788.

43. *Boston Gazette*, October 26, 1789.

44. *Connecticut Courant*, November 2, 1789.

45. *Diaries of George Washington*, ed. Donald Jackson and Dorothy Twohig (Charlottesville, VA, 1979), vol. 6, 114.

46. *General Advertiser* (Philadelphia), May 19, 1791.

47. Henderson, *Washington's Southern Tour*, 119, 130, 153–56.

48. *Gazette of the United States*, November 21, 1789.

49. *Diaries of GW*, vol. 6, 112.

50. Ibid., 111.

51. Quoted in Henderson, *Washington's Southern Tour*, 65–66.

52. A thorough account of the controversy in Virginia can be found in Pauline Maier, *Ratification: The People Debate the Constitution, 1787–1788* (New York, 2010), 255–319.

53. Quoted in Henderson, *Washington's Southern Tour*, 66.

54. *Boston Gazette*, November 2, 1789.

55. Henderson, *Washington's Southern Tour*, 91.

56. *General Advertiser*, May 19, 1791.

57. Ibid.

58. *Dunlap's American Daily Advertiser*, June 1, 1791.

59. *Independent Chronicle*, October 29, 1789.

60. *Maryland Journal*, May 31, 1791.

61. See Craig Koslofsky, *Evening's Empire: A History of the Night in Early Modern Europe* (Cambridge, UK, 2011), 95. Also see A. Roger Ekirch, *At Day's Close: Night in Times Past* (New York, 2006).

62. GW Papers, Presidential Series, vol. 2, 1.

63. *Gazette of the United States*, October 21, 1789.

64. *General Advertiser and Political, Commercial, Agricultural and Literary Journal*, May 11, 1791.

65. The best discussions of these topics are Rosemarie Zagarri, *Revolutionary Backlash: Women and Politics in the Early American Republic* (Philadelphia, 2008), and Linda Kerber, *Women of the Republic: Intellect and Ideology in Revolutionary America* (Chapel Hill, NC, 1997).

66. *Diaries of GW*, Vol. 5, 490.

67. Ibid., 480.

68. *Gazette of the United States*, May 25, 1791.

69. GW Papers, Presidential Series, vol. 8, 415.

70. Ibid., vol. 10, 109.

71. Isaac Weld, *Travel through the States of North America* (London, 1799), letter 6, 60.

72. *General Advertiser*, May 19, 1791.

73. *Diaries of GW*, vol. 5, 480, 490.

74. *Dunlap's American Daily Advertiser*, June 24, 1791.

75. For his personal count of women at receptions, see *Diaries of GW*, vol. 6, 111, 116–17, 120, 124, 129, 130, 131, 137, 139, 141, 142, 151.

76. My interpretation of women and politics draws on Catherine Allgor's provocative essay, "Margaret Bayard Smith's 1809 Journey to Monticello and Montpelier: The Politics of Performance in the Early Republic," *Early American Studies* (Winter 2012): 30–68.

Also helpful was Simon P. Newman, "Principles or Men? George Washington and the Political Culture of National Leadership, 1776–1801," *Journal of the Early Republic*, 12 (1992): 477–507.

77. *New-Hampshire Recorder* and the *Weekly Advertiser*, November 2, 1789.

78. *Gazette of the United States*, October 31, 1789.

79. William H. Sumner, "Some Recollections of Washington's Visit to Boston," *New England Historic-Genealogical Society* 14 (1860): 161.

80. *General Advertiser*, June 1, 1791.

81. *Maryland Journal*, May 31, 1791.

82. Ibid., November 10, 1789.

—CHAPTER V: THE NEW ENGLAND TOUR—

1. *Writings of George Washington*, ed. John C. Fitzpatrick (Washington, DC, 1931–1944), vol. 30, 448–49.

2. Ibid., 442.

3. *New York Daily Gazette*, October 12, 1789.

4. *Diaries of George Washington*, ed. Donald Jackson and Dorothy Twohig (Charlottesville, VA, 1979), vol. 5, 461.

5. Cited in Merrill Jensen, *The Founding of a Nation: A History of the American Revolution, 1763–1776* (New York, 1968), 634.

6. *Diaries of GW*, vol. 5, 463.

7. Ibid., 470.

8. Ibid., 464, 467.

9. Ibid., 467.

10. T.H. Breen, *The Marketplace of Revolution: How Consumer Politics Shaped American Independence* (New York, 2004); Kariann A. Yokota, *Unbecoming British: How Revolutionary America Became a Postcolonial Nation* (New York, 2011).

11. Isaac Weld, *Travels through the States of North America* (London, 1799), 12. Also see Charles S. Grant, *Democracy in the Connecticut Frontier Town of Kent* (New York, 1971); Alan Taylor, *William Cooper's Town: Power and Persuasion on the Frontier of the Early American Republic* (New York, 1995); and Woody Holton, *Abigail Adams* (New York, 2010).

12. Cited in Cathy D. Matson and Peter S. Onuf, *A Union of Interests: Political and Economic Thought in Revolutionary America* (Lawrence, KS, 1990), 157.

13. For an excellent account of economic thinking in the early republic, see Drew R. McCoy, *The Elusive Republic: Political Economy in Jeffersonian America* (New York, 1980).

14. GW Papers, Presidential Series, vol. 1, 263–64.

15. Quoted in Stephen Decatur Jr., *Private Affairs of George Washington: From the Records and Accounts of Tobias Lear, Esquire, His Secretary* (Boston, 1933), 9.

16. *Diary of GW*, vol. 5, 479. Also see the Records of the Second Congregational Church, Beverly, Massachusetts, Beverly Historical Society and Museum, Beverly, Massachusetts.

17. Cited in Perry Walton, *The Story of Textiles: A Bird's-Eye View of the History of the Beginning and the Growth of the Industry by Which Mankind Is Clothed* (New York, 1936), 164.

18. GW Papers, Presidential Series, vol. 1, 323.

19. Ibid., 260–61.

20. Diary of GW, vol. 5, 468.

21. Ibid., and Decatur, *Private Affairs*, 79.

22. *Daily Advertiser*, November 14, 1789.

23. Diary of GW, vol. 5, 468.

24. Cited in Chester M. Destler, "The Hartford Woolen Manufactory: The Story of a Failure," *Connecticut History* 14 (1974): 12. Also see Hartford Woolen Manufactory Papers, 1788–1796, Box 1, "A General Account of Goods, Unwrought Materials, & Implements

made, purchased & sold for account of the Hartford Woolen Manufactory, Connecticut Historical Society, Hartford."

25. *Popular Science Monthly* 39 (August 1891): 462; Destler, "The Hartford Woolen Manufactory," 12–18; and David John Jeremy, ed., *Henry Wansey and His American Journal*, 1794 (Philadelphia, 1970), 68.

26. GW Papers, Presidential Series, vol. 3, 195–96. Also see William Cooper Howells, *Recollections of Life in Ohio from 1813 to 1840* (Cincinnati, 1895).

27. T.H. Breen, *Tobacco Culture: The Mentality of the Great Tidewater Planters on the Eve of Revolution* (Princeton, NJ, 1985).

28. GW Papers, Presidential Series, vol. 3, 192–93.

29. *Writings of GW*, vol. 30, 463.

30. GW Papers, Presidential Series, vol. 3, 195.

31. Ibid., vol. 5, 563.

32. Ibid., vol. 7, 225–26.

33. *Diaries of GW*, vol. 5, 472.

34. Alfred F. Young, *Liberty Tree: Ordinary People and the American Revolution* (New York, 2006), 50; William M. Fowler, *The Baron of Beacon Hill: A Biography of John Hancock* (Boston, 1980).

35. Gaillard Hunt, *Writings of James Madison* (New York, 1904), 270.

36. Cited in Pauline Maier, *Ratification: The People Debate the Constitution, 1787–1788* (New York, 2010), 160.

37. Fowler, *Baron of Beacon Hill*, 267–72; Henry Cabot Lodge, *Boston* (London, 1891), 174–75.

38. *Writings of GW*, vol. 30, 451–52.

39. "The Diary of Samuel Breck, 1823–1827," *Pennsylvania Magazine of History and Biography* 103 (1979): 93.

40. GW Papers, Presidential Series, vol. 4, 217.

41. Ibid., 212–13.

42. *Independent Chronicle*, October 29, 1789.

43. *Diaries of GW*, vol. 5, 472–73.

44. *Gazette of the United States*, October 28, 1789.

45. GW Papers, Presidential Series, vol. 4, 213.

46. Quotations from P. J. Marshall, *Remaking the British Atlantic: The United States and the British Empire after American Independence* (Oxford, 2012), 72.

47. *Gazette of the United States*, October 31, 1789.

48. *Diaries of GW*, vol. 5, 473–74.

49. Mark Anthony De Wolfe Howe, *Boston, The Place and the People* (New York, 1924), 127–28; Decatur, *Private Affairs*, 79–81; GW Papers, Presidential Series, vol. 4, 228–29.

50. "Diary of Samuel Breck," 93.

51. Cited in Douglas Southall Freeman, *George Washington: A Biography* (New York, 1954), vol. 6, 244.

52. *Diaries of GW*, vol. 5, 476.

53. Cited in Freeman, *George Washington*, vol. 6, 244–45.

54. Howe, *Boston*, 127–28; Fowler, *Baron of Beacon Hill*, 276–77.

55. *Independent Chronicle*, October 29, 1789.

56. Seth Ames, *Works of Fisher Ames* (New York, 1869), vol. 1, 73, Ames to Thomas Dwight, October 21, 1789.

57. Ibid., 74. Ames to Dwight, October 30, 1789.

58. "Diary of Samuel Breck," 94.

59. John Adams to Abigail, November 1, 1789, in Margaret A. Hogan, et al., eds., *Adams Family Correspondence* (Boston, 2007), vol. 8, 432; and see Kenneth A. Lockridge, *Literacy in Colonial New England: An Enquiry into the Social Context of Literacy in the Early Modern West* (New York, 1975).

60. *Correspondence of Samuel Blachley Webb*, ed. Worthington Chauncey Ford (New York, 1894), vol. 3, 142.

61. *Independent Chronicle*, October 22, 1789.

62. Ibid., October 29, 1789.

63. *Herald of Freedom*, October 23, 1789.

64. *Massachusetts Spy*, November 5, 1789.

65. *Independent Chronicle*, October 22, 1789.

66. Ibid., October 29, 1789.

67. Mary Smith Cranch to Abigail Adams, November 1, 1789, in Hogan, et al., eds., *Adams Family Correspondence*, vol. 8, 433.

68. *Diaries of GW*, vol. 5, 477.

69. *Maryland Journal*, November 13, 1789.

70. Ibid., November 10, 1789.

71. Quoted in Thomas C. Amory, *Life of James Sullivan* (Boston, 1859), vol. 1, 256.

72. *Independent Chronicle*, October 22, 1789.

73. Mary Smith Cranch to Abigail Adams, October 23, 1789, in Hogan, et al., eds., *Adams Family Correspondence*, vol. 3, 428.

74. Harold Kirker, *The Architecture of Charles Bulfinch* (Cambridge, MA, 1969), 23–24.

75. *Connecticut Courant*, November 2, 1789; *Maryland Journal*, November 13, 1789 (Boston) *Independent Chronicle*, October 29, 1789.

76. *Independent Chronicle*, October 29, 1789.

77. Frederic C. Detwiller, "Thomas Dawes: Boston's Patriot Architect," *Old Time New England* 68 (1977): 5–6.

78. *Diaries of GW*, vol. 5, 475.

79. Many newspapers carried accounts of the parade, but the fullest can be found in the *Connecticut Courant*, November 2, 1789.

80. "Reflections on Titles, Preeminence, and Ceremonies," *Massachusetts Magazine* 2 (January 1790): 94–96.

81. *Boston Gazette*, October 26, 1789.

82. "Diary of Samuel Breck," 94–95.

83. GW Papers, Presidential Series, vol. 4, 552–53.

84. See Charlene Bangs and Kenneth R. Bowling, *Birth of the Nation: The Federal Congress, 1789–1791* (Lanham, MD, 2002); and Joseph J. Ellis, *Founding Brothers: The Revolutionary Generation* (New York, 2000), chaps. 2, 3.

85. GW Papers, Presidential Series, vol. 5, 396–97, vol. 6, 280.

86. "Journal of William Loughton Smith, 1790–1791," in *Proceedings, 1917–1918, Massachusetts Historical Society*, vol. 51, 39.

87. GW Papers, Presidential Series, vol. 4, 585.

88. *Massachusetts Spy*, August 26, 1790.

89. *Newport Herald*, August 19, 1790.

90. Ellen Smith and Jonathan D. Sarna, "Introduction: The Jews of Rhode Island," in George M. Goodwin and Ellen Smith, eds., *The Jews of Rhode Island* (Waltham, MA, 2004), 2–3.

91. Cited in Carl Bridenbaugh, *Peter Harrison: First American Architect* (Chapel Hill, NC, 1949), 1. See Rockwell Stensrud, *Newport: A Lively Experiment, 1639–1969* (Newport, 2006), 163.

92. Marilyn Kaplan, "The Jewish Merchants of Newport, 1749–1790," in Goodwin and Smith, eds., *Jews of Rhode Island*, 22–23.

93. *Columbian Magazine: or, Monthly Miscellany*, "A Tour to the Eastern States" (September 1789): (October 1789): 535.

94. Stensrud, *Newport*, 163.

95. GW Papers, Presidential Series, vol. 6, 286.

96. Ibid., 285. The statement on toleration was so powerfully argued and elegantly written that some historians have concluded that it must have been the work of Thomas Jefferson. There is no proof of his authorship, and in any case, it was Washington who delivered the response to the members of the Touro congregation. The current state of this address is not clear. The controversy over access to Washington's response and over the physical care of the manuscript is discussed in "Notes," *Publication of the Rhode Island Jewish Historical Association* 16 (November 2011): 131–46. On Locke and toleration, see Alan Ryan, *On Politics* (New York, 2012), vol. 2, ch. 13.

—CHAPTER VI: SIGNS OF TROUBLE—

1. Stephen Decatur Jr., *Private Affairs of George Washington: From the Records and Accounts of Tobias Lear, Esquire, His Secretary* (Boston, 1933), 209–10. Also see Terry W. Lipscomb, *South Carolina in 1791: George Washington's Southern Tour* (Columbia, SC, 1993), 3–4.

2. GW Papers, Presidential Series, vol. 5, 96.

3. Cited in Archibald Henderson, *Washington's Southern Tour, 1791* (Boston, 1923), 7.

4. GW Papers, Presidential Series, vol. 8, 361.

5. A good account of these negotiations can be found in Joseph J. Ellis, *Founding Brothers: The Revolutionary Generation* (New York, 2000), 48–80.

6. GW Papers, vol. 7, 211, 236–37.

7. "Journal of William Loughton Smith, 1790–1791," in *Proceedings, 1917–1918, Massachusetts Historical Society*, vol. 51, 70, 71.

8. GW Papers, vol. 7, 211.

9. Ibid., 584.

10. "Itinerary for the Southern Tour," in ibid., 472–85.

11. GW Papers, vol. 8, 59–60.

12. Ibid., 278–79.

13. Ibid., 265.

14. George Washington to Robert Cary & Co., September 28, 1760, in *The Writings of George Washington*, ed. John C. Fitzpatrick (Washington, DC, 1931–1944), vol. 2, 350. Also see Bruce A. Ragsdale, "George Washington, the British Tobacco Trade, and Economic Opportunity in Pre-Revolutionary Virginia," *Virginia Magazine of History and Biography* 97 (1989): 143.

15. See the appendix, "Hiding in Plain Sight."

16. T.H. Breen, "Horses and Gentlemen: The Cultural Significance of Gambling among the Gentry of Virginia," in *Puritans and Adventurers: Change and Persistence in Early America* (New York, 1980), 148–63.

17. Quoted in Henderson, *Southern Tour*, 19; GW Papers, Presidential Series, vol. 6, 425–26.

18. Quoted in Lipscomb, *South Carolina*, 3.

19. GW Papers, Presidential Series, vol. 8, 35.

20. *Diaries of George Washington*, ed. Donald Jackson and Dorothy Twohig (Charlottesville, VA, 1979), vol. 6, 99.

21. Ibid., 100.

22. Ibid., 100–101.

23. *Federal Gazette and Philadelphia Evening Post,* April 9, 1791; *Massachusetts Spy*, April 21, 1791.

24. GW Papers, Presidential Series, vol. 8, 18; also 38–39.

25. *Diaries of GW*, vol. 6, 103–7.

26. Ibid., 107.

27. Quoted in Henderson, *Southern Tour*, 44.

28. GW Papers, Confederation Series, vol. 3, 300. Also see Joel Achenbach, *The Grand Idea: George Washington's Potomac and the Race to the West* (New York, 2004).

29. Ibid., Presidential Series, vol. 1, 300–301.

30. Robert J. Kapsch, *The Potomac Canal: George Washington and the Waterway West* (Morgantown, WV, 2007), 49–57; Wayland Fuller Dunaway, "History of the James River and Kanawha Company," *Studies in History, Economics, and Public Law* 104 (1922): 241–486.

31. Douglas R. Littlefield, "The Potomac Company: A Misadventure in Financing an Early American Internal Improvement Project," *Business History Review* 58 (1984): 565.

32. *Diaries of GW*, vol. 4, 9–10. Also see Grace L. Nute, ed., "Washington and the Potomac: Manuscripts of the Minnesota Historical Society, 1769–1796," *American Historical Review* 28 (1923): 705–22.

33. For the full text, see *Magazine of History* 100 (1924): 213–14.

34. GW Papers, Confederation Series, vol. 2, 69.

35. Douglas Southall Freeman, *George Washington: A Biography* (New York, 1954), vol. 6, 15; Ella May Turner, *James Rumsey: Pioneer in Steam Navigation* (Newton, KS, 1930), 64; David G. Allen, *James Rumsey, American Inventor* (Clarksburg, WV, 2008).

36. Langhorne Gibson Jr., *Cabell's Canal: The Story of the James River and Kanawah* (Richmond, 2000), 42–43.

37. "Journal of William Loughton Smith, 1790–1791," in *Proceedings, 1917–1918, Massachusetts Historical Society*, vol. 51, 65.

38. Quoted in Gibson, *Cabell's Canal*, 42.

39. *Diaries of GW*, vol. 6, 109.

40. James Read to William Jackson, May 1, 1791, Washington Papers, Library of Congress, online digital collection.

41. GW Papers, vol. 8, 277.

42. Ibid., 301.

43. See Henry Wiencek, *An Imperfect God: George Washington, His Slaves, and the Creation of America* (New York, 2003), 315–17.

44. GW Papers, Presidential Series, vol. 8, 67.

45. Ibid., 131–32 (emphasis added).

46. Ibid., 85.

47. George Washington Parke Custis, *Recollections and Private Memoirs of George Washington* (Bridgewater, VA, 1859), 422–24. Also see Decatur, *Private Affairs*, 190.

48. GW Papers, Presidential Series, vol. 8, 202, 232. Also see Joseph E. Fields, ed., "Worthy Partner," in *The Papers of Martha Washington* (Westport, CT, 1994), 231.

49. Cited in Ron Chernow, *Washington: A Life* (New York, 2010), 605.

50. Wiencek, *Imperfect God*, 320–29.

51. GW Papers, Presidential Series, vol. 8, 132.

52. Cited in Fritz Hirschfeld, *George Washington and Slavery: A Documentary Portrayal* (Columbia, MO, 1997), 70.

53. GW Papers, Retirement Series, vol. 2, 16.

54. Fields, ed., "Worthy Partner," 389.

55. Cited in Hirschfeld, *George Washington*, 71.

56. See David Bromwich, *The Intellectual Life of Edmund Burke: From the Sublime and Beautiful to American Independence* (Cambridge, MA, 2014).

57. Quoted in John Keane, *Tom Paine: A Political Life* (Boston, 1995), 291.

58. Edmund Burke, *Reflections on the Revolution in France*, ed. L. G. Mitchell (Oxford, 1993), 33. Also see Alan Ryan, *On Politics* (New York, 2012), bk 2, 616–51.

59. Three valuable examinations of Paine's life and works are Eric Foner, *Tom Paine and Revolutionary America* (New York, 1976); John Keane, *Tom Paine: A Political Life* (Boston, 1995); and Harvey J. Kaye, *Thomas Paine: Firebrand of the Revolution* (New York, 2006).

60. Thomas Paine, *Rights of Man* (Mineola, NY, 1999), 78.

61. Ibid., 92.

62. Cited in Foner, *Tom Paine*, 218.

63. GW Papers, Presidential Series, vol. 8, 362–63.

64. Ibid., 166–67.

65. Ibid., 163–64.

66. *Papers of Thomas Jefferson*, ed. Julian Boyd (Princeton, NJ, 1982), vol. 20, 290–97.

67. "Publicola," *Columbia Centinel*, June 8, 1791.

68. See the appendix on the coach's strange history after Washington's death.

69. GW Papers, Presidential Series, vol. 8, 265–66.

70. Ibid., 358.

71. Ibid.

72. Ibid., 358–59.

73. *Diaries of GW*, vol. 6, 158.

74. For more on these divisive issues, see James Roger Sharp, *American Politics in the Early Republic: The New Nation in Crisis* (New Haven, 1993).

—APPENDIX—

1. George Washington Parke Custis, *Recollections and Private Memoirs of George Washington* (Bridgewater, VA, 1859), 424–25.
2. Mary Stevens Beall, *The Story of the Washington Coachee and of the Powel Coach* (Washington, DC, 1908), 24.
3. Ibid., 36–37.
4. Ibid., 30–31.
5. Elizabeth Donnan and Leo F. Stock, eds., *An Historian's World: Selections from the Correspondence of John Franklin Jameson* (Philadelphia, 1956), 1.
6. Ibid., 116.
7. Beall, *Story*, 24–25.

Photograph Credits

1. Photograph by the author.
2–5. Courtesy of the Library of Congress.
6–8. Courtesy of the American Antiquarian Society.
9. Courtesy of the Yale University Art Gallery.
10. Courtesy of the City of Charleston, South Carolina.
11. *Massachusetts Magazine*, 1789.
12. Courtesy of the American Antiquarian Society.
13–14. Courtesy of the Touro Synagogue Congregation Jeshuat Israel.
15. Courtesy of the Museo Thyssen-Bornemisza/Scala/Art Resource, NY.
16–17. Courtesy of the Mount Vernon Ladies' Association.
18. Mary Stevens Beall, *The Story of the Washington Coachee and of the Powel Coach Which Is Now at Mount Vernon.*
19–20. Courtesy of the Mount Vernon Ladies' Association.

Index

Index

Washington, George (*cont.*)
  family crest of, 218
  health crises of, 67–70, 160, 190,
    200
  historical reenactment of, 253
  humor of, 24
  Humphreys' attempted biography
    of, 29
  namesakes of, 197
  personal characteristics of, 5, 6–7,
    34, 41, 43, 48–50, 61–62, 64–65,
    68, 87, 96, 98–99, 116, 121–22,
    151, 163, 175, 190, 222, 227,
    234, 249–50
  political realism of, 7
  popularity of, 2, 4–5, 17, 30, 41,
    86–87, 113, 184
  Rights of Man dedicated to,
    242–43
  in scheme to transport slaves out
    of Philadelphia, 232–39
  strong federal union espoused by,
    1, 2, 3, 4, 7–10, 12, 22, 25, 31,
    41, 81, 83–109, 159, 161, 163,
    177, 207, 210, 217, 225, 227,
    238, 248, 250
  as symbolic of new nation, 5, 70,
    128
  wealth of, 49, 50, 78, 194, 217
  westward expansion espoused by,
    83–84, 105, 156, 207, 223–30
Washington, George, journeys of, 1
  author's retracing of, 8–11
  ceremonies for, *see* welcoming
    ceremonies
  end of, 103
  entourages for, 13–15, 25, 28, 71,
    256

  expenses of, 74–75
  general rules of conduct on, 70–81
  goals of, 2–4, 17, 25, 81, 83, 102,
    129
  GW's optimistic appraisal, 160–61,
    197–98, 247–50
  heroic presentation of, 15–16, 34,
    50, 73, 125–27, 186, 193, 210
  initial idea for, 25–26, 64–67
  North-South competition in, 211
  onset of, 3, 69, 107
  as political theater, 15–16, 43–82,
    111, 129–34, 164, 210, 217, 250
  public lodgings used for, 73–78,
    134, 178, 213–14
  republican values reflected in,
    70–78, 124, 129, 141, 155, 163,
    188–89, 190, 195–96, 198
  signs of trouble in, 207, 248–49
  successes and triumphs of, 155–57,
    159–206
  see also inaugural tour; New
    England tour; Rhode Island
    tour; Southern tour; *specific
    states, cities and towns*
Washington, George, presidency of:
  apprehensions and misgivings of,
    40–41
  challenge of presidential
    presentation for, 12, 29, 37,
    43–82, 167–68, 210, 250
  determining an appropriate title
    for, 43, 51–60
  election of, 26, 28
  first term of, 1, 3, 4, 43, 54, 160,
    176, 199, 209, 210–11
  formal public receptions hosted
    by, 61–64

About the Author

T.H. Breen was the founding director of the Nicholas D. Chabraja Center for Historical Studies and the William Smith Mason Professor of American History at Northwestern University. He is currently the James Marsh Professor-at-Large at the University of Vermont. He has taught at Yale University, Oxford University, Cambridge University, and the California Institute of Technology.

Breen is the author of a dozen monographs and collections, three of which received awards: *Imagining the Past: East Hampton Histories*, *Tobacco Culture: The Mentality of the Great Tidewater Planters on the Eve of Revolution*, and *The Marketplace of Revolution: How Consumer Politics Shaped American Independence*.

Composer T. J. Anderson and poet Yusef Komunyakaa transformed Breen's essay "Making History," a study of the end of slavery in Massachusetts, into a full-length opera entitled *Slip Knot*.

Breen has received research support from the Guggenheim Foundation, Humboldt Foundation, MacArthur Foundation, National Humanities Center, Colonial Williamsburg, and the Huntington Library. He has contributed to the *Times Literary Supplement*, the *New York Review of Books*, the *New York Times*, and the *American Scholar*. Breen and his wife, Susan, live in Greensboro, Vermont.